The ART of Avoiding a Train Wreck

Tips and Tricks for Launching and Operating SAFe Agile Release Trains

Em Campbell-Pretty and
Adrienne L. Wilson

First published in 2019 by Em Campbell-Pretty & Adrienne L. Wilson

© Pretty Agile
The moral rights of the author have been asserted.
This book is a SpiritCast Network Book.

Author:

    Campbell-Pretty, Em & Wilson, Adrienne L.

Title:

    The ART of Avoiding a Train Wreck; *Tips and Tricks for Launching and Operating SAFe Agile Release Trains*

ISBN:

    978-0-359-59445-0

Subjects:

    1. Organisational Effectiveness, 2. Agile Software Development, 3. Information Technology – Management, 4. Computer Software – Development

All rights reserved. Except as permitted under the Australian Copyright Act 1968 (for example, a fair dealing for the purposes of study, research, criticism or review), no part of this book may be reproduced, stored in a retrieval system, communicated or transmitted in any form or by any means without prior written permission. All enquiries should be made to the publisher at em@prettyagile.com

Cover Design: Bliss Inventive
Editor: Anita Saunders

Disclaimer:

The material in this publication is of the nature of general comment only, and does not represent professional advice. It is not intended to provide specific guidance for particular circumstances and it should not be relied on as the basis for any decision to take action or not take action on any matter which it covers. Readers should obtain professional advice where appropriate, before making any such decision. To the maximum extent permitted by law, the author and publisher disclaim all responsibility and liability to any person, arising directly or indirectly from any person taking or not taking action based on the information in this publication.

Praise for *The ART of Avoiding a Train Wreck*

"Implementing SAFe in a large organization is never an easy task, unless you have a dedicated coach to guide you. Em and Adrienne are amazing guides and with this book you can feel just as if they are with you, guiding you the whole way with tips and tricks and warnings of pitfalls to avoid before you fall into them. This is a book I wish I had when I was taking my first steps into the world of SAFe."
—**Inbar Oren**, SAFe Fellow and Principal Consultant, Scaled Agile, Inc.

"If you are thinking of launching an ART DON'T! Until you read this book. It is filled with great experiential learning and advice as well as tips to avoid a train wreck. This is a must read for anyone planning on launching a train!"
—**Joe Vallone**, SPCT and SAFe Fellow, Scaled Agile, Inc.

"Whether you are adopting SAFe or launching your first Agile Release Train, Em and Adrienne's book is a must-read. Don't get derailed, instead, learn from two renowned experts and gain practical insights into how to best lead a successful enterprise Lean-Agile transformation."
—**Richard Knaster**, SAFe Fellow, Principal Consultant, Author SAFe *Distilled Book* series

"*The ART of Avoiding a Train Wreck* applies a practical and empathetic approach to the ins and outs of actually applying SAFe. It shines an emphasis on the people, and shares real-world success, tools for success, and anti-patterns that we can all learn from. Much gratitude to Em and Adrienne for sharing their stories, and their hearts with us."
—**Jennifer Fawcett**, SAFe Fellow, Scaled Agile, Inc.

"Launching and managing agile release trains isn't easy. Organizations encounter a variety of bumps and challenges along the way. Thanks to Em and Adrienne, there is now an owner's manual with practical instructions and expert tips to ensure they don't get stuck in the mud!"

—**Marc Rix**, SAFe Fellow, Scaled Agile, Inc.

"By far, the best real-life guide to implementation I have ever read! This book is an absolute required read for any enterprise who wants to get it right and more so for those who may have started on the wrong foot and need a self-help guide to correct."

—**Scott Frost**, SAFe Fellow, SPCT and Business Agility Advisor, Accenture | SolutionsIQ

"I have known Em since the dawn of Scaled Agile Framework. She is dedicated, has a witty sense of humour and is always dead serious when it comes to Agile Release Trains and how to set up those correctly. She is passionate on things like teamwork and getting organizations to perform at their best. This book is full of gold nuggets from one of the very first pioneers on getting Scaled Agile set up and running.

"Most organizations that I have met who would like to start their journey on SAFe are really nervous on the potential pitfalls that they might not recognize before it is too late. A seasoned coach is the best thing you can have to avoid those pitfalls in the first place, and this book is a fast pass access to senior coach knowledge. If you are a SAFe SPC and your job is to set up a train or trains, this book is a must.

"*The ART of Avoiding a Train Wreck* is filled with advanced level knowledge like how to apply Impact Mapping with Epics and a fun and easy way to prioritize a train's problems. It also has some expert-level knowledge on how to integrate Lean UX correctly in your train and tips to run events for globally distributed ARTs. Em does a huge service for the entire SAFe community by making this knowledge available in very easy-to-read handbook format."

—**Dr. Maarit Laanti**, SPCT4 and founder Nitor Delta

Praise for *The ART of Avoiding a Train Wreck*

"*The ART of Avoiding a Train Wreck* was outstanding; it was a privilege to read. I have learned of multiple new books that I need to go read after reading some of the references. I absolutely loved the amount of practical advice provided. I live in a world where we still have projects, teams work overtime when needed, and we still need to meet some waterfall expectations due to external forces. I left this book feeling hopeful with a number of new ideas to try as opposed to feeling guilty because my culture is a little slower to evolve."
—**Robin Yeman**, SPCT Candidate and Lockheed Martin Space Fellow

"The number of times that I have said that SAFe is a Framework NOT a Prescription, in fact if I had a penny for every time I said it I would be a wealthy man. Every time I have implemented SAFe it has always been different because you have to use your brain (it is not a one-two-three-step guide) and then you need to apply it to the organisation context. And as Dean Leffingwell told me, 'If you are still doing the same thing a year later, then you are doing it wrong because you are not inspecting and adapting based in relentless improvement.'

"At last, Em and Adrienne captured their many learnings from launching Agile Release Trains over many years, including not only learnings that I completely agree with (absolutely bloody right moments!) but many that are new insights for me as well. It also includes 'SAFe says this but our experience says that'. It is full of practical insights of avoiding a Train Wreck but more importantly how to set the train up on the right tracks, e.g. how to run an Epic Workshop, what to watch out for in PI Planning and some real 'gotchas' to avoid. Plus laced with some great anecdotes.

"A must-read for all SAFe Program Consultants."
—**Darren Wilmshurst**, SPCT, Director and Head of Consulting, Radtac Ltd

"Em & Adrienne's book definitely fills a gap in the SAFe literature and the literature about Lean & Agile transformation in general. It gives you a very good impression of how a healthy transformation feels like and what to do to get there. It's not just a cookbook of how to do a proper transformation, though there are a lot of good tips you can follow, but it tells a story you can relate to taken from everyday life in transformations.

This is a must read for everyone who wants to run a transformation on their own, but even seasoned transformation coaches will probably get interesting perspectives with this well told narration.

I had a good time reading it and I think my time was very well invested."
—**Dr. Wolfgang Brandhuber**, SPCT at Kegon AG

"Em has produced another amazing book filled with pragmatic, real-world guidance on how to use the SAFe framework in real life. Highly recommended for anyone working in a multi-team environment delivering complex products or services."
—**Carl Starendal**, SPCT at We Are Movement

"Introducing something like Agile or even the Scaled Agile Framework (SAFe) with its Agile Release Trains to an organisation is hard. It is a real change, a real organisational development effort, a journey with a lot of challenges to overcome.

"If you are successful you helped your organisation to become more agile, lean and—most important—more competitive in an ever-faster-changing world. You will have a lot of stories to tell and experiences to share with those who are going to start their own expedition into the wild land of Agile and Lean.

"With their book *The ART of Avoiding a Train Wreck* Em and Adrienne are providing great insights on how to start your first Agile Release Train, including a lot of interesting Anecdotes and 'Protips'. They also clearly state where there are potential train wrecks waiting—some of them they have experienced themselves.

"I really enjoyed reading the book. I liked the writing style and learned a lot. I will be recommending it in all my future training classes and

Praise for The ART of Avoiding a Train Wreck

to my consulting clients as it provides a lot of value, especially to people in charge of implementing SAFe in their organisations."

—**Felix Rüssel**, SPCT and Partner at KEGON AG (Germany)

"I absolutely loved the real, practical insights and honest reflections in *The ART of Avoiding a Train Wreck*! Several times throughout reading it I was scribbling notes to go and experiment with right away! I would recommend that any aspiring SPC, RTE or executive leading a transformation reads this book to help bring some practices to life and avoid some of the pitfalls that we have all been through at one time or another!"

—**Aaron McKenna**, Business Agility and Digital Transformation Engineer, McKenna Consultants

"*Tribal Unity* for me was a gentle introduction into the world of Agile Release Trains. It was like hopping onto a steam train to explore breathtaking mountain territory. Em's storytelling ability really brought SAFe to life for me and helped me understand why it was important and how I could practically apply it in my own context. *Train Wreck* is a whole other level. If *Tribal Unity* was a mountain adventure, *Train Wreck* is a bullet train! Em and Adrienne pull no punches as they describe their extensive experience launching and leading Agile Release Trains. The Anecdotes, Cautions, and Protips back up everything they claim, and they are not afraid to share the good, the bad and the awkward.

"I found myself nodding my head either fervently in agreement or to say 'Oh, that happened to me too—sigh'. What I love about *Train Wreck* is that it consists of 15+ years of compiled experience that proves the importance, as well as the 'how to', of scaling Agile well, leadership buy-in, and investment in Agile capability."

—**Emma Sharrock**, author *The Agile Project Manager*

"*The ART of Avoiding a Train Wreck* is a very hands-on and pragmatic book. Em and Adrienne's stories are very realistic and do not only depict the ideal world. As a SAFe practitioner, I can relate to many of them as we have gone through some of the good ideas as well as the wrecks they describe. I can also see where we might have taken shortcuts in some areas and it gives me ideas for areas of improvements. This is the book to read for anyone interested in launching their first train, but also for anyone embarked on a SAFe journey who wants to step back and assess its current way of working and get inspired. Finally, I find it is accessible to non-native English speakers."

—**Cécile Auret**, Agile Change Agent in a French Government Agency

"Agile coaches, you're going to appreciate this book! It's chock-full of practical ways to enhance the standard SAFe guidance on launching Agile Release Trains, as well as the every-important "why" behind the guidance. For example, how to keep the team readouts from being boring; how business leaders can truly engage the teams when discussing the business value of program increment (PI) objectives; and how to handle the unexpected and at times unavoidable mid-PI change in priorities. I particularly appreciate the guidance on what battles to win early on versus which ones can be won in subsequent PIs, insight into how the ART will feel a year into its journey, and many reminders of the core lean principles and how they apply. Of course, this book also includes references back to standard SAFe tools and resources, as well as tips and tricks for making the SAFe ceremonies run even smoother! I am excited for this book to be available to the people working with SAFe, so they can benefit from the useful experience-based ideas within."

—**Lynn Winterboer**, Lean-Agile Servant Leader, Educator, and Coach

"*The Art of Avoiding a Train Wreck* helped me recognize some of the missteps our ARTs had made along the way. The easy-to-understand Case Studies and Anecdotes provide immediate patterns and practices you can implement to get your Trains back on track. Within two weeks, I was able train multiple RTEs and coaches to implement some specific Protips outlined in the book. This helped to reset and improve our Inspect and Adapt and Program Increment

Praise for The ART of Avoiding a Train Wreck

Planning ceremonies. Thanks to this book, we now have a roadmap of practices to implement when our next PI starts."

—**Jeffrey Smith**, SAFe Program Consultant

"Implementing any kind of transformation is challenging. It is challenging because the organisation is often so ingrained in their current ways of doing things and blind by their own flawed logic that they fail to see that what used to work no longer meets the needs of today. This means the people who are leading the transformation need to take the opportunity to learn from practitioners who have successfully transformed teams and organisations repeatedly to the point that they can consistently produce the same level of success. These practitioners understand the challenges and the cost constraints that organisations face when undergoing an organisation wide transformation. Experience and real know-how take years to accumulate, and no doubt, there are many lessons learned in the process, some are very costly. In *The ART of Avoiding a Train Wreck*, Em and Adrienne show many of the lessons learned, some learned in a very hard way so that you can enjoy a smoother ride and avoid train-wreck along the way."

—**Sonya Yeh Spencer**, Professional Agilist & Practitioner, NLP Trainer & Coach

"I loved reading The ART of Avoiding a Train Wreck- the pointers and "Caution, train wreck ahead!" are awesome - makes it very easy and fun to read. It is a great resource for anyone looking to tackle the many complex and layered problems and challenges an enterprise presents, all while using real world challenges."

—**Teresa Simmermacher**, SAFe Program Consultant and Agile Coach

"Interesting and an easy read! Em and Adrienne have done a great job of making what can be a very dry subject interesting. The Anecdotes make it a very practical guide to implementing an Agile Release Train. In my experience, it sometimes gets tricky when the SAFe Framework meets the already existing processes in an organisation. If the Finance and PMO cannot be part of the initial rollout it becomes difficult to implement the framework as is. This book provides practical solutions to get around these situations and implement 'SAFe' in the real world. I also like the candid explanations of the process, sometimes learning through failures. I love the 'Potential Train Wreck Ahead' sections which will help readers to avoid some of the pitfalls already experienced by Em and Adrienne."

—**Shobha Kanherkar**, SAFe Agile Transformation Leader

"*The ART of Avoiding a Train Wreck* does a solid job of calling out the usual pitfalls that an organisation that has embarked on implementing the Scaled Agile Framework may run into. The experience of Em and Adrienne shows through and will allow the reader to be on the lookout for similar potential failures as they work through forming and maintaining solid Agile Release Trains. This book should enable the reader to lead the change more efficiently and proactively. There are additional tips and activities which can bring a lot to the implementation plan."

—**Rebecca Davis**, iSPCT Candidate at a Fortune 10 Company

"*The ART of Avoiding a Train Wreck* is a must-read for new and seasoned SPCs, RTEs, Product Managers, Architects, Scrum Masters wanting to know how run great trains and avoid the track-works or worse train wrecks! I look forward to my copy being dog-eared and covered in post it notes."

—**Claire Sanders**, SAFe Program Consultant

"The freely revealed body of knowledge from Scaled Agile Inc is worthwhile, but a bit hard to grasp. This great work by Em finally makes it intuitive and approachable."

—**Håkan Lovén**, SAFe Program Consultant, Avega Group

"This book offers advice and insight how to get the absolute best out of SAFe model. The book is rooted in the learnings from the authors' real-life SAFe experiences. A great way to avoid a couple of speed bumps on your SAFe journey."

—**Anna Virolainen**, Senior Agile Coach, OP Financial Group

In memory of Em's mum Ros McCarthy.
1947-2017

Acknowledgements

There are so many people without whom this book would not have been possible.

The folks on all the Agile Release Trains we have had the pleasure of working with—thank you for letting us be a part of your world and for letting us share your stories.

Dean Leffingwell, thank you so much for taking time out from your SAFe Summit preparations to review our book and write such a wonderful foreword.

The contributors who provided anecdotes for inclusion in the book: Maarit Laanti, Darren Wilmshurst, Aaron McKenna, Claire Sanders, Cécile Auret, Robin Yeman, Michael Stump, Melissa Hay, Carl Stardenal, Marc Rix and Sonya Yeh Spencer.

The reviewers: Scott Frost, Cécile Auret, Aaron McKenna, Emma Sharrock, Jennifer Fawcett, Claire Sanders, Brian Adkins, Shobha Kanherkar, Lynn Winterboer, Robin Yeman, Jeffrey Smith, Maarit Laanti, Darren Wilmshurst, Melissa Hay, Carl Stardenal, Anna Virolainen, Rebecca Davis, Felix Rüssel, Wolfgang Brandhuber, Candy Durfee, Michael Stump, Debbie Brey, Marc Rix, Inbar Oren, Teresa Simmermacher, Chad Moore, Joakim Sundén, Sonya Yeh Spencer, Anna Virolainen, and Håkan Lövén—thank you for taking time out of your busy schedules to provide us with constructive feedback and additional thoughts. This book is better because of you.

Dave Thompson and the crew from the Inspirational Book Writers Retreat and the SpiritCast Network. Thank you for flexing with us as the book grew, and the timelines extended! As always, your support has been priceless!

Table of Contents

Praise for The ART of Avoiding a Train Wreck .... *iii*
Acknowledgements .... *xiii*
Table of Contents .... *xv*
Foreword by Dean Leffingwell .... *xix*
Preface by Em Campbell-Pretty .... *xxi*
Preface by Adrienne L. Wilson .... *xxv*

Part 1 – Introduction 7
    Going All In 10
    The Right ART for Right Now 21
    Before You Buy Your Ticket 26
    Chapter Summary 40

Part 2 – Laying the Tracks 41
    Preparing for *Leading SAFe®* Training 43
    Designing the Agile Release Train 48
    Principles for Designing the Agile Teams 61
    Working With Vendors 77
    Specialist Roles 80
    What About Me? 110
    Who's on First? 114
    W.R.A.P. 120
    Planning the ART Launch 121
    Training the Product Organisation 126
    Chapter Summary 129

Part 3 – Preparing the Cargo 131
Understanding the SAFe® Requirements Model 132
Identifying the Program Epics 134
Defining the Program Epics 135
Program Epic Prioritisation 149
ART Design Validation 157
Impact Mapping Epics Into Features 158
Defining Features 161
Completing the Lean Business Case for an Epic 168
Prioritising Features 170
Allocating Feature to Teams 174
Case Study: But my "Epic" has a Fixed Scope Business Case! 176
Chapter Summary 183

Part 4 – Setting the Timetable for the Train 185
Program Increments 186
Sprints 190
ART Sync 192
System Demo 195
Load the Cargo on Cadence 196
Tribal Unity Events 196
Innovation and Planning (IP) Sprint 200
Chapter Summary 203

Part 5 – All Aboard! 205
Our Quick-Start Pattern 207
Logistics 210
Scrum Master Training 213

Table of Contents

    Team Day 214

    Team Training 220

    Program Increment (PI) Planning 228

    What Happens After PI Planning? 280

    Chapter Summary 282

Part 6 – Staying on the Tracks 283

    The Program Kanban 284

    Sprinting 308

    Operationalising the Chapters 317

    Executing the Innovation and Planning (IP) Sprint 317

    Adding Teams to the Train 337

    Speeding up the Train with DevOps 339

    Chapter Summary 341

SAFe Travels 343

Appendix 345

    PI Planning Stationery 345

    Checklist for Avoiding a Train Wreck 347

Contributors 353

Bibliography 357

About the Authors 361

    Em Campbell-Pretty 361

    Adrienne L Wilson 363

Also by Em Campbell-Pretty 365

Index ....

Foreword by Dean Leffingwell, creator of SAFe®

SAFe™ Fellow Em Campbell-Pretty has been with us since pretty much (no pun intended) day one. I've always appreciated her unique combination of inquisitiveness, her challenging nature, and her commitment to continuous learning and getting things right. Like most of our Fellows, Em constantly pushes the envelope of SAFe, explores new areas, adds value, and occasionally discovers that some things are already better reflected in SAFe as written. We don't mind when people push the boundaries; in fact, that is the basis of our science and we look for that quality in our SAFe Fellows.

Coming from a non-technical background, Em brings a strong business leadership perspective to this book and the larger challenge of building business solutions, reminding us all that launching real business solutions involves a lot more than the bits we developers tend to focus on. Here, she draws on the experience of hundreds of engagements to write what may be the most practical book ever written about SAFe. She is aptly aided in this endeavor by Aerospace Engineer and SPCT Candidate Adrienne Wilson.

This book is gritty and down in the trenches; it provides a real-world view of the challenges in implementing an Agile Release Train (ART) and the organizational change that comes with it. In SAFe, we don't spend a lot of time describing what not to do—if we did, the Framework would be twice as big—but knowing what doesn't work, why it failed, and how to avoid it in the future can be an enterprise saver. Em and Adrienne have also tested and learned from many early compromises, the ones you often have to make to get started with SAFe... you can't find this practical, real-world experience just anywhere, and this book is filled with pithy vignettes and challenges.

Em and Adrienne do a phenomenal job of focusing on the core of SAFe, what we term Essential SAFe, and the act of launching an Agile Release Train through the Implementation Roadmap. And when that works well, the other areas—from building large solutions to thinking about the portfolio to improving the performance of Agile Teams—will likely come along for a fun ride.

Because of that perspective, I highly recommend Em and Adrienne's book and its guidance to help 'keep your trains on the tracks'. They bring in the human side of a tribe in the generic sense as a form of an ART. They provide the specific, practical, topical, day-to-day guidance that a leader, SAFe Program Consultant (SPC) or Release Train Engineer (RTE) needs to successfully launch an ART.

This book is truly essential reading for anybody launching an ART and I highly recommend it to everyone involved in a SAFe implementation. I'd also like to personally thank Em for this book and her ongoing and valuable contributions to the field.

'Pretty' good book Em!

Dean Leffingwell
Creator of SAFe®
Author of *SAFe Distilled*, *SAFe Reference Guide*, *Agile Software Requirements* and *Scaling Software Agility*
Boulder, Colorado
12 September 2019

Preface by Em Campbell-Pretty

In December 2011, I was a General Manager working in Finance at a large Australian telecommunications company. My primary role was the business owner of a multi-year, multi-million-dollar program of work intended to enhance the Enterprise Data Warehouse (EDW). The technology delivery teams tasked with delivering on this program of work were using "Agile," or as I came to understand it, "Wagile."[1]

There were five or six of these "Wagile" teams, working quite independently on what was a single interdependent program of work. Each team had its own approach, different sprint lengths, different ways of defining the backlogs, different quality standards, different methods for planning and estimating work, and, of course, each team was its own unique shape and size. As the business owner of the program, I found it was very difficult to understand how the program was progressing.

December 2011 marked two years since I had pitched the business case for the EDW program to the CEO and received his endorsement to proceed. It had been a long and painful two years and we had very little to show for our efforts. In hindsight, it was like I was feeding a money fire. The technology team would request funding for the next tranche of work, I would reluctantly approve the funding, the technology team would light a match and set the money alight and then come back for more money. Surely there had to be a better way ...

So that summer when I headed to Bali for my end-of-year vacation, I was looking for answers as to how to make agile work at scale. As has always been my habit, I turned to Amazon looking for books that might contain the answers. Dean Leffingwell's *Scaling Software*

---

[1] Wagile is a term used by agilists to describe waterfall dressed up as Agile.

gility[2] had been doing the rounds amongst some of the agile folks where I worked so on their recommendation, I downloaded it on my kindle and started reading.

Figure 1 - Me reading in the pool in Bali.

It was the notion of the Agile Release Train[3] that caught my attention; the idea of teams being aligned to a common mission and common cadence was really appealing. Maybe, just maybe, this approach would help my program of work ...

When I returned to work in January 2012 my whole world changed. There was a "spill and fill"[4] that resulted in my job ceasing to exist.

---

[2] Dean Leffingwell, *Scaling Software Agility: Best Practices for Large Enterprises* (Boston: Addison-Wesley, 2007), Kindle edition.
[3] To learn more about Agile Release Trains or ARTs check out: https://www.scaledagileframework.com/agile-release-train/ (Accessed 8 April 2019).
[4] For non-Aussie readers: A spill and fill is a restructuring process whereby a range of positions in a workplace are made redundant and the employees filling those positions must reapply for the smaller number of newly created positions. Source: https://www.smh.com.au/public-service/spill-and-fill-a-fairer-way-to-shed-employees-20130805-2r928.html (Accessed 20 August 2019).

I was strongly encouraged to try one of the newly created roles, General Manager of Strategic Delivery. Sounds fancy, I know. Believe me, it was not fancy at all. It was, in fact, essentially the "head of the money fire." A job that the organisation had been unable to find someone suitable (or perhaps more accurately someone willing) to take. A job I wasn't really sure I wanted at all but also the job that would change my life.

As you may be aware *Scaling Software Agility* and its oddly named sequel, *Agile Software Requirements*,[5] contain the initial thinking behind the Scaled Agile Framework® (SAFe®).[6] It was with these books in hand that I used my new role to launch Australia's first SAFe Agile Release Train (ART). This ART would become the source of two official SAFe case studies and the inspiration for my first book *Tribal Unity*.[7]

The results we achieved over my two years leading this ART were well beyond my greatest expectations:

- Employee Engagement (eNPS) from -49 to +56
- Stakeholder NPS from -100 to +50
- Frequency of Release from once a quarter to once a week
- Cycle Time from 12 months to 3 months
- 95% decrease in production defects

This ART also taught me many lessons, but none more important than the words of W. Edwards Deming:

---

[5] Dean Leffingwell, *Agile Software Requirements: Lean Requirements Practices for Teams, Program, and the Enterprise*. (Boston: Addison-Wesley, 2011), Kindle edition.
[6] SAFe and Scaled Agile Framework are registered trademarks of Scaled Agile, Inc.
[7] Em Campbell-Pretty, *Tribal Unity: Getting from Teams to Tribes by Creating a One Team Culture*. (SpiritCast Network, 2017).

*"I should estimate that in my experience most troubles and most possibilities for improvement add up to the proportions something like this:
94% belongs to the system (responsibility of management)
6% special"*[8]

Our results were achieved almost exclusively by changing "the system" (i.e. the way the work works, environment, policies, standards, etc.). People are often surprised to learn that no specific people changes were made in achieving these results.

By the beginning of 2014, it was time for a new challenge. I needed to know if the pattern was repeatable and to my surprise and joy it was!

Over the past eight years, I have had the great privilege of launching dozens of Agile Release Trains impacting the work lives of thousands of people. It has not always been rainbows and unicorns, but it has been incredibly fertile soil for experimentation and learning. Through this book I hope to be able to help and inspire you to get your train on the tracks and keep it there by sharing both the train wrecks and the proven success patterns I have observed while riding the SAFe railways.

---

[8] W. Edwards Deming, *Out of the Crisis*, (Cambridge: MIT Press, 1982) p. 315.

Preface by Adrienne L. Wilson

In 2013, the organisation I was working at was an interesting blend of telecom meets aerospace. At this point I had spent about 17 years of my career building all manner of cockpit avionics solutions anywhere from flight critical guidance systems to far less critical navigation solutions for the pilots.

One of the Project Managers that had joined the company was a SAFe Program Consultant (SPC)[9] and he pitched the idea of adopting SAFe to the organisation. Sure enough, they decided they wanted to go SAFe. Right about this time I was having a conversation with the General Manager of the business about needing a challenge ...

I remember being in a particular meeting with that SPC and he saw me coaching a team on the finer points of hardware and software design considerations for aircraft certification. I was a Senior Program Manager at the time who was running the most complex programs the organisation had in flight. I had a lot of domain experience and knew how to build complex embedded systems, get them certified and deployed on an aircraft. It wasn't long after that meeting I was asked to be this thing called a Release Train Engineer (RTE)[10].

Fast forward to 2014 in Boulder, Colorado and it was time for me to get my SPC, too. Scale Agile had started the SAFe Program Consultant Trainer (SPCT)[11] program and would-be SPCTs had to

---

[9] To learn more about SAFe Program Consultants check out: https://scaledagileframework.com/safe-program-consultant/
[10] To learn more about the Release Train Engineer role in SAFe check out: https://www.scaledagileframework.com/release-train-engineer-andsolution-train-engineer/ (Accessed 19 June 2019).
[11] To learn more about the SAFe Program Consultant Trainer check out: https://www.scaledagile.com/spct-certification-requirements/ (Accessed 22 September 2019).

come back and watch Dean Leffingwell teach *Implementing SAFe*. It was in this class Dean kept asking SPCT Candidate "Em" what she thought. Over and over, "Em, what you do think?" I decided I needed to meet this Em. Later that evening at a happy hour Em and I finally got to have a conversation. Little did either of us know we'd end up in business together three years later!

One part of Em's story that really resonated with me was wanting to find out if the success I was seeing at this organisation was able to be replicated. SAFe became a passion for me so much so I left the aerospace industry and took a role as an RTE at a medical IT company. That position ended up growing into a much bigger role, but I was wanting yet another challenge. I was toying with the idea of starting my own business when I got a push from the universe and got laid off while at the 2016 SAFe Summit! That same day I got my first SAFe consulting engagement and voila, my consulting business was born!

A year later, Em and I reconnect at the 2017 SAFe Summit. It wasn't long after that I took her up on her offer to work with her team in Australia. We started comparing war stories about the really big messes we had seen organisations inflict on themselves either through getting bad advice or trying to implement SAFe on their own. Em had shared a few years back she was thinking about another book to help with this problem. I could immediately see the need for the book from my own experiences then and told her she should write it. She didn't get around to it for one reason or another until the universe intervened again and we found ourselves with an unusual week with no client engagements. Off we went to write this book.

I have had the great honour of working with organisations as big as the Fortune 5 to just a few hundred people in countless industries around the world launching a lot of Agile Release Trains. I'm really fortunate to do what I love with a great team.

It's my hope that as you wade your way through this book, you'll find some tips for implementing SAFe, some pitfalls to avoid, and maybe a little fun along the way.

Introduction

This book is for those who are thinking about implementing the Scaled Agile Framework (SAFe) and/or launching Agile Release Trains[12] (ARTs). It is also for those who have launched ARTs, coached or led ARTs, and are looking for ways to course correct or uplift.[13] If you are looking to be "sold" on SAFe, this is probably not the book for you. You would probably be better served by taking a *Leading SAFe* class,[14] then if you want to learn more, this book would then be a good option.

The ART of Avoiding a Train Wreck is not intended as an introduction to SAFe, nor a substitute for taking a *Leading SAFe* class, an *Implementing SAFe*[15] class, or reading *SAFe Distilled*.[16] The intent of this book is to build on the knowledge you have gained from the classroom, your own reading, or experience in the workplace by sharing war stories and success patterns to aid you in jumping aboard your next Agile Release Train. As we introduce SAFe concepts in the book we have endeavoured to include links in the footnotes to the related articles on scaledagileframework.com for those who need a quick refresher.

---

[12] To learn more about Agile Release Trains in SAFe check out: https://www.scaledagileframework.com/agile-release-train (Accessed 8 April 2019).

[13] If your train has completely derailed, you might like to use this book as a guide to reset your ART. Depending on how many corners were cut in the initial ART launch (or since then) we often find the most effective remediation is a total reboot.

[14] To learn more about *Leading SAFe* check out: https://www.scaledagile.com/certification/courses/leading-safe/ (Accessed 29 August 2019).

[15] To learn more about *Implementing SAFe* check out: https://www.scaledagile.com/certification/courses/implementing-safe/ (Accessed 29 August 2019).

[16] Richard Knaster and Dean Leffingwell, *SAFe 4.5 Distilled: Applying the Scaled Agile Framework for Lean Enterprises (2nd Edition)*, (Addison-Wesley, 2018).

The ART of Avoiding a Train Wreck

I wrote this book in collaboration with Adrienne Wilson covering the patterns we developed before we met (sharing war stories, if you will) and the practices we have refined or created since we started working together towards the end of 2017. Hence, you will find an interweaving of content from me (Em) and us depending on the topic.

The focus of this book is success patterns for launching and operating a SAFe Agile Release Train and therefore mainly covers tips and tricks related to Essential SAFe.[17] We have tried to highlight where a Solution Train[18] or Portfolio SAFe[19] may require a different tack but this guidance is by no means exhaustive.

Don't feel you have to read the entire book end to end. It was written with the expectation that many readers will choose to work their way through the book a section at a time, in parallel with an ART launch.

Throughout the book you'll also see some icons that are designed to bring your attention to key learnings we have had.

> Where you see this coffee cup, we will be sharing **Anecdotes** from one or both of our perspectives, as well as anecdotes shared with us by other SAFe practitioners.

---

[17] To learn more about Essential SAFe check out: https://www.scaledagileframework.com/essential-safe/ (Accessed 8 April 2019).
[18] To learn more about the Solution Train in SAFe check out: https://www.scaledagileframework.com/solution-train/ (Accessed 29 August 2019).
[19] To learn more about the Portfolio level in SAFe check out: https://www.scaledagileframework.com/portfolio-level/ (Accessed 29 August 2019).

Introduction

Caution! Potential Train Wreck Ahead!
Look for this icon for cautionary tales and common mistakes we have witnessed, and our advice on how to avoid them.

Next to this icon you will find a **Protip**. Between the two of us we have over 15 years of experience with SAFe. Here are some of the best ideas we have tried and succeeded with.

When scaling agile, globally distributed ARTs are almost inevitable. These ARTs have a unique set of challenges that need to be considered. Next to this icon you will find our **Tips for Globally Distributed ARTs**.

Some ARTs are launched without their funding model being changed from project funding to value stream funding.[20] This may not be ideal, but we know it is a reality for many Agile Release Trains. Next to this icon we will share tips and tricks for being **SAFe in a Project Driven World**.

This book has seven sections designed to help you on your journey from thinking about launching an Agile Release Train to running a full operational ART.

---

[20] To learn Funding Value Streams with SAFe check out: https://www.scaledagileframework.com/lean-budgets/ (Accessed 30 August 2019).

Ticket to Ride

Besides being a great lyric from a Beatles song, this first section briefly covers the things you might like to consider before committing to launching an ART. The primary focus is on attaining executive buy-in, choosing your first ART, and determining how you will measure success.

Laying the Tracks

In this section we will talk about the considerations when constructing your ART, including guidance for deciding on roles and the teams, and the system of people around the train with the goal of setting the launch date!

Preparing the Cargo

Before the Agile Release Train can be launched, we need to create, refine, and prioritise the work. This section will help you understand the taxonomy of requirements in SAFe and approaches to decomposing the work so that it is ready for Program Increment Planning.

Setting the Timetable for the Train

With your train defined and your cargo ready, it is time to schedule the cadence-based events that will keep your train on the track after launch.

All Aboard!

It's finally here! It is time to launch the train! We will deep dive on how to prepare for the big dance that is Program Increment Planning. We will share how to get your people ready for this event by focusing on team formation and role specific training. We will provide guidance on logistics as well as a step-by-step guide to facilitating the event itself, including many tips and tricks we have learned over the years.

Staying on the Tracks

The train has left the station! So, now what? In this section we talk about the operational rhythms to keep the train healthy including the designing a Kanban system, facilitating SAFe ceremonies and our own operational learnings. At the end of this section you would have completed one full Program Increment (PI)[21].

SAFe® Travels

Well, you've done it. You've launched your Agile Release Train and completed some number of PIs! Here are some final thoughts from us to keep you pointed in the right direction.

Just a few more things to talk about before we send you on your way. We have chosen to use the term Sprint rather than Iteration. While SAFe moved from using Sprint to Iteration in 4.0 we have found the term Sprint to be the more common vernacular.

If you enjoyed this book, please consider providing a review on Amazon and/or Goodreads. The number of reviews and ratings on Amazon have a huge impact on the reputation of a book.

You can also join the conversation on LinkedIn at The ART of Avoiding a Train Wreck Community of Practice: http://bit.ly/TrainWreckCoP

All aboard! Please keep your hands and feet inside the book at all times ...

---

[21] For more information on Program Increments check out: https://scaledagileframework.com/program-increment/ (Accessed 22 September 2019)

PART 1

TICKET TO RIDE

So, you think you want to launch an Agile Release Train? But do you really? Are you ready? Are you REALLY ready? Let's find out!

Before you can launch an Agile Release Train you will need to determine which train to launch. For an organisation of less than one hundred people, this is likely to be fairly straightforward as there will probably only be one ART! For most other organisations working out where to start can be more complicated.

The official Implementation Roadmap from the folks at Scaled Agile Inc[22] (SAI) outlines a typical adoption pattern for the Scaled Agile Framework,[23] where step three is "Identify Values Streams and ARTs." (See Figure 2) In my experience an organisation takes one of two paths when travelling this roadmap: they either follow the steps roughly as outlined or they jump straight to "Prepare to Launch"! There is no right or wrong approach here but the path you choose and the steps you travel upon it will have an impact on the success of your ART. It is also important to note that the roadmap is not a "one and done" journey; you will continuously revisit steps on the roadmap as you experiment and learn.

---

[22] The providers of the Scaled Agile Framework (SAFe): https://www.scaledagile.com/about/about-us/ (Accessed 9 April 2019).
[23] Richard Knaster, *SAFe Distilled*, p. 234.

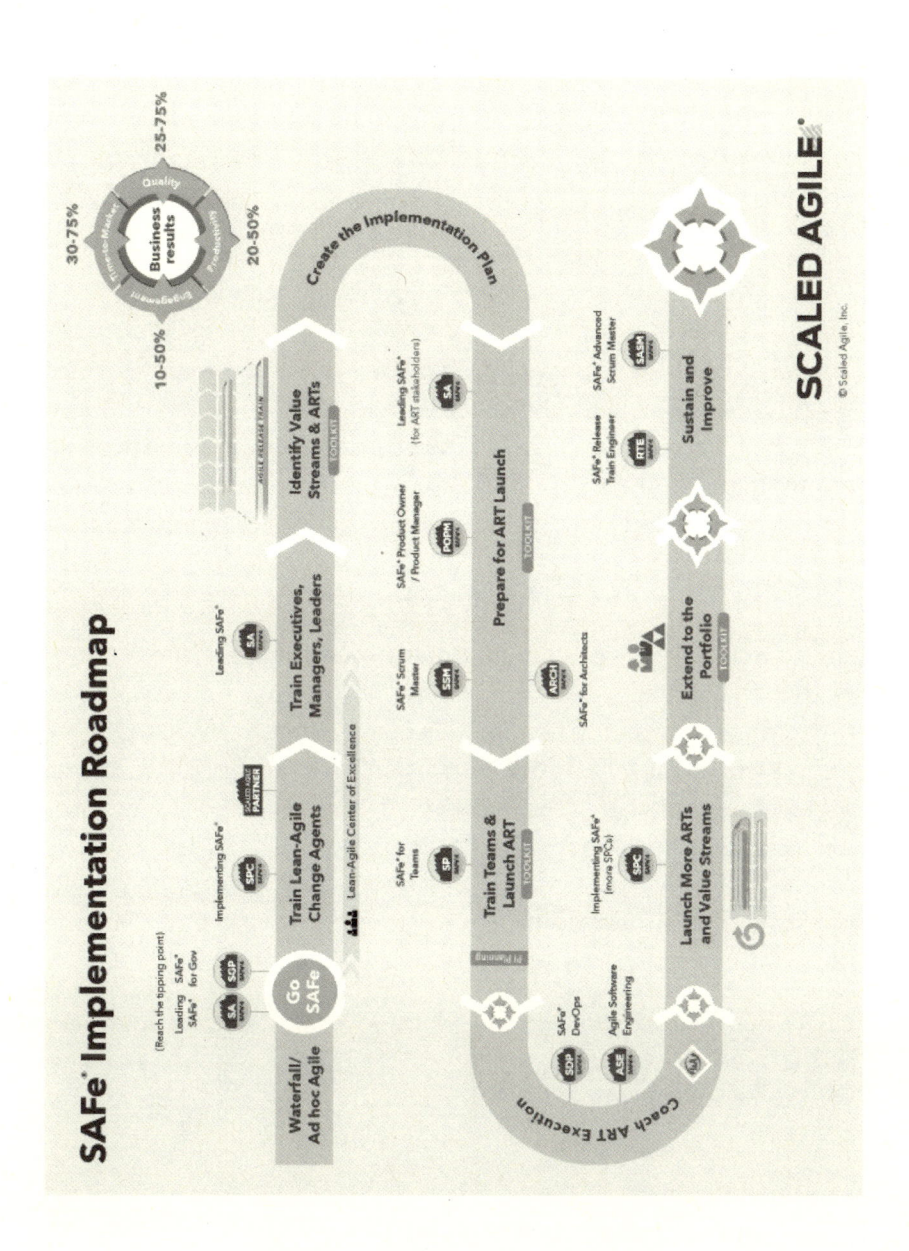

Figure 2 - The SAFe Implementation Roadmap[24]

---

[24] See: https://www.scaledagileframework.com/implementation-roadmap/ (Accessed 7 April 2019).

Going All In

The first path is perhaps less typical and more idealistic. Some influential senior executive inside the organisation wakes up one morning and declares to all and sundry, *"We are going SAFe!"* followed by the battlefield cry, *"CHARGE!"*

This influential senior executive was most likely inspired by a *Leading SAFe* class, an article they read on the internet, or some top-tier consulting company. With any luck they then seek out an experienced SAFe Program Consultant (SPC)[25] and/or a Scaled Agile Partner[26] to help them and the broader organisation navigate the roadmap.[27] Then they make their first critical move to invite the CEO and their Leadership Team to attend a *Leading SAFe* class.

Leading SAFe® for the C-Suite

At this point, many of you (and many of my clients) have decided we are completely nuts. Perhaps you are asking, "What CEO in the **real world** is going to take a *Leading SAFe* class? What CEO in the **real world** can take two days out of their schedule to attend a *Leading SAFe* class?" My response: *"... one that recognises they have a moral obligation to understand how they are asking their organisation to change before inflicting that change upon the organisation."* The shadow of a leader is transparent; if they do not go to training, people won't see it as important either.

I have had many organisations ask me over the years to conduct a shorter, special executive briefing to cover the bases of SAFe because the executives can't possibly find two days to attend *Leading SAFe*.

---

[25] To learn more about the SAFe Program Consultant certification check out: https://www.scaledagile.com/certification/courses/implementing-safe/ (Accessed 15 June 2019).
[26] See: https://www.scaledagile.com/find-a-partner/ (Accessed 15 June 2019).
[27] Is it just me or would subway map be a more apt name for an approach to launching trains?

Ticket to Ride

> **Em's Anecdote**
> In a time before there was a *SAFe Executive Workshop*, I had a client convince me to give their executive team a two-hour briefing on SAFe to "tide them over" until they could schedule a two-day *Leading SAFe* class. I walked them through *SAFe Foundations*[28] and answered their questions as best I could in the time box. About half the attendees followed through on their promise to attend *Leading SAFe*. One of the executives that didn't told a LACE[29] member they did not need to attend the class as "Em" had given them a special, shorter briefing. 🐧 Safe to say, I never made this mistake again.

> **Darren's Anecdote**
> *"Darren, you have clearly not read my name badge; I am a very important person and I haven't got time to come to your two-day training class! Plus, I wouldn't be where I am today if I didn't already have the 'training.' For heaven's sake, I'm a senior exec!!"* Then I came across someone who was the most senior person in a government organisation and said this in his New Year's Message:
> *There are three core ingredients for successful change but most importantly a learning culture including the leadership, where those with the most influence must do as much, or more, learning than anyone else.*
> Priceless—use his quote all the time.

---

[28] This has been superseded by the Introducing SAFe® 4.6 PowerPoint https://www.scaledagileframework.com/videos-and-presentations/ (Accessed 15 June 2019).

[29] LACE stands for Lean-Agile Centre of Excellence. To learn more, see: https://www.scaledagileframework.com/lace/ (Accessed 15 June 2019).

The folks at Scaled Agile provide the *SAFe Executive Workshop*[30] toolkit to SPCs for this exact scenario. This workshop is designed to help the organisation reach the "tipping point."[31] However, in our view, this workshop is constructed as a catalyst to help executive teams appreciate that they can't learn the framework in a few hours and therefore they need to make time to attend a *Leading SAFe* class!

These days if we are pushed for a "special briefing" we offer the *SAFe Executive Workshop* as an option. Accompanied by the following caveat: *"The SAFe Executive Workshop is designed to convince your executive team to commit to taking the two-day Leading SAFe class. Are you sure you want to ask your time-poor executive team to spend half a day with us, so that I can convince them that they need to spend two more days with us?"* Much to my surprise, some folks answer this question with a yes. The end result being the executive team does both the half day "briefing" and then agrees to attend *Leading SAFe*!

While not every CEO in every organisation I have worked with has taken a *Leading SAFe* course, many have. I think the best response we have ever had to the question of making time was the CEO that said to us, *"If I can find two days to sit on a plane to travel to a business meeting I can find two days for this."* Whether you get the CEO and their leadership team in the room or not, there is one thing that is for sure: the breadth and success of your SAFe transformation will be determined by the span of influence of the most senior brought-in leader in the organisation.

Occasionally, the resistance to this *Leading SAFe* class for the executives doesn't come from the executives themselves, but

---

[30] The SAFe Executive Workshop is available to SAFe Program Consultants via the SAFe Community portal https://www.scaledagile.com/spc-resources/ (Accessed 15 June 2019).

[31] To learn more about Reaching the Tipping Point with SAFe check out: https://www.scaledagileframework.com/reaching-the-tipping-point/ (Accessed 29 August 2019).

from people who work for them and have taken the class. Many are horrified that we would dare to suggest an executive team take such a detailed class. In our experience, with the right facilitators, *Leading SAFe* can hold its own at almost any level of the organisation.

The key is getting the right people in the room. A C-Suite attending this class as a team will have a very different experience than a group of frontline leaders, because they bring a different perspective to the classroom, asking different questions of both the instructors and their peer group. *Leading SAFe* is about starting the change process and doing this as a group can have a massive impact.

> **Caution! Potential Train Wreck Ahead!**
> It is important to choose wisely when selecting the instructor(s) for this executive *Leading SAFe* class. You will likely only get one shot at this. I once had a client contact me to ask my advice on accepting free *Leading SAFe* training from one of their incumbent vendors. The vendor in question was not a Scaled Agile Partner and had little to no experience with SAFe. I suggested that no one gives away anything valuable for free and that in their shoes I would respectfully decline the offer. After all, the true cost of training is never the instructors, it is the cost of putting the executive team in a room for two days!
>
> As is often the way with these things, they ignored my ironically free advice and proceeded with the "free" training. A number of months later, we were engaged to launch an ART at this same organisation. When we met with the ART's stakeholders many of them were quick to tell us about the awful "free" SAFe training that they had been made to sit through.
>
> In an unexpected twist, some of the ART's stakeholders chose to do the class again with us. The resulting excitement was infectious, and the message spread quickly that our training was

The ART of Avoiding a Train Wreck

different. A number of executives followed suit and came to our classes, but others just weren't willing to give up another two days. Unfortunately, what had been done could not be undone. Our sponsors had used up all their political capital getting executives to attend the "free" class.

Protip
A question we get asked a lot is how do you find the right instructor? One approach that we find our clients use is to "test drive" the trainer by attending one of their public SAFe classes before you put them in front of your executive team.

The other consideration when weighing up the value of getting executives to join a *Leading SAFe* class is how their attendance, or lack thereof, will be perceived by the broader organisation. As SAFe is rolled out to the organisation, *Leading SAFe* will be delivered time and time again. In each class the instructors will share the *SAFe Implementation Roadmap* and the importance of Lean-Agile Leaders being lifelong learners.[32] Inevitably the class will ask *"Have our leaders taken this class?"* How would you like the *Leading SAFe* instructors at your organisation to answer this question? Honestly, we hope!

Em's Anecdote
When it comes to displays of leadership following a *Leading SAFe class*, the business executive that had never heard of "scum"[33] before takes the cake.[34] Not only did she take the class, and learn about Scrum, but she also took the exam and proudly

---

[32] Richard Knaster, *SAFe Distilled*, p35.
[33] I think she meant Scrum!
[34] For those outside the US to "take the cake" is to be the most outstanding in some respect, either the best or the worst.

displayed her *SAFe Agilist*[35] certificate in her office. Oh boy, did that create a buzz in the organisation!

Michael's Anecdote

I once had a C-Level executive and their direct reports spend two days in *Leading SAFe* directly followed by a one day *Value Stream Workshop*[36]. The C-Level executive made it mandatory for all direct reports to attend. The first morning of *Leading SAFe*, the message spread in the organisation that the leadership team is attending a two-day training and that this is a serious initiative that is backed by the leadership team up to the top.

Perhaps the most important reason to get the enterprise's most senior executives into a *Leading SAFe* class is that we need them to participate in identifying the organisation's value streams and *Leading SAFe* provides them with the base knowledge and the principles by which to do this. In line with SAFe guidance we like to spend a day with the executive leadership group immediately following *Leading SAFe* to agree how value flows through the organisation. We then subsequently define and prioritise the value streams and the potential ARTs.[37]

---

[35] This is the certification that Scaled Agile Inc. provides to those who have both taken a *Leading SAFe* class and passed the *SAFe Agilist* exam.
[36] For more information on the Value Stream Identification Workshop check out:https://scaledagileframework.com/identify-value-streams-and-arts/ (accessed 22 September 2019)
[37] SAFe Program Consultants can use the SAFe Value Stream and ART Identification Toolkit to facilitate this workshop: https://www.scaledagile.com/spc-resources/ (Accessed 15 June 2019).

> **Protip**
> If you do manage to schedule a *Leading SAFe* class with an executive team and find that you have a handful of "spare seats" it's best not to allocate them to Scrum Masters or Project Managers or anyone not part of this peer group. This will constrain the conversation as there will be some questions and debates that the executives (quite rightly) won't want to have outside their peer group.

Identifying the Value Streams

The standard *SAFe Value Stream and ART Identification Workshop*[38] takes the organisation's leaders on a journey that starts with acknowledging the existing silos and identifying the operational value streams.[39] Executive participation is fundamental to achieving an aligned outcome here. The next step in the workshop is to get a more detailed understanding of the operational value streams, so that we can see the people that do the work, the systems that they use, and the flow of information. Once we see the systems, we can identify the people who build, enhance, support, and maintain the systems, thereby identifying the development value stream(s). If the development value stream contains in excess of 125 people, we then split the value streams into multiple Agile Release Trains.

---

[38] SPCs in good standing can download the toolkit for the *SAFe Value Stream and ART Identification Workshop* from: https://community.scaledagile.com (Accessed 15 August 2019).

[39] To learn more about identifying value streams check out: https://www.scaledagileframework.com/identify-value-streams-and-arts/ (Accessed 19 June 2019).

> **Protip**
> At the start of the *Value Stream Workshop* identify the goal the organisation wants to achieve. Alignment and transparency on the goal(s) is as important as alignment and transparency in the execution. Once the goal(s) are agreed you will also want to understand how they measure it and then baseline it to show the progress of the change. Having the goals identified at the beginning will also help and guide the discussion about the Value Streams.

> **Michael's Anecdote**
> In one *Value Stream Workshop* the group declared that they did not need to discuss the goal as everyone was clear that the goal was "Time to Market." I asked for five minutes and split the room into smaller groups and every group had to write down their definition of "Time to Market." Every group had a completely different understanding of what it meant, how to measure it, where they were at that point, and where they wanted to go.

The key to success is getting the right participants in the room without having so many participants you can't get anything done.[40] You need people who know:

- How the business works operationally, the people who operate the business and the systems they use
- The technology landscape, what systems support what operational processes, and how those systems fit together
- The names of the specific people who develop, support, and maintain the systems.

---

[40] While the largest group we have done this with was up over thirty people, 12 or less is what we usually aim for.

This will probably be a combination of executives, middle managers, frontline managers, and a variety of architects. In larger organisations this is likely to be a lot of people. For example, when running a *Value Stream Identification Workshop* with a group of executives in a large organisation, it is unlikely they will be able to talk to specific systems and individuals. That level of detail is rarely at an executive's fingertips. If you do end up with a large group consider splitting the workshop so that the first one is focused on defining and prioritising the value streams and the second session is focused on splitting the priority value streams into ARTs, prioritising the ART(s), and laying out the initial implementation plan. As was the case with the executive team the participants in the second Value Stream and ART Identification Workshop should also take a Leading SAFe class before the workshop.

> **Em's Anecdote**
> The more I do this the more I understand why Mike Rother and John Shook titled their book on value streams *Learning to See*.[41] Organisations are always surprised by these visualisations. One client identified approximately five hundred people working across 60+ systems when mapping one of their value streams and concluded: *"No wonder we can't deliver anything* (See Figure 3)."

---

[41] Mike Rother and John Shook, *Learning to See: Value Stream Mapping to Create Value and Eliminate Muda*, (Brookline: The Lean Enterprise Institute, 1999).

Figure 3 - A five-hundred-person, 60-system Value Stream

For larger value streams the above pattern is repeated at the ART level until we can see the specific named individuals that work on the development value stream. Our goal is to leave the workshop knowing which ART we will start with and when we want to launch it. We also like to have agreed on the ART's Business Owners,[42] know the specific names, location, and skill sets of the people who do the work, and have identified candidates for the key ART roles of Release Train Engineer,[43] Product Manager,[44] and the System

---

[42] To learn more about the Business Owner role in SAFe check out: https://www.scaledagileframework.com/business-owners/ (Accessed 7 April 2019).

[43] To learn more about the Release Train Engineer role in SAFe check out: https://www.scaledagileframework.com/release-train-engineer-and-solution-train-engineer/ (Accessed 19 June 2019).

[44] To learn more about the Product Manager role in SAFe check out: https://www.scaledagileframework.com/product-and-solution-management/ (Accessed 19 June 2019).

Architect.[45] We like to refer to these three ART Leaders as the Trifecta, or as one client likes to call them, "the power of three."[46]

> **Protip**
> When choosing which ART to start with, I like the advice Dean Leffingwell gave my SPC class: *"Find the worst-performing part of the organisation and start there. If you manage to make an impact there, then the rest of the organisation will sit up and take notice."* I also like to think that if it is truly broken you probably can't make it any worse, so it is the safe choice (pun intended!).

> **Caution! Potential Train Wreck Ahead!**
> Some larger companies (e.g. Fortune 50) seriously struggle with right-sized ARTs as most have hundreds and sometimes thousands of people working on large solutions and have such trouble finding enough people to guide the dozen ARTs they should have that they end up choosing ARTs in the 200 –400 people range. They are trapped by their bias (and sometimes what the consulting firms have convinced them) that more people are better when sometimes taking one hundred people "out of an ART" would result in better outcomes and faster flow. I know of at least one instance in which "sub trains" spontaneously emerged out of a 20+ team ART.

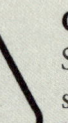

---

[45] To learn more about the System Architect role in SAFe check out: https://www.scaledagileframework.com/system-and-solution-architect-engineering/ (Accessed 19 June 2019).

[46] We have also heard the Trifecta referred to as: the Troika, Triad (although in many parts of the world this is the name of an organised crime syndicate!), the Holy Trinity, the holy triad (apparently this plays well in Sweden as they are "so secular") and the triforce (from the Zelda games).

The Right ART for Right Now

The second and, in our experience, far more common path organisations take on their first journey down the SAFe implementation roadmap is when a single leader wakes up one morning and decides they are going to solve the woes of their department or program with an Agile Release Train!

This often results in the ART not being aligned to the value stream or perhaps representing only a portion of the value stream.[47] According to the Scaled Agile Framework: *"Value Streams represent the series of steps that an organization uses to build Solutions that provide a continuous flow of value to a customer."*[48] There are many SAFe enthusiasts that are diametrically opposed to ARTs that are not value stream aligned. Personally, I am a little more pragmatic.

The Scaled Agile Framework talks about two types of ARTs: a feature area ART and a subsystem ART. Feature area ARTs are generally value stream aligned while subsystem ARTs are generally aligned to applications or platforms.[49] While the value stream aligned ART is unparalleled in its ability to decrease time to value, it is not without its perils. Most value stream aligned ARTs will require buy in from multiple department heads as the value stream crosses many organisational silos. Which means the people and teams for the ART will be sourced from those multiple departments.

---

[47] For more information on identifying Value Streams and potential ARTs go to: https://www.scaledagileframework.com/identify-value-streams-and-arts/ (Accessed 7 April 2019).
[48] See: https://www.scaledagileframework.com/glossary/#V (Accessed 15 June 2019).
[49] See: https://www.scaledagileframework.com/identify-value-streams-and-arts/ (Accessed 22 August 2019).

> **⚠ Caution! Potential Train Wreck Ahead!**
>
> I have on more than one occasion witnessed a perfect value stream aligned ART fall to pieces because the ART was designed by one department head in isolation. When it came time for other departments to contribute teams to the ART their managers flatly refused. This almost always seems to result in the ART hiring additional people with the missing skill sets so that they can deliver on their mission, which tends to create system integrity issues in due course.
>
> Of course, a *Leading SAFe* class attended by all the department heads potentially impacted by an ART followed by a joint Value Stream and ART Identification Workshop would go a long way to avoiding this sort of problem.

In some cases, the ART you have the political cover to launch may not be aligned to a value stream and that is perfectly okay in most circumstances. For example, if you can form cross-functional teams within the constraints of your own organisation and those teams can deliver meaningful value to real users, who am I to argue? After all, I started with an ART aligned to an Enterprise Data Warehouse, which I think we can all agree was a more technology aligned than value stream aligned approach. However, these teams must at a minimum have a shared mission or some reason to collaborate.

In *Project to Product*, Mik Kersten suggests that the key to identifying value streams is having a well-defined customer and that the customer could be an external or internal user of the product. He goes on to state, "Value streams are composed of all of the activities, stakeholders, processes, and tools required to deliver business value to the customer." This includes business stakeholders and support teams.

> **Em's Anecdote**
> One organisation we have delivered a number of SAFe classes for created their ARTs off the back of an organisational restructure that was not in any way value stream aligned. In fairness they were doing the best they could with the hand they had been dealt but the result was a bunch of teams with no interdependencies struggling to find value in ART events like the System Demo. Meanwhile, the dependencies between the ARTs made their solution board "look like a spider web"!

> **Caution! Potential Train Wreck Ahead!**
> If you choose to launch a subsystem ART, it is important that you proceed with your eyes wide open. First, consider if your ARTs customer is a system rather than people and if so try and look for an alternative. For example, ARTs consisting solely of API[50] or ESB[51] teams will struggle without a connection to a user or a customer. It's hard to hold a story writing workshop when you don't understand why you are building something or why it's important, let alone trying to write "user stories" from the perspective of an inanimate object! If your circumstances still dictate this is the only option, then so be it.
>
> Second, be prepared for your ART to be dismantled in the future. Should your ART be wildly successful it will likely spark broader organisation interest in SAFe! Hopefully this leads to the design of more value stream aligned ARTs. These new ARTs will likely need team(s) from your ART, potentially resulting in your original ART ceasing to exist. Knowing this, will you be prepared to let the teams go?

---

[50] API stands for Application Program Interface.
[51] ESB stands for Enterprise Service Bus.

> **Protip**
> When the technical integrity of the system itself is critical, or in need of attention, a subsystem centric ART may be a better choice. For example, when there is a lot of technical debt or a lack of clear architectural guidelines, creating a subsystem centric ART with strong feature teams (teams that can deliver any feature[52] on the subsystem) is a good choice. It certainly presents less of a risk to the structural integrity of the (sub)system in the short term. It creates a path whereby when the time is right you have technically capable feature teams that can join feature-aligned ARTs with less risk. In this move, those feature teams on the subsystem centric ART would now look like component teams on a feature-oriented ART. Over time you should look to cross-skill the folks on these component teams to the point that you can reshape the teams on the ART into feature teams.

Start where you are and evolve to feature teams

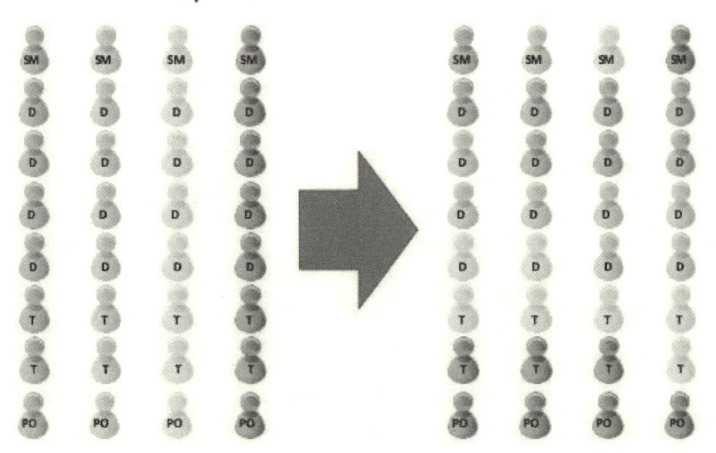

Figure 4 - Start with component teams, focus on cross-skilling within these teams then move to feature teams later.

---

[52] To learn more about Features in SAFe check out: https://www.scaledagileframework.com/features-and-capabilities (Accessed 31 August 2019).

SAFe in a Project Driven World

One struggle many organisations have when launching their first Agile Release Train, is access to value stream funding.[53] If you can't get agreement for this can you still launch an ART? In my view, absolutely. It may not be the most strategic ART, but it may well be the "right ART for right now".

A challenge that the project funded ART might encounter is the stability of funding. Projects are notorious for lump sum funding. Teams are ramped up and ramped down on demand, making maintaining persistent teams impossible. One way to address this it to have your PMO or finance team to do some analytics on the average labour spend on the system(s) related to the ART over the last few years. This number is often very similar year on year. You can then use this data to reverse engineer what size train you need to be able to deliver on a yearly program of work of x million dollars.

The other approach I have used to solve for this is to quite simply start with where you are. Form the train based on the current workforce and see how you go. Whichever approach you use resist the urge to add or remove teams every time you get under pressure to deliver or the work looks to be drying up. Remember stability is the goal here.

Another variant of the project funded ART is when the project (or program) is the Agile Release Train. This tends to occur when someone has a multi-million-dollar, multi-year program of work that they want to deliver using agile. Stable funding can be less of a challenge here as the Project (or Program) is probably funded. However, you will need to make sure the spend profile is not pre-defined as a slow ramp up, a huge workforce at the peak followed by a slow ramp down.

---

[53] To learn funding Value Streams with SAFe check out: https://www.scaledagileframework.com/lean-budgets/ (Accessed 30 August 2019)

Regardless of whether your approach to SAFe is "go all in" or just "the right ART for right now," everyone starts with an ART and that is what we hope to help you do with this book.

Before You Buy Your Ticket

Just one more, well, maybe two more things before you buy your ticket for the Scaled Agile Railway. You need to know your why, your driver for change and what you hope to achieve. It can be very hard to motivate people to change if they can't see the reason for it. Is your goal to improve time to market? Or do you hope to improve morale? Or perhaps the quality of your product is your primary concern? If you are struggling to answer this question, another approach is to think about what hurts. Ask yourself, where is the pain? Pain is often a motivation for change.

Empathy Interviews

To help the executive team concretise their case for change we conduct empathy interviews. These are short 1:1 sessions with the executives that head up the business units, functional silos, Enterprise PMO, support organisations, etc. The goal is to attain an appreciation of the challenges the organisation is facing, confirmation from the Leaders that they see and feel these challenges, and their aspirations for SAFe. Ideally these sessions will take place before the executive *Leading SAFe* class, enabling you to help the organisation create connections between the problems they are facing and the opportunity that SAFe offers to address these challenges.

Some examples of the types of questions we ask include:

- ❏ What **goal(s)** are you hoping that SAFe will help your organisation achieve?
- ❏ What do you hope to **accomplish** by implementing SAFe and/or launching an Agile Release Train?
- ❏ What **problems** are you hoping SAFe/the ART will address?
- ❏ What **benefits** are you hoping to achieve by using SAFe/launching an ART?

❏ What **organisational issues** are you hoping to address with SAFe/the ART?
❏ What is the **current situation** in the organisation?
❏ What is the **future state** you desire?[54]

Understanding how the organisation hopes to improve also informs what metrics should be baselined and tracked.

Baseline Metrics Before You Start

If you do nothing else before you start this journey—baseline your metrics! At some point in the not-too-distant future you are going to be asked, how do you know your Agile Release Train is making a difference? For you the answer might be obvious—it just feels better. It was very much that way for me with my first ART. Metrics weren't the first indicator that things were better, it was the changes in behaviour.

> **Aaron's Anecdote**
> For me, this has been one of my biggest learnings over the past few years. If you do not baseline your metrics, when the ART hits a tough spot in terms of delivery, technical challenges, etc. I find that it's all too easy for people who are not 100% bought in to the change to say, *"It's SAFe's fault that we aren't delivering."* If I had got the baseline metrics earlier, then I could dispel the myth quickly by showing the tangible improvements! It also keeps the transformation team focused on the key things to improve—the goal is not to "be really good at SAFe," it's to improve quality, time to market, etc.!

---

[54] Adapted from: Jean Tabaka, *Collaboration Explained: Facilitation Skills for Software Project Leaders*. (Upper Saddle River: Pearson Education, 2006). Kindle Edition. Location 2228.

> **Em's Anecdote**
>
> When I first took over the EDW delivery organisation, my days were spent dealing with escalations, trying to drum up work for my teams, and trying to stem the tide of staff exits. I knew SAFe was making a difference when my phone stopped ringing off the hook with escalated complaints about not delivering, demand started to increase, and people were queuing up to join the team, not exit it!
>
> The other really telling behaviour change was when our sponsors lost interest in holding monthly governance meetings. Apparently if you are delivering on your commitments governance meetings are less interesting to executives! Perhaps the most obvious observable change that gave me confidence that we were getting better was the delivery of working software! In the context of my first train this was nothing short of a miracle!

While the changes in behaviour I observed were enough to convince me we were making a difference, management will always want metrics.

Below are some of the metrics we like to use when launching Agile Release Trains, many of which you may recognise as also being recommended in the Scaled Agile Framework article on metrics.[55]

Employee Net Promoter Score (eNPS)

The Employee Net Promoter Score (eNPS)[56] is part of the Net Promoter System (NPS).[57] NPS is a customer loyalty measurement

---

[55] You can find the SAFe guidance on metrics at: https://www.scaledagileframework.com/metrics/ (Accessed 18 June 2019).

[56] To learn more about the Employee Net Promoter Score http://www.netpromotersystem.com/about/employee-engagement.aspx (Accessed 18 June 2019).

[57] To learn more about the Net Promoter System check out: http://www.netpromotersystem.com/ (Accessed 29 August 2019).

identified by Fred Reichheld and some folks at Bain. When understanding drivers of customer loyalty, they determined that: *"Very few companies can achieve or sustain high customer loyalty without a cadre of loyal, engaged employees."*

Employee NPS is measured by asking the question: "On a scale of 0 to 10, where 0 is not at all likely and 10 is extremely likely, how likely are you to recommend working on [insert ART name] to a friend or colleague?" Those who answer 9 or 10 are classified as promoters, those who respond 7 or 8 are classified as passives and those who respond with a 6 or below are classified as detractors. The eNPS score is calculated by subtracting the percentage of detractors from the percentage of promoters.[58] You should be expecting eNPS to increase as a result of launching your ART.

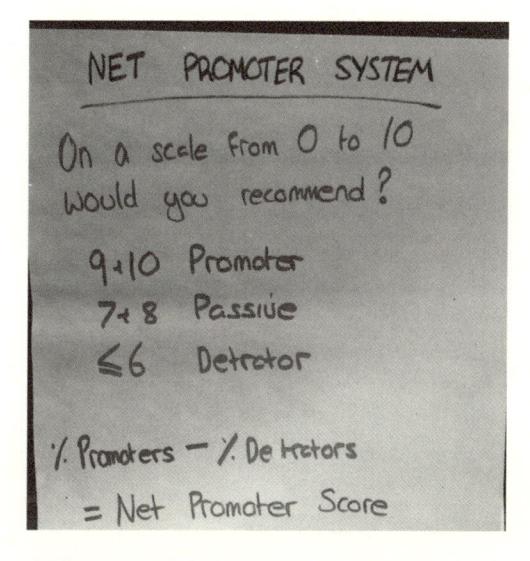

Figure 5 – Calculating the Net Promotor Score

---

[58] You can find my template for capturing eNPS in *Tribal Unity*. (see Location 1314 in the Kindle Edition)

Case Study:
Measuring Team Happiness

When I accepted the role leading the EDW delivery team, I knew my biggest challenge was going to be customer engagement. As you know I had been an unhappy customer of the EDW delivery team for a number of years. I was going to have to change the business perception of our ability to deliver if we were going to survive.

I came across the idea of employees NPS (eNPS) when researching the Net Promoter System (NPS). Having worked in market and customer research in a previous life, my curiosity had been sparked by my employer's adoption of NPS. My research led me to the book behind the Net Promoter System, Fred Reichheld's *The Ultimate Question 2.0*.[59] In reading the book the message that spoke to me the loudest was *"You can't create loyal customers without first creating loyal employees."*[60] Or as I like to phrase it: "Happy teams lead to happy customers."

The companies referenced in the book asked their employees: *"On a scale of zero to ten, how likely is it you would recommend this company (or this store) as a place to work?"* followed by an open-ended question like *"What are the primary reasons for your score?"* This made a stark contrast to the 70-question yearly Employee Engagement Surveys (EES) I was used to my employer sending out. In addition to being long and infrequent, they were also incomplete as only permanent staff were invited to participate.

Inspired by what I had read I launched my quarterly team eNPS survey, with a simple three-question questionnaire administered via SurveyMonkey. The results were nothing short

---

[59] Fred Reichheld, T*he Ultimate Question 2.0: How Net Promoter Companies Thrive in a Customer-Driven World*, (Boston: Harvard Business Review Press, 2011).
[60] Reichheld, T*he Ultimate Question 2.0*, p. 126.

> of phenomenal. In 18 months, we moved from -49 to +53. The real value in eNPS is not so much the numerical score as it is the feedback to the open-ended question. Sometimes it will be confronting, sometimes it will be exceedingly pleasing. The key is to learn from it.[61]

Employee Retention

This is a rather traditional metric that your HR people probably already have and track. Keep an eye on it as retention should stabilise and then start to increase as your ART becomes better with the new way of working. If this doesn't happen, it is often a sign that something is not quite right with your ART. It might also be interesting to compare retention in parts of the organisation using ARTs versus those that are not.[62]

Stakeholder Net Promoter Score (NPS)

This is my take on NPS for the stakeholders[63] of your ART. We use the same approach as outlined in eNPS, but this time the question is *"On a scale of 0 to 10, where 0 is not at all likely and 10 is extremely likely, how likely are you to recommend the delivery services of [insert ART name] to a friend or colleague?"* You should also expect to see this go up over time.

---

[61] Adapted from: http://blog.prettyagile.com.au/2013/11/measuring-team-happiness.html (Accessed 23 August 2019).
[62] Thanks, Candy Durfee, for the inspiration for this one.
[63] We use the term stakeholder here as many organisations don't consider internal customers to be customers. Ideally, we would not need to make this distinction. For more on this topic check out Chris Matts' blog post: There are no stakeholders in (Scaled) Agile: https://theitriskmanager.com/2019/07/28/there-are-no-stakeholders-in-scaled-agile/ (Accessed 29 July 2019).

Feature Lead Time

Once you have your ART(s) up and running you should be able to capture lead time[64] for features,[65] where lead time is calculated as the total time from when the train first receives the feature to the time when the features is deployed to production. When we launch ARTs, we usually create a Program Kanban system[66] to visualise the flow of feature through the ART (this will be covered in more detail later). If you track the flow of the features through the Kanban this will give you lead time data. You should expect to see lead time decrease once your ART has been up and running for a while.

Baselining lead time might be challenging as you probably don't have features at the beginning of your SAFe journey. In this case, my advice is to measure the lead time of your current equivalent. Another way I have seen this done is by mapping the development value stream. This can be done very informally by taking a pencil and a sheet of A3 paper and walking the process.[67] Noting the steps, the time they take to execute and the wait times between each step. You can then revisit this map periodically, updating it and hopefully showing a reduction in cycle time. Alternatively, the *SAFe DevOps* class[68] includes this exercise and/or Karen Martin's book *Value Stream Mapping*[69] provides a detailed workshop guide.

---

[64] While historically we used to use the term cycle time for this, we have found that everyone has a different definition of cycle time, so we decided to use the term lead time instead as this seems less controversial.
[65] To learn more about features in SAFe check out: https://www.scaledagileframework.com/features-and-capabilities/ (Accessed 18 June 2019).
[66] You can learn more about this at: http://blog.prettyagile.com.au/2015/03/leaning-into-safe-with-feature-flow.html (Accessed 22 July 2019).
[67] Mary Poppendieck and Tom Poppendieck, *Lean Software Development: An Agile Toolkit*, (Addison-Wesley, 2003) p. 11.
[68] To Learn more about the *SAFe DevOps* class check out: https://www.scaledagile.com/certification/courses/safe-devops/ (Accessed 22 July 2019).
[69] Karen Martin and Mike Osterling, *Value Stream Mapping: How to Visualize Work and Align Leadership for Organization Transformation*, (McGraw-Hill Education, 2013).

Frequency of Release or Deployment

This one looks at how frequently you deliver outcomes to your customers. Often articulated as frequency in a period, e.g. once a year, or twice a quarter, etc. For many traditional organisations this is dictated by the enterprise release cycle. Depending on your context, you might need to make the DevOps distinction between deploying to the end target versus releasing to your customer. In some instances, your customer may not appreciate frequent releases, or it may not make sense in your context (e.g. releasing to an aircraft is very different than releasing to a website). But you should expect to see one or both of these increase in frequency.

> **Aaron's Anecdote**
> This is my favourite metric! I have found that by focusing on this you start to improve so many other things around it. Teams worry that if we release more frequently, then we need to improve the quality, then they worry about the length of time for regression, so they automate, then they worry about the length of time to deploy and release, so they get support to tackle CAB[70], etc. It's a great metric to promote other great behaviours.

Escaped Defects

This is a count of defects that make it to production, or "escape" your system. While there are lots of different ways you could approach this, I find tracking of production found defects to be more objective than tracking defects in non-production code. These can also be easier to track as when a customer finds a defect there is usually a ticketing system that the defect is logged in. Two common approaches are to capture the number per release or the number per PI. You should expect to see this decrease.

---

[70] CAB stands for Change Approval Board

> **Caution! Potential Train Wreck Ahead!**
> In a code base with a lot of technical debt,[71] you may find that your identification of defects increases in your early PIs as teams become more disciplined about recording defects they find while working on new features. While ideally these defects would have been fixed as they were discovered, we have a view that if a defect will require enough work that it will impact the specific feature or sprint objectives being worked on at the time then teams should choose to record the defect for future prioritisation. This way the entire team can see the defect and the Product Owner can make a responsible decision about prioritising it while maintaining balance for the committed prioritised objectives.

Test Automation

If your Agile Release Train is software or hardware related, then you will want to baseline your level of test automation. This is your total number of automated tests as a percentage of your total number of tests (manual and automated). Some organisations will start with a zero and may take some time to get started with test automation but keeping it visible on your list of metrics will help bring focus. Of course, we are looking to have the percentage of automated tests increase over time due to both the creation of automated tests and the removal of manual tests.

---

[71] To understand more about Technical Debt, check out: https://en.wikipedia.org/wiki/Technical_debt (Accessed 24 August 2019).

> **Caution! Potential Train Wreck Ahead!**
> We have seen organisations take up a pattern where automating tests happens in the sprint after a story is implemented or, there is a dedicated automation team which is responsible for automating everything. Both patterns have challenges. For the first one, you are building technical debt every sprint and have to burn it down in the next. For the second scenario, the throughput of the train will increase there by building more technical debt that one team can possibly burn down.

A better pattern is for automation skills to be developed in each team so that each team doesn't create more technical debt. We recommend changing the Story and Feature Definition of Done (DoD)[72] so that the automation of tests happens with in the sprint.

Ratio of "Doers" vs "Non-Doers"

Another interesting metric to baseline and track is the percentage of people "doing the work" as a proportion of the people who work in the department. "Doers" tends to be defined as people who define, build, test, and deploy (i.e. Agile teams including the Scrum Masters), making everyone else a "non-doer." You should expect to see the ratio of doers increases.

Market Performance

If your ART is aligned to a Product or Service monetised by your company, you might also find it interesting to baseline the current market performance of that product or service. Some examples include Volume of Sales, Services in Operation, and Market Share. In a similar but perhaps more daring approach the folks at TomTom used Share Price to demonstrate the value of SAFe in the Agile2014

---

[72] To learn more about the Definition of Done in SAFe check out the section on the *Scalable Definition of Done:* https://www.scaledagileframework.com/built-in-quality/ (Accessed 29 August 2019).

presentation *Adopting Scaled Agile Framework (SAFe): The Good, the Bad, and the Ugly.*[73]

Some metrics you won't be able to baseline before you start but you can start tracking once you begin executing your first program increment.

Cost per Story Point

This one will be tricky to baseline prior to launching the ART as you may not be using story points and, if you are, you probably don't use normalised estimation[74] yet. It is, however, worth knowing the labour cost of the ART for a PI and deciding how you will record story point data so you can baseline this at the end of PI1. The idea is that I know the cost of the people working on the ART and I know the historical velocity of the ART and therefore I know the cost per story point.

As simple as all this sounds, there are some nuances that may or may not be material but will certainly make your numbers more defendable. To learn about our approach to calculating Cost per Story Point check out our Cost Per Story Point White Paper: http://bit.ly/CostPerPointWP

> **Caution! Potential Train Wreck Ahead!**
> Do not under any circumstances <u>ever</u> let this be used as a team level metric. I also would not advocate allowing this to be used to compare trains. If nothing else variances in labour costs for different skill sets will make this nonsensical. If you are concerned about misuse report the trend rather than specifics. Remember, if you make this a KPI it will be gamed and then it will become useless.

---

[73] See: https://static.sched.com/hosted_files/agile2014/79/1359_TomTom_Agile_v4.pdf (Accessed 18 June 2019).
[74] To learn more about normalised estimation in SAFe check out: https://www.scaledagileframework.com/iteration-planning/ (Accessed 18 June 2019).

> **Protip**
> Almost any cost-based metric will be difficult to prove, and you will almost certainly be asked how you calculated it. One of the ways I have backed up my assertions with respect to reduced cost per story point is by triangulating that data to see if other approaches to calculating cost reduction yield similar results. One such "test" is to take a "project" or epic that was originally estimated using a traditional or waterfall method and look at the actual costs after delivering it using SAFe. While by no means perfect, it may help support your argument that costs are decreasing.

Program Predictability Measure

In addition to the self-assessments, SAFe offers the Program Predictability Measure[75] as a way to measure agility. Personally, I see this more as a measure of predictability rather than agility, but then again, I don't believe in trying to measure agility!

This seems to be one of the most commonly missed parts of SAFe. To be able to calculate this you need to capture the Business Value of the Team PI Objectives at PI Planning.[76] Sometimes this gets skipped due to time pressure and other times the organisation deliberately skips this as it is perceived as "too subjective." Of course, it is subjective, but I figure this is mitigated by ensuring the people who provide the Business Value at PI Planning are the same people who provide the "actual" value rating as part of the Inspect and Adapt.[77]

---

[75] See the section on *Lean Portfolio Metrics*: https://www.scaledagileframework.com/metrics/ (Accessed 18 June 2019).
[76] To learn more about PI Objectives in SAFe check out: https://www.scaledagileframework.com/pi-objectives/ (Accessed 22 July 2019).
[77] To learn more about Inspect and Adapt in SAFe check out: https://www.scaledagileframework.com/inspect-and-adapt (Accessed 22 July 2019).

> **⚠ Caution! Potential Train Wreck Ahead!**
> The other trap I see organisations fall into is changing the objectives and the business value during the PI, as it is not the team's fault that "the business" changed their mind. Correct! It is also not the team's fault when the system is unpredictable! If you stick to using the objectives from PI Planning the PI Predictability Measures will reflect the health of the entire system—both the team's delivery on commitments and the business's commitment to the process. If you change the objectives, you no longer have a measure of predictability!

Agile Maturity

Armed with all the above metrics, it is my hope that you will be able to avoid the dreaded Agile Maturity metric. Measuring Agile maturity has never made any sense to me. Agility is not the goal! The goal is the delivery of value in the shortest sustainable lead time. In addition to the Program Predictability Measure, SAFe offers the Program and Team Self Assessments as a way to measure agility.[78] The problem with using self-assessments to measure Agile maturity is it destroys the true value of the self-assessment, which for me is in taking the time to reflect and identify areas for improvement (more on this topic later).

As the popular proverb says: "What gets measured, gets done." So, if you turn the self-assessments into a measurement or KPI then I have no doubt your train's Agile maturity will increase on paper, but I am less convinced they will actually be improving. In fact, I have often found that as the team's Agile maturity increases their self-assessment scores decrease as they become more aware of what good looks like!

---

[78] SAFe provides a template for both team and train self-assessments: https://www.scaledagileframework.com/metrics/ - P6 and https://www.scaledagileframework.com/metrics/ - T4 (Accessed 18 June 2019).

So please, whatever you do, don't try and measure Agile maturity and if you must please do not use self-assessments for this purpose. Instead, focus on NPS, cycle time, escaped defects, and test automation. Moving these numbers is a sign you are headed in the right direction.

> **Caution! Potential Train Wreck Ahead!**
> The other metric we recommend avoiding is velocity. This is another example of what gets measured gets done. Velocity is the term used by Agile team to describe the number of story points they delivered in the previous sprint(s). The simplest way for a team to double their velocity is to double their estimates! This is not helpful, especially if we want the team to use velocity for capacity planning (which we do in SAFe!).

As Jeffrey Liker said in *The Toyota Way*: *"It is advisable to keep the number of metrics to a minimum. Remember that tracking metrics takes time away from people doing their work. It is also important ... to discuss the existing metrics and immediately eliminate ones that are superfluous or drive behaviours that are counter to the implementation of the lean future state vision."* [79]

With our first train identified and our metrics baselined it is time to lay down the tracks by designing the teams and key program roles for the Agile Release Train.

---

[79] Jeffrey Liker, *The Toyota Way: 14 Management Principles from the World's Greatest Manufacturer*. (McGraw-Hill Education, 2004), Kindle Edition. Location 5282.

Chapter Summary

In this chapter we explored:

- The trade-off between value stream aligned ARTs and the "right ART for right now";
- The importance of getting executives to attend Leading SAFe training;
- Having clarity on the organisation's motivations for "going SAFe" and approaches to surfacing those reasons;
- Starting the journey to launching an ART with Leading SAFe and the Value Stream and ART Identification Workshop;
- Tips for conducting the Value Stream and ART Identification Workshop and;
- Baselining the current state metrics before we launch the ART and what metrics to avoid.

PART 2
LAYING THE TRACKS

"Train everyone. Launch trains."[80]

---

[80] See: https://www.scaledagileframework.com/train-teams-and-launch-the-art/ (Accessed 11 August 2019).

The first step in launching an Agile Release Train is always the same—a *Leading SAFe* class for the key leaders that will be needed to support the Agile Release Train. As a rule, we look to identify between 12 and 20 leaders from both business and technology to attend this class. Our goal is to create shared understanding of SAFe, it's shared taxonomy and commence the process of joint problem solving. A *Leading SAFe* class delivered face to face and attended by a co-located, cross-functional team is an opportunity to embrace the principles behind the Agile Manifesto.[81] Remember, the teams will always ask *"Did our leaders take this class?"* What better way to respond than to be able to say, *"Yes, as a cross-functional team with their peers from across the organisation!"* This is also a step towards bridging the great divide that often exists between "the business" and "technology."

> **Caution! Potential Train Wreck Ahead**
> There is an all-too-common pattern whereby "IT" wants to "get their ducks in a row" before they include "the business." They take *Leading SAFe* without their business counterparts and sometimes even try to do value stream identification and ART design without them. *"We want to draft it and do the heavy lifting without them because they won't have the patience"* OR *"We do not want them to see the IT messiness."* Honestly, the business already knows IT is messy; they see the lack of delivery! Business teams are often just as messy. Everyone needs to learn together. The *Leading SAFe* class is a "forcing function" for the conversation that needs to happen in order to move toward agility. It's about ALIGNMENT.[82]

Depending on how you got here and how close you are to knowing the specifics of the ART, multiple *Leading SAFe* classes may be required. We like all of the managers with people on,

---

[81] See: http://agilemanifesto.org/ (Accessed 18 June 2019).
[82] Thanks to Scott Frost for reminding us of this potential train wreck!

Laying the Tracks

or impacted by, the new Agile Release Train to attend *Leading SAFe* as a group. Train. We refer to this class as the *ART Leading SAFe*. In addition to these managers you should endeavour to include the Business Owners, potential RTEs, Product Managers, Product Owners, System Architects, and members of the ART Shared Services[83] team.

> **Protip**
> If you are going to have people from your vendors on the ART it is probably wise to train their leaders, too. It will be good for the sponsorship community of the ART to take the class with the vendor so that they can start to talk about how they will start to work differently. It will hopefully also start a conversation around technical agility practices[84] and the lean-agile mindset.

Preparing for *Leading SAFe*® Training

An investment upfront in high-quality training has a multiplier effect. Failure to invest upfront also has a multiplier effect—in the other direction![85]

Choosing an Instructor

As we have already discussed, choosing the right instructors to deliver your *Leading SAFe* classes is important. Many organisational change agents choose a path I refer to as a "deal with the devil." Despite having no experience with SAFe and never having delivered

---

[83] To learn more about Shared Services in SAFe check out: https://www.scaledagileframework.com/shared-services/ (Accessed 15 August 2019).
[84] For more on Lean-Agile mindset check out: https://scaledagileframework.com/lean-agile-leadership/ (Accessed 22 September 2019)
[85] Thanks to Emma Sharrock for the reminder!

any training in the past, they ask their employer to fund them attending *Implementing SAFe* so that they can get their SAFe Program Consultant (SPC) certification. The employer agrees on the condition that this newly minted SPC delivers the required SAFe training for the ART launch. The change agent thinks this is a fine deal; after all, how hard could this training lark be?

At the end of the four-day *Implementing SAFe* class panic sets in. We see it all the time. There is a little thought bubble that appears over their head that says, *"How can I possibly train others in SAFe when the full extent of my SAFe knowledge is four days in a classroom?"* However, the deal has been struck and there is often no way out for these folks. In our experience, this scenario rarely ends well.

> **Protip**
> The best advice I can give you is to find someone who has real-world practical experience launching ARTs to either deliver the class for you or pair with you to deliver the class. When an internal and an external SPC deliver a class together, you get the internal view and experience as well as the industry view and comparison from the external one which is a win-win for the organisation.

Logistics

The number of participants and the venue you choose for your class is also important. *Leading SAFe* scales to forty-two participants; however, it is nearly impossible to cover all the material in two days with forty-two different voices in the room. Unless the client is willing to invest in a three day class, we will cap our classes at twenty-four people with a strong preference to keeping class sizes below 20. In countries where most people are not native English speakers, we will generally default to three-day classes even with smaller groups. At the other extreme with a class smaller than 12 the PI Planning simulation will be a struggle.

Laying the Tracks

You will want a room that can be set up cabaret style,[86] with plenty of space to move between tables. Your organisation's board room might be "free," but it will make for a compromised training experience.

You should also cater the event. This does not need to be a three-course sit-down meal; in fact, that would be best avoided. But making it easy for people to get to good quality nutrition, without leaving the venue, will help keep break times under control. This is also a valuable networking opportunity for the attendees. A wonderful side effect of having your students eat together is that "we become fonder of people and things we experience while we are eating."[87] And my wife would want me to remind you to make sure to ask folks about food allergies before the class!

Give people advance notice of the class. There is nothing worse than being asked to clear your schedule with one- or two-days' notice. Even when participants manage to clear their calendars, they often end up needing to step out of the room for calls or meetings that could not be moved. This does not create a space in which people can focus on learning.

> **Adrienne's Anecdote**
> At one client site training invitations were often sent out 48 hours before the class because they couldn't get a room booking! Unsurprisingly, the classes were rarely full and key people often couldn't make it. This resulted in us needing to run additional classes, and the timeline for the ART launch coming under pressure.

---

[86] For US-based readers cabaret style seating is the same as "rounds."
[87] Mary Lynn Manns and Linda Rising, *More Fearless Change: Strategies for Making Your Ideas Happen*, (Boston: Addison-Wesley, 2015), Kindle Edition. Loc 2509.

> **Em's Anecdote**
> Make sure the people attending class are being supported by their management. There is one client I work with where people are routinely pulled out of classes by their managers to deal with "emergencies" and this client is not a hospital emergency room! Holding the class offsite can sometimes help with this.

> **Protip**
> Sharon Bowman, the creator of Training from the Back of the Room,[88] recommends "priming" your students before a class. *"Neuroscientific studies have shown that the human brain will accept new information more readily when it has been 'primed' beforehand. This means that trainers need to offer learners ways to explore content before the actual class or training occurs."*[89] One of the ways we do this is by sharing the SAFe Introduction White Paper[90] with our students before the class.

Setting the Stage

Have whomever is sponsoring the class open up the day by providing some organisational context. I have completely lost count of the number of times I have been engaged to deliver classes to people who have no idea why they are there and what, if any, plan the organisation has with respect to SAFe. It will also

---

[88] Sharon Bowman, *Training from the BACK of the Room! 65 Ways to Step Aside and Let them Learn*, (San Francisco: Pfeiffer, 2008).
[89] See: https://bowperson.com/2015/03/priming-getting-the-brain-ready-to-learn/(Accessed 27 August 2019).
[90] The SAFe Introduction White Paper is available to download at: https://www.scaledagile.com/resources/safe-whitepaper/ (Accessed 27 August 2019).

be important for this leader to acknowledge these people are busy, but this training is important. It is essential to get people into an open and learning mindset to get the maximum return on investment from the class.

Encourage Students to Sit the Exam

I always tell my classes that even if they do not value certification they should study for and attempt the exam, ideally within seven days of the class, as it will assist with their retention of the material. This is the start of their learning journey.[91]

> **Em's Anecdote**
> A number of years ago I attended a *Coaching Agile Teams* class with Lyssa Adkins and Michael Spayd. They wrote the numbers 10, 24, 7 on the whiteboard then asked the class what it meant. Of course, none of us had the foggiest clue! They explained that adult learners retain less than 10% of classroom training. A way to increase this retention to 80%+ is to follow the 10 24 7 formula:

- When teaching a concept talk for 10 minutes or less and get the learners to take action by using the learning in an activity;
- 24 hours after learning a concept review it; do something to recall what happened yesterday and;
- 7 days after learning a concept do something to re-activate what you learned.

---

[91] The team at Scaled Agile Inc. say that based on their data the earlier people take the exams the more likely they are to pass.

The approach aligns with the *Training from the BACK of the Room*[92] thinking that underpins the design of many SAFe classes including *Leading SAFe*.

> **Cécile's Anecdote**
> We feel certification is part of the learning journey. Employees are strongly encouraged to take the certification exam no matter the training, even when the exam is in English. About one third of the people are sadly demotivated by the language barrier. We usually have good feedback from the people who do it.

We organise a one-hour presentation for the future trainees a couple of weeks before the session so that expectations are set on the prerequisites and the certification work. We also organise conference call meetings to discuss their questions and difficulties once they are in the middle of their preparation. For SAFe training, this is an opportunity for them to learn how to use the website to deepen their understanding of the concepts.

Designing the Agile Release Train

Designing trains is always more art than science, no pun intended! In this section we will explore the key ART leadership roles, team design principles, and specialist roles.

ART Leadership Roles

Business Owners

In *Leading SAFe* the Business Owners are described as "key stakeholders on the Agile Release Train." This has always struck me as rather vague. I like to think of the Business Owners as the sponsors for the ART. A community of between three and six

---

[92] *Training from the BACK of the Room* is Sharon Bowman's "brain-based" approach to adult learning. She has written a number of books on this topic.

business <u>and</u> technology leaders that have some sort of commercial responsibility for the value stream(s) the ART belongs to. In some cases, this is as simple as repurposing an existing steering committee.

As you contemplate who the right Business Owners are for your ART, SAFe suggests you ask the following questions:

- Who is ultimately responsible for the business outcomes?
- Who can steer this ART to develop the right solution?
- Who can speak to the technical competence of the solution now and into the near future?
- Who should participate in planning, help eliminate impediments, and speak on behalf of development, the business, and the customer?
- Who can approve and defend a set of Program Increment (PI) plans, knowing full well that they will never satisfy everyone?
- Who can help coordinate the efforts with other departments and organisations within the enterprise?[93]

While there is no right or wrong answer, I would encourage you to also consider the practical aspects of the Business Owner role. At a minimum they need to attend every PI Planning[94] and Inspect and Adapt workshop[95] for the ART. In a large enterprise with a dozen or more ARTs, this probably means the Business Owners are not the C-Suite! By the same token, I would expect the Business Owners to be more senior than (or at minimum peers of) the Trifecta. The ideal Business Owners are people the Trifecta can safely escalate to with the confidence that actions will be taken. Business Owners can also change or be added as your ART evolves.

---

[93] See: https://www.scaledagileframework.com/business-owners/ (Accessed 19 June 2019).
[94] To learn more about PI Planning in SAFe check out: https://www.scaledagileframework.com/pi-planning/ (Accessed 16 July 2019).
[95] To learn more about the Inspect and Adapt workshop in SAFe check out: https://www.scaledagileframework.com/inspect-and-adapt (Accessed 16 July 2019).

The Trifecta

The ART Leadership, often referred to as the Program Team or, as we like to call them, the Trifecta, consists of the Release Train Engineer, Product Manager, and System Architect. Getting the right people in these roles can make or break your ART.

> ⚠ **Caution! Potential Train Wreck Ahead!**
> Sometimes the Trifecta can turn into a three-headed monster! Especially when one struggles to see the value the other(s) are bringing to the ART. A possible cause of this is what Adam Grant refers to as responsibility bias in his book *Give and Take*.[96] Responsibility bias occurs when we exaggerate our own contribution relative to others. While in some instances this can be ego driven, it is also a natural by-product of information discrepancy. *"We have more access to information about our own contribution than the contributions of others. We see all of our own efforts, but we only witness a subset of our partners' efforts. When we think about who deserves the credit, we have more knowledge of our own contributions."*[97]

One way I like to address this is to have the Trifecta hold regular retrospectives to reflect on how they are working together. Another exercise that might be useful is Empathy Mapping.[98] Have each role put themselves in the shoes of the other and complete an empathy map. This can be very eye opening.[99]

---

[96] Adam Grant, *Give and Take: Why Helping Others Drives Our Success*, (London: Weidenfeld & Nicolson, 2013). Kindle Edition.
[97] Adam Grant, *Give and Take:* p. 82
[98] To learn more about Empathy Mapping check out: https://www.innovationgames.com/empathy-map/ (Accessed 29 August 2019).
[99] Adapted from: http://blog.prettyagile.com.au/2014/05/release-train-engineer-batman-or-wonder.html (Accessed 29 August 2019).

Release Train Engineer (RTE)

When it comes to identifying an RTE[100] for the ART my advice is simple: Find the person you trust to lead a team of fifty to one hundred people <u>and</u> facilitate the delivery of an annual program of work in the vicinity of $5 – 20 million USD.

More often than not the folks that end up in RTE roles are ex-Program Managers. This doesn't mean every Program Manager will make an awesome RTE, but there is a reality that Program Managers are used to dealing with delivery complexity and organisational red tape and these skills are useful to an RTE. The right Program Manager for the RTE role will have a learning mindset. Some of the best RTEs I have worked with have been self-educators, or what Dean Leffingwell would call "lifelong learners." They read books, follow blogs, attend conferences, and sign up for training. They are also humble. They know what they don't know, and they ask for help.

Most RTEs I have worked with have been part of the technology delivery organisation. While I like to think this does not have to be a rule, RTEs I have seen sourced from "the business" have struggled to make the mental shift from "poacher to gamekeeper."[101] Although, upon reflection, it is not so much their background as it is their current reporting line that appears to be the root cause here. On the top of reporting lines, we have often debated the pros and cons of the RTE being a line manager. This is a very context-specific puzzle but, in most cases, it is probably better that they are not people managers. Especially if they are only the people leader for a subset of the ART.

---

[100] To learn more about the Release Train Engineer (RTE) role in SAFe check out: https://www.scaledagileframework.com/release-train-engineer-and-solution-train-engineer/ (Accessed 19 June 2019).
[101] For US-based readers "poacher turned gamekeeper" means a person's job has changed so that they now have authority over the same sort of people that they were themselves before.

Em's Anecdote

A number of years ago I was engaged by one of Australia's largest banks to help a program manager take his program Agile. He had inherited a waterfall program that had been running for six years. His job was to drop the final releases and turn the delivery organisation Agile. Just one problem—he knew nothing about Agile. I will always remember our first meeting. After explaining to me the position he was in his first question was *"What books should I read and what training do I need to do?"* I thought I had struck gold. This NEVER happens! I usually find myself trying to convince leaders that they need to invest in self-education and this guy volunteered in our first meeting and followed through! This is the type of leader that makes an excellent RTE.

Adrienne's Anecdote

One thing I look for a lot in an RTE is someone who will demonstrate and take the time to build a culture of fun and delivery excellence. We want this person to command a presence in a room and foster a sense of one mission, one team. This person will be stretched out of the gate because RTEs don't grow on trees so they will need to look upon learning new things with enthusiasm. I know when I first stepped into the role, I knew it was big and I had a lot of learning to do. I was also wishing I had never had that conversation with my General Manager about needing a challenge. What's that phrase—be careful what you ask for? Just know that this person will make mistakes and continue to support them as they start to flex their newly forming muscles.

Later when I was looking for three RTEs as part of launching a Solution Train[102] big bang style, I had the luxury of hiring one that had a very strong program management background and two others that were from technical backgrounds. I sent them on their SPC course together because I needed them to be a team. They learned from each other and filled in each other's gaps. So, when you are thinking about that Solution Train and all of those RTEs you will need to find, consider how to create teaming moments for them as well.

Last thoughts on RTEs. There is only one on the train and this role needs to be positioned in the organisation so that they have enough political capital that they are seen as equals to the leaders of business and technology organisations. They have the clout by title and position, but they shouldn't need to use it. I really like the role being a Director level. I was and my RTEs were too. It's a significant role and should be compensated accordingly.

Maarit's Anecdote

When I am hiring RTEs I look for three things. First, the person must have been working in a bigger organisation so long that they have a systemic understanding how the organisation works and how they can improve the organisation as a system. Typically, this comes via a former project/program manager/line management role and years of expertise. Secondly, I look for someone who is willing to leverage the work they do via other people/groups. These are people who are willing to give credit to others and teach them as they work.

---

[102] To learn more about Solution Trains in SAFe check out: https://www.scaledagileframework.com/solution-train/ (Accessed 10 September 2019)

These people have really good social skills, and they are good problem-solvers. As an RTE you often end up solving personality clashes between people; you need to understand both sides and be able to coach people into solutions that take the organisation forward. Thirdly, I am looking for people who truly have internalised an agile and lean way of working, and are willing to keep on educating themselves, just like Em described.

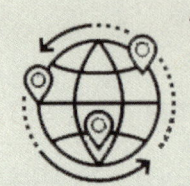

Tips for Globally Distributed ARTs
If your development teams are offshore the right location for your RTE is probably with the offshore development teams. Many organisations have the opposite instinct as they see the RTE through a more traditional program management lens and prefer the RTE to be the voice of the ART at head office instead of the servant leader the ART needs.

Product Management

My approach to sourcing Product Managers[103] is fairly similar to my approach to the RTE role. For me the person(s) in this role needs to be trusted by the organisation to make the right priority calls over an annual program of work of $5 – 20M USD and they really should come from the business.

The Product Manager(s) needs to be able to articulate the vision and product roadmap for the ART. True Product Managers tend to be obsessed with the latest technologies, and all new cool things the organisation has the potential to create. They earn the respect of the train by knowing their product domain inside and out.

---

[103] To learn more about the Product Manager role in SAFe check out: https://www.scaledagileframework.com/product-and-solution-management/ (Accessed 19 June 2019).

Laying the Tracks

If the ART covers multiple customer segments, or multiple product lines, you may want to have a Product Manager for each. Should that happen the Business Owners of this train will need to decide how the capacity[104] of the train should be split so that the Product Managers don't have to guess.

> **Caution! Potential Train Wreck Ahead!**
> If you happen to have a train with as many "products" as you do teams, or thereabouts, this does not mean your ART should have a Product Manager for each. I would struggle to think of a scenario where more than three Product Managers makes sense, and in most cases one or two should suffice. Probably the most common reason I have seen for multiple Product Managers has been some sort of consumer vs business split.

> **Adrienne's Anecdote**
> One Solution Train I relaunched at an insurance company was particularly challenging. The Product Managers were from the technology and were trusted by the technology leaders. I wouldn't go so far as to say that the business didn't trust them, but we could see that the technology Product Managers were more comfortable with working and prioritising the technology part of backlog versus prioritising with a lens of running a business, not surprisingly.

---

[104] For more information on capacity allocation check out: https://scaledagileframework.com/program-and-solution-backlogs/ (accessed 22 September 2019)

When we put in Solution Managers[105] from the real business and they started coaching the Product Managers on the priorities of the business the Product Managers did not listen. These technology-based Product Managers needed to be coached to understand that the Product Manager role in SAFe has a business fiduciary responsibility to it and therefore they needed the Solution Managers' input if they were going to be successful in the role. This was also the first time where the business was putting both hands on the wheel and started steering. Prior to this, there was a great divide between the business and technology.

Tips for Globally Distributed ARTs
If your organisation is distributed it is typical for Product Management to be co-located with the rest of the product organisation rather than with development. If the Product Manager is not co-located with their ART or the product organisation this is just hard for everyone and best avoided.

SAFe in Project Driven World
If your ART is funded by a multitude of individual projects, then the role of the Product Manager as envisaged by SAFe is likely to be compromised. One of two models tend to apply in this situation. Either the Product Manager is what I would have called in my life before SAFe the Business Owner of the application or domain, or sometimes there is no Product Manager at all.

---

[105] To learn more about the Solution Management role in SAFe check out: https://www.scaledagileframework.com/product-and-solution-management/ (Accessed 10 September 2019)

Application/Domain Business Owner as Product Manager

Project funded trains and system centric trains tend to go hand in hand. Probably the most common instantiation of this I have seen is the Digital Agile Release Train. This is where the "digital" program ring fences all of the online and mobile development and creates an ART. This ART often excludes people working on the backend systems such as mainframes.

Product Management comes from Digital but many of the projects are funded by the other business units. In these scenarios, I have often had the Product Manager provide Product Owners and the project sponsors provide Feature Owners.[106] Work arrives in the form of a project. Sometimes that means it arrives with a scope and a budget already defined! Some of these projects will be able to be delivered by the ART, some will need inputs from other domains, and some will consider the ART an external dependency.

When the work of the train is funded by projects and those projects are not sponsored by the Product Manager (or their management) then product management can become a toothless tiger. In this scenario the Product Management role is heavily skewed towards negotiating priorities and protecting the congruency of the solution. The features are accepted by both Product Management and the Feature Owner.

Pipeline Manager instead of Product Manager

The alternative is an ART without a true Product Manager. This usually goes hand in hand with a subsystem ART. For example, if the scope of the ART was an Enterprise Data Warehouse, then the projects could be championed by any part of the organisation from the channels through to product management and beyond. In this scenario it is sometimes not possible to identify a Product Manager, so we have used a

---

[106] The Feature Owner concept is elaborated later in this chapter.

> Pipeline Manager[107] instead. You can think of this as a Program Manager for the ART, that facilitates backlog readiness and prioritisation of epics.

System Architect

Identifying the System Architect(s)[108] can also be tricky. It seems to me that every organisation has a different view of the role of architecture and when you ask which of their architects has the best knowledge of the systems that underpin the ART the answer can be anything from there are nine of them or there are none! Of course, neither of these answers are overly helpful. In my experience the System Architect(s) are perhaps best described as domain architect(s).

> ⚠️ **Caution! Potential Train Wreck Ahead!**
> Every once in a while, I encounter an organisation with no architects for the given domain. While this is quite clearly the organisation's reality, that does not make it a good idea. You will need to find someone to at least wear the System Architect hat as the teams are going to need direction. If your ART makes it all the way to PI Planning without a System Architect be prepared for some pain. The teams will have questions, and someone will need to be able to answer them!

---

[107] To read more about the Pipeline Manager: http://blog.prettyagile.com.au/2014/03/launching-agile-release-train-while.html

[108] To learn more about the System Architect role in SAFe check out: https://www.scaledagileframework.com/system-and-solution-architect-engineering/ (Accessed 19 June 2019).

> **Maarit's Anecdote**
> I have also encountered organisations that do not have a System Architect role in place. Usually the result is lots of technical debt and spaghetti code in the system under development. Development may be painfully slow. In one recent client case we put all architects in the teams: when the pain grew too hard, one of them started crying that we need to get an understanding what the whole system does and how we can start developing its future. He came and proposed a number of changes benefitting the whole ART. My thesis is that people with motivation and passion will grow to the needed role—when you make the pain (i.e. the need) evident, the right people with the right mindset will emerge.

Ideally the ART has a single System Architect; however, if the ART consists of many systems and technologies it may not be practical to expect a single person to understand all of them. In this case the most responsible choice is to have just enough architects so that the train can function. Depending on the breadth of your ART there may be more than one but there is unlikely to be nine! Of course, if there is more than one architect, they will need to work closely together and stay in alignment so as to not provide contradictory (and frustrating) advice to the teams.

> **Caution! Potential Train Wreck Ahead!**
> If the organisation continues to push the ART to have four or more architects, I would consider this a "smell."[109] Often it is a sign that the Archi-

---

[109] In his book *Refactoring*, Martin Fowler introduced the term smell to refer to something that may not be right. Just because something smells doesn't mean there's a problem; it does mean, though, that further investigation is warranted. https://www.mountaingoatsoftware.com/articles/toward-a-catalog-of-scrum-smells (Accessed 24 June 2019).

tects are "in the weeds," possibly writing detailed design documents or doing code reviews instead of providing guidance on the wholesale changes required to the system. Remember in SAFe we want to achieve a balance between "intentional architecture" provided by the System Architect(s) and "emergent design" from the teams.[110]

Em's Anecdote
In one organisation I worked with, there were as many "architects" as there were teams; in fact, I think it is possible there were more! In this organisation they were called "solution architects." Similar to the example above they were deep in the design detail. We knew we needed their expertise, so we decided to have them join the teams as Technical Leads, with the expectation that they would support the team not only with design but also through coding. For many this meant knocking off some rust as they hadn't coded in many years.

The right System Architect[111] is going to advocate for the inclusion of technical enablers in the Program Backlog.[112] They will define the Architectural Runway[113] for the train, in collaboration with

---

[110] To learn more about Agile Architecture in SAFe check out: https://www.scaledagileframework.com/agile-architecture/ (Accessed 24 June 2019).

[111] To learn more about the System Architect in SAFe check out: https://scaledagileframework.com/system-and-solution-architect-engineering/ (Accessed 22 September 2019)

[112] To learn more about the Program Backlog in SAFe check out: https://www.scaledagileframework.com/program-and-solution-backlogs/ (Accessed 24 June 2019).

[113] To learn more about the Architectural Runway in SAFe check out: https://www.scaledagileframework.com/architectural-runway/ (Accessed 24 June 2019).

the technical leads. This will be informed by Product Management vision and roadmap for the ART. The System Architect will need to be pragmatic in balancing the ART's technical needs with business priorities. System Architects are most effective when they don't think in terms of their title and really look for areas to help the train deliver. There is no place for ivory tower architects in SAFe.

> **Protip**
> Consider making the System Architect the Product Owner for the System Team.[114] This should help keep the System Architect grounded in the reality of the health of the system that Agile teams are working with. If your System Architect is not already a DevOps advocate this will help get them thinking about the benefits of continuous integration and delivery.[115]

Principles for Designing the Teams

With the Business Owners and Trifecta identified it is now time to look at the rest of the train, starting with the stars of the show—the Agile teams!

When we design trains and teams, we impact people's lives. We need to be conscious of this when we decide who to include in the conversation. You need people in the room who actually know the people doing the work as there will always be questions about skill sets and current responsibilities that need to be answered. Often this is the line managers of the people involved or sometimes the Project

---

[114] To learn more about the System Team in SAFe check out: https://www.scaledagileframework.com/system-team/ (Accessed 27 August 2019).
[115] To learn more about SAFe's Continuous Delivery Pipeline check out: https://www.scaledagileframework.com/continuous-delivery-pipeline (Accessed 24 June 2019).

Managers from inflight projects that are likely to be delivered by the ART. I would also expect the Trifecta to be involved in these discussions.

Everyone Has a Role Day One

Where possible, I like to start the conversation about ART design by identifying everyone already working on the system, value stream, or set of projects that are considered in scope for the Agile Release Train. The goal is to make sure you see the people contributing to the "as is" delivery process clearly and to ensure we find a home for everyone in the new world. While it is possible, and maybe even likely, that you will not need all the people you have today in your new world you should be cautious about randomly culling people. I also think it sends a terrible message to the organisation if every time a train is launched some significant percentage of the workforce is laid off.

Some organisations are still eager to change or reduce the existing workforce. Traditional management training has conditioned many leaders to believe the root cause of their organisation's performance challenges is the people. Of course, as lean-agile leaders and students of Deming we know better: "People are already doing their best; the problems are with the system."[116] If you are struggling to get the organisation to buy into this, introduce them to the NUMMI case study, a joint venture between General Motors and Toyota that completely transformed the performance of a GM factory, with 85% of the original unionised workforce still intact.[117]

---

[116] Richard Knaster, *SAFe Distilled*, p. 29.
[117] This short video, introduced to us by Katie Anderson, provides an excellent summary: https://courrier.jp/news/archives/81220/ (accessed 27 June 2019).

Caution! Potential Train Wreck Ahead!

Taking the organisation's current state and mapping it into the team of teams that will become the Agile Release Train can be confronting for organisations. In one instance this resulted in a train of feature teams, where each team had two business analysts, two functional analysts, one developer, and no tester. One of the Business Owners was horrified at the skill mix. Why do we have so many analysts and so few developers and testers? I was quick to explain the train skill mix was a reflection of the existing organisation. I think it would be fair to say this was eye-opening for him!

Maarit's Anecdote

The most horrifying example of this is an organisation that outsourced all their software development "because software is not our core competence." Software is the future! Implementing more and more functionality using software is a mega trend. One of the "trains" proposed by this organisation had over one hundred managers and two doers!

An organisation chart is an easy way to hide the problems and set the blame on "developers being lazy." When you look at the organisation from an ART perspective you will start to see the linkage between the people you have in the organisation and the results you get.

Avoid Keeping or Creating Project Centric Teams

Sometimes ARTs are formed by merging a set of Agile projects and Agile project teams into a train. This tends to create a scenario whereby the team's identity is synonymous with the project they are working on. The business folks who own the project feel that they "own" the team. While there is something nice about teams having a close relationship with their business sponsors, it starts to become awkward when enterprise priorities dictate that the team work on a feature that doesn't come from that sponsor's backlog!

> **Aaron's Anecdote**
> I've got this wrong a few times by assuming that a client's current Program of work/project is equal to an ART. This is often an easy win as people already have roles, teams assigned, work intake structure, and a goal/mission. However, taking this "easy win" gets the train out of the station quickly BUT down the line reinforces existing habits and cultural norms (project-based mentality and silos, etc.). I have also quickly realised that the teams are missing key people, teams have many external dependencies, and after the initial buzz of SAFe, need a lot of course corrections and eventually a train relaunch to get right. The negative PR of "our existing program/project isn't working because of SAFe" is a tough reputation to shake off moving forward!

Bias to Feature Teams Over Component Teams

In our experience a better pattern is to form generic feature teams that work on the agreed priorities, regardless of which "project" they belong to or who is sponsoring the work. I refer to this approach as creating "evenly matched feature teams." For this to work the organisation has to be willing to invest in cross-skilling as we often start with a team of individuals with different specialisations and very limited, if any, generalisation. In most cases the train's backlog will not contain a set of features that will evenly utilise every team member's specialisation, therefore some members will need to start learning new skills from the very first sprint of the very first program increment.

Laying the Tracks

> **Protip**
> For teams with extremely diverse skill sets and little to no overlap, we recommend they try Mob Programming. *"Mob Programming is a software development approach where the whole team works on the same thing, at the same time, in the same space, and at the same computer."*[118] This is a proven approach to learning that accelerates cross-skilling and enhances quality. While it might sound expensive the benefits far outweigh the cost.[119]
>
> In *Mob Programming: A Whole Team Approach*, Woody Zuill and Kevin Meadows list some of the benefits they have observed with mob programming:
>
> - We are no longer waiting for answers to questions because the people with the answers are sitting and working with us on the same thing.
> - With everyone reviewing the code continuously the code was of much better quality.
> - Things got done sooner with the whole team focusing on one thing at a time.
> - Rather than trying to be productive we were learning to be effective.[120]
>
> When starting to experiment with Mob Programming, Woody and Kevin recommend starting with simple coding exercises (known as coding katas) in a coding dojo format, for a couple of hours a couple of times a week.[121]

---

[118] Woody Zuill and Kevin Meadows, *Mob Programming: A Whole Team Approach*, (Leanpub, 2016), p. 4.
[119] See case study: https://blog.prototypr.io/100-of-the-team-in-a-mob-for-12-months-taking-mob-programming-a-couple-of-steps-further-62d1e9962f37 (Accessed 29 August 2019).
[120] Woody Zuill, *Mob Programming*, p. 61.
[121] Woody Zuill, *Mob Programming*, p. 26.

One of the great advantages of "evenly matched feature teams" is flexibility. "Evenly matched feature teams" pulling from a single backlog is an application of Don Reinertsen's Principle of Queuing Structure: Serve pooled demand with reliable high capacity servers.[122]

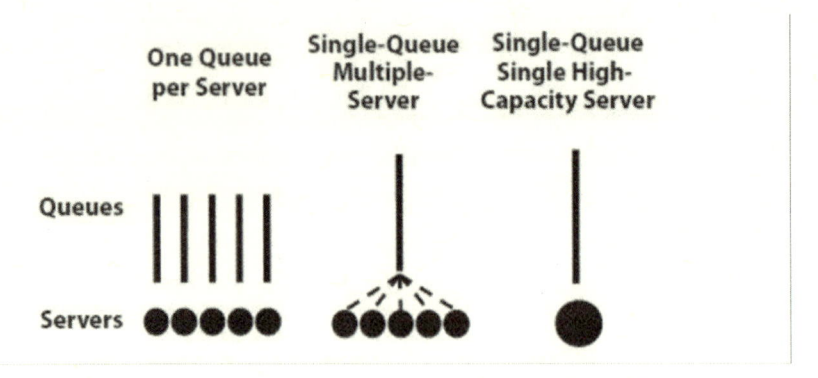

Figure 6: Queuing System Structures

> **Em's anecdote**
> I once had an ART working on an epic with a fixed regulatory deadline. This ART's features were dependent on work being delivered by other programs. Initially, we had 12 weeks to deliver; however, the upstream programs slipped eight weeks. As we had "evenly matched feature teams" we were able to increase the number of teams working on our features and deliver in four weeks, meeting the regulatory deadline.

---

[122] Donald G. Reinertsen, *The Principles of Product Development Flow: Second Generation Lean Product Development*, (Redondo Beach: Celeritas Publishing. 2009). Kindle Edition p. 64.

> **Caution! Potential Train Wreck Ahead!**
> Not every leader in every organisation is going to be okay with the idea of their "highly paid" specialists spending time cross-skilling and working outside their specialisation. Their traditional management training has wired them to believe that this is an uneconomical choice. This is an example of what *This is Lean* calls the efficiency paradox.[123] Anytime you can make a flow efficient decision versus a resource efficient decision you will deliver outcomes faster.

> **Claire's Anecdote**
> I once worked with an ART with cross-functional teams who serviced the various and numerous incoming requests of the business. Not all of this work constituted "perfect" features: using all of the teams' specialisations in just the right proportion. The leaders knew this would be the case when the feature teams were created but failed to tell their people that they were expected to cross-skill. This left specialist team members unclear on how to help the team deliver without contravening what they thought their managers wanted and measured. This left the teams disgruntled and disempowered.

Keep Team Sizes to 7 +/- 2

While we prefer feature teams over component teams[124] there is often a tension between having all the skills necessary to deliver

---

[123] Niklas Modig and Pär Åhlström, *This is Lean: Resolving the Efficiency Paradox*, (Rheologica, 2013). Kindle Edition.
[124] To learn more about organising by feature or component check out: https://www.scaledagileframework.com/features-and-components/ (Accessed 15 June 2019).

a feature and keeping the team size to 7 +/- 2. Whilst the Scrum Guide[125] and SAFe advocates for team size to be 3 to 9 plus a Scrum Master and Product Owner, I prefer 7 +/- 2 including the Scrum Master and Product Owner. For me this is a matter of simple maths; the larger the team the harder it is to communicate within the team.[126] A team of 11, as advocated by the Scrum Guide, has 55 communication channels, whereas a team of 9 only has 36. I know which team I would prefer to be a member of!

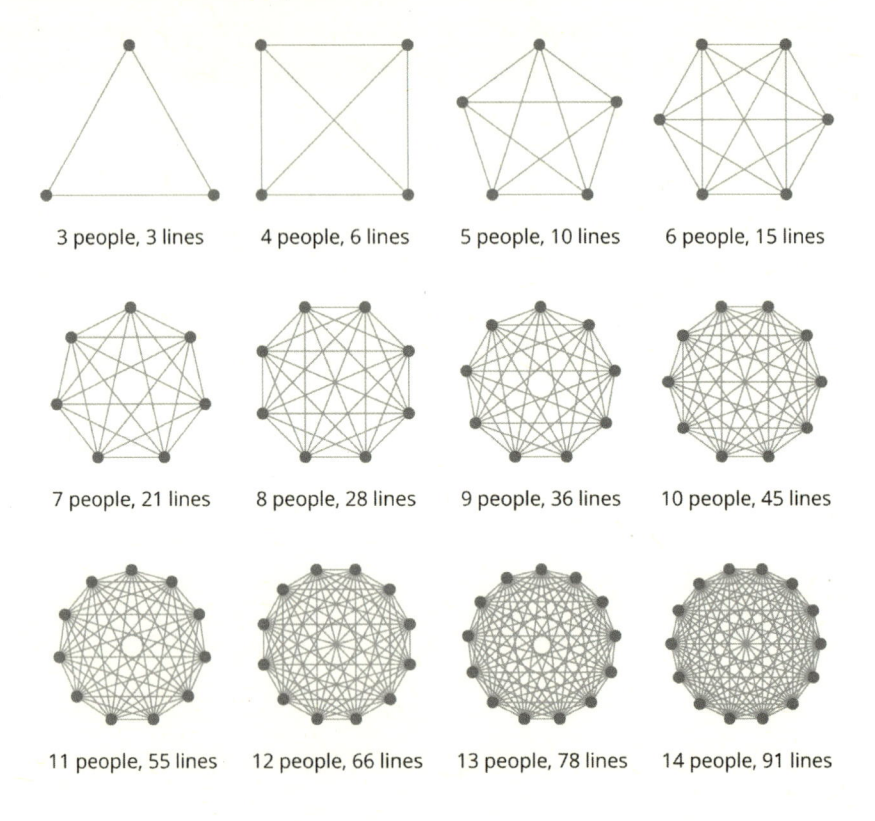

3 people, 3 lines   4 people, 6 lines   5 people, 10 lines   6 people, 15 lines

7 people, 21 lines   8 people, 28 lines   9 people, 36 lines   10 people, 45 lines

11 people, 55 lines 12 people, 66 lines 13 people, 78 lines   14 people, 91 lines

Figure 7 - Lines of communication for different sized groups[127]

---

[125] See: https://www.scrumguides.org/scrum-guide.html (Accessed 8 April 2019).
[126] Em Campbell-Pretty, *Tribal Unity*, p. 6.
[127] Em Campbell-Pretty, *Tribal Unity*, p. 6.

Laying the Tracks

When determining the skill mix for the teams, we start this conversation by creating nine blank spaces running vertically down a whiteboard, representing the largest possible team construct. We fill the top three positions with Product Owner, Scrum Master, and Technical Lead. Then, fill the bottom position(s) with a Test or Quality Engineer. Next, we list out all the other skill sets involved in delivering on the ARTs mission and if there are more than four or five, we explore what combination of feature and component teams make sense for this ART. If there are less than this, we start to determine what mix of skill sets each team will need.

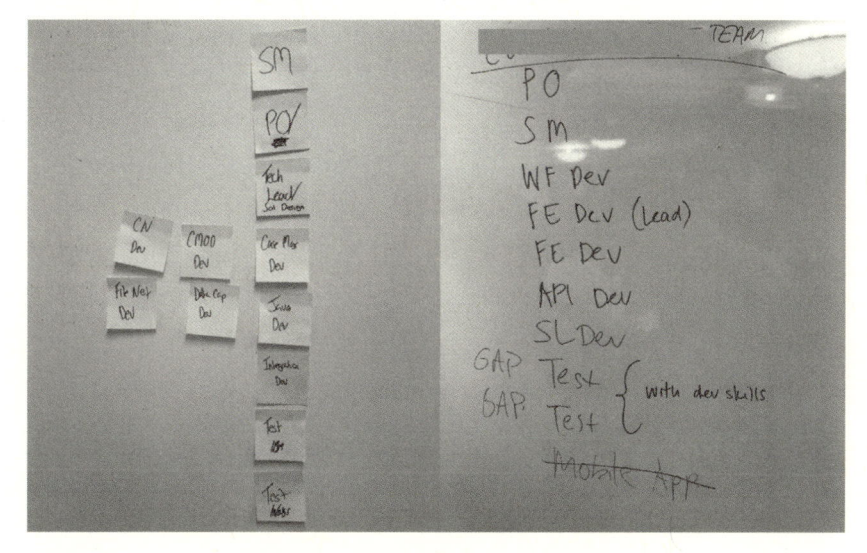

Figure 8 - Examples of Team Designs

Location, Location, Location

Ideally, we want teams to be co-located. While this is not always possible it is always preferable. It is very hard to team with people you rarely, if ever, get to spend facetime with. Video conferencing is better than nothing, but it is no substitute for in-person, face-to-face conversation. Different time zones, languages, and the quality of the video conferencing facilities all add to the difficulty of teams in a distributed team.

Caution! Potential Train Wreck Ahead!
Traditionally trained leaders are likely to consider collocated teams an uneconomical choice. Often both labour and business premises are considered to be cheaper in offshore locations, while the benefits of colocation are perhaps more intangible—clearer, faster communication, less handoffs, better quality, and short cycle times.[128]

Protip
The exception to my tough stance on colocation is the completely distributed team on the same or similar time zone. In this scenario the playing field is level. All communication is via video conferencing, phone, chat, or email and there are no second-class citizens.

Maarit's Anecdote
To my surprise, when I ran a survey within one organisation I was working with, the people who said agile has helped them, most were the ones in distributed teams. Yet everyone on distributed teams was complaining—so how was this possible? I went on and interviewed some of the teams. *"Now we have a joined backlog, and we speak daily,"* they said. *"This is a ton better than in the past where we were not sure what was expected of us and ended up doing the wrong things."* Later this organisation learned that co-located teams have faster velocity, so it went through a massive change and co-located all teams.

---

[128] To learn more about how counterintuitive calls can help lean leaders achieve ambitious targets check out *The Lean Strategy* by Michael Ballé et al. Thanks to Cécile Auret for the book recommendation.

Include Support Wherever Possible

If application development is separate to application support, then consider including both groups in your ART design. I have never seen anything good come from separating "bug fixing" from the application development teams. Our mantra is "you broke it, you fix it." Meaning that "bugs" are returned to the team that created them.

> **Adrienne's Anecdote**
> One organisation I was working at was considering having one entire train for maintenance support. From an economic perspective can you imagine how much capacity the organisation was willing to allocate in a year to fixing issues? The other issue is a cultural one. What would it mean to be on one of the teams on the maintenance train? Are they not good enough to be on product development trains? Are you allowed to make bugs if you're on the product development trains? Isn't the maintenance train context switching all the time and learning the new implementations after the fact? Fortunately, they didn't go down this path. Instead, we developed a process to triage the bugs with the Product Managers and created a Kanban system for the teams to pull from a prioritised queue of bugs.

There is no one-size-fits-all approach to integrating development and support on a single team and there are always a lot of really context-specific considerations. In the simplest scenarios we can distribute the support folks across the teams so that every Agile team has someone from support. We can then ask the teams to cross-skill with this person in the same way as they do with any other role on the team. This works best when the support teams are co-located with the delivery teams and their role is more triage and bug fix than batch monitoring.

Some of the more complex scenarios may require a longer runway to solve. For example:

- The support teams being located in a different building/country/time zone to development. In this scenario, your teams might go from co-located to distributed due to the inclusion of a remote operations person. In this scenario the logistical challenges of having one remote team member may well outweigh the benefit of having support team members on each team.

- The support team members have different contractual arrangements to the development team member that include evening and weekend shift work. Ideally, you would want all team members to have the same arrangements, thereby spreading the burden of afterhours work across the team. Depending on the personal circumstances of the team members this may not be a practical option and therefore it might be fairer on all concerned to have the support team operate as a component team on the ART.

Em's Anecdote
An alternative to moving support into the development teams might be shifting some responsibilities. I once worked with an ART where development was completely separate to support, as support was outsourced and offshore. In order to operate in line with the "you broke it, you fix it" mantra we decided that the Agile teams would need to provide "warranty support" for all their code for three months post an accepted "zero defect" release to production. Later we also discovered that the primary source of uncontrolled changes to the codebase was the production support team. To fix the problem we changed the responsibilities so that all code changes were made by the development teams on the train.

Design With Index Cards Not Spreadsheets

Often well-intended SPCs will try to design the ART using the Team Roster spreadsheet in the Program Increment Toolkit.[129] We prefer to design ARTs using index cards on a physical wall. One index card per person. Each card will usually state the person's name, core skill set, physical location in the world, and business unit. A spreadsheet might be a useful tool for creating the initial list of names and recording the final outcome, but it just doesn't cut it if you want an interactive and participatory discussion to take place.

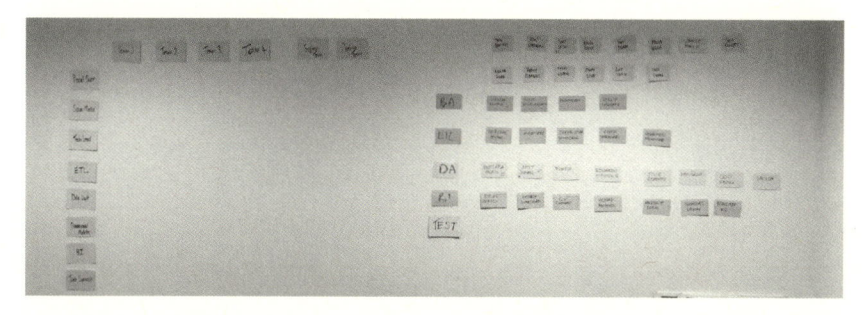

Figure 9 - The blank team grid is on the left and all of the existing team have their names written on the cards on the right side ready to be mapped into teams. In this example colour is used to indicate skill set

We usually start by creating a blank grid, with the team roles down the left-hand side and team 1 through "n" across the top. We then try to create feature teams by placing index cards on the wall. Using index cards means we can quickly and easily move things around when considering various "what if" scenarios. This visualisation approach can be very powerful, especially with some well-considered colour coding choices. Often, I will use colour to differentiate skill set, but I have also used it to identify location and employer depending on the scenario.

---

[129] The SAFe Program Increment Toolkit is available for download by all SPCs in good standing via community.scaledagile.com. (Accessed 16 July 2019).

The ART of Avoiding a Train Wreck

> **Em's Anecdote**
> With one client we used colour to indicate employees and another for vendor staff and the organisation learned that not a single permanent member of the technology team was contributing to delivering product. Apparently, this was news to them!

Figure 10 - Coloured index cards to show vendors (pink) and employee (blue/green)

Coloured index cards can also help with identifying missing skill sets, such as one train I encountered recently with six teams and only two testers! I have also tended to use blank pink cards to represent vacancies. As the vacancies are filled the cards are replaced and we can see our progress towards filling the teams at a glance.

Figure 11 - Pink cards indicate vacant roles.

A Person Can Only Be on One Team and Everyone is 100% on the ART

For some organisations this design principle is a showstopper. They are quick to tell me that they can't possibly have people dedicated to teams, it is a business imperative that people work on 10 to 20 "projects" at once! This is an excellent opportunity to have a discussion about the cost of context switching. *"Any person assigned to more than three tasks will lose at least half of their time to switching."*[130] If the organisation is not ready to start thinking about reducing its Work In Process (WIP)[131] then it might not be ready to move to Agile ways of working.

---

[130] Gerald M. Weinberg, *Why Software Gets In Trouble: Software Quality Series: Vol. 2*, (Leanpub, 2017).

[131] To learn more about the importance of limiting work in process (WIP) check out SAFe Principle #6: https://www.scaledagileframework.com/visualize-and-limit-wip-reduce-batch-sizes-and-manage-queue-lengths/ (Accessed 15 July 2019).

The ART of Avoiding a Train Wreck

When using index cards to design the ART you can visualise the people who are not 100% dedicated by folding cards in half for 50%, tearing out a corner to represent 75% and folding it in four to represent a 25% time commitment to the ART.

> **Adrienne's Anecdote**
> When working with one client on ART design the half and quarter cards illustrated how they had created a model of half-time people on every piece of work to try to get it all done. It also became obvious that there was only one part-time tester. The cause of the volume of defects found by their customers also became clearer!

Figure 12 - A potential ART with quarter, half- and three-quarter-time people on teams

Working With Vendors

One of the most common questions I am asked when teaching SAFe classes is how to work with vendors. There is no "one size fits all" answer as it depends on how the organisation is contracting with the vendor.

Time and Materials (T&M)

A time and materials engagement, also known as staff augmentation, definitely makes things simpler. These engagements are likely to be for named individuals to fill specific roles. The vendor does not own any of the delivery risk, therefore they do not feel compelled to "project manage" the engagement and they work within whatever delivery approach you choose.

> **Caution! Potential Train Wreck Ahead!**
> There was an ART I launched where 50% of the team came from the same vendor that had the production support contract. When the production support team could not solve an issue the vendor manager would come and tap the development team to work on the problem after hours. This meant people on the train were being asked to work at an unsustainable pace. In other instances, people were asked by the vendor manager to work on production support tasks instead of their team backlog, letting down their team and resulting in the organisation paying twice for the "bug fix", once through the production support contract and again through the T&M development contract!

Outcome-Based Contracts

The traditional fixed cost, fixed time, deliverables-based contract is probably the worst scenario. In my view, if you already have this style of contract in place you cannot then dictate your vendor's delivery approach and still hold their "feet to the fire" to deliver on the fixed cost, fixed time, deliverables-based contract.

> **Em's Anecdote**
> Some of the worst "train wrecks" I have witnessed were the result of vendors being both stubborn and mistreated. Their client pulled the rug out from under them after an outcome-based contract had been signed by insisting the vendor's people join the teams on a new Agile Release Train. In one instance the vendor flatly refused to provide developers to the teams, instead offering up business analysts who would "gather requirements" for the developers. This resulted in every sprint going something like:
>
> - Days 1 and 2: Write stories and record them an Agile tool.
> - Days 3 to 8: The separate offsite vendor developer team would re-type the stories into their local Jira instance and develop the stories.
> - Days 9 and 10: The stories are returned to the Agile team to "test" and "demo" with very mixed results.
>
> Unsurprisingly this program delivered about a year later than initially planned.

Contract an Entire Agile Release Train

While I prefer staff augmentation, some organisations are fundamentally opposed to this model. A middle ground that might be interesting is having your vendor provide an ART, while your organisation provides Product Management and then uses the discipline of PI Planning to agree on the "deliverables" on a PI by PI basis. The challenge with this model is that it can start to become a mini/quarterly version of the fixed scope, fixed cost and fixed time contract with all of the same pitfalls this model entails.

Contract Teams

Another middle ground could be contracting cross-functional teams. As with contracting an entire ART this approach could also start to become a series of mini fixed scope, fixed cost and fixed time contracts. A possible mitigation here could include keeping the Scrum Masters as full-time employees co-located with the vendor teams.

> **Protip**
> No matter which vendor model you have you must bring your vendors on the journey. Create a "vendor as partner" culture. Train them on SAFe and help them see the case for change. Remember to include the vendor teams in you eNPS surveys.

> **Adrienne's Anecdote**
> One of the best examples of this we have seen was a CIO that called a meeting with all the vendors impacted by the ART, the internal technology leaders responsible for the ART, and their SAFe partners. She briefed everyone on her expectations that we all work together to launch her organisation's first Agile Release Train. She also invited the vendor account managers to join *Leading SAFe* training so that they could better understand the new paradigm.

> **Maarit's Anecdote**
> Once I had a chance to interview a really talented RTE who was responsible for an ART that was formed from multiple subcontractors working together. *"I made sure from the beginning,'* she said, *"that no one is going to get any credit if we fail; so, if we fail, we fail together. I also made sure that we did some team building exercises so that people felt they were primary in this train and the company where they came from was a secondary thing. The people in the train need to take an ownership on the results they deliver,"* she said. *"That is the only way a subcontracted train can work well."*

> **Melissa's Anecdote**
> In a train sprinting Wednesday to Tuesday we had a team who were mostly co-located. The industry was very small with skill specialisation that was hard to come by. As a result, we ended up with a number of independent contractors across the train. We treated them just like any permanent employee as we were all committed in long term teams. One contractor lived interstate and wanted to work remotely. After some negotiation, we arrived at a cadence for onsite versus remote. She flew in for the last day of the sprint and first day of the next sprint (at her own expense) and then work remotely in between. This enabled the team to demo, retro and sprint plan together every fortnight. In between we would use video conferencing for all team rituals including the stand-up where she was live on camera waving from her balcony every morning!

Specialist Roles

Scrum Masters

Often the first big debate in any ART design workshop is the topic of Scrum Masters.[132] If the organisation is not already using some form of agility, they probably don't have Scrum Masters but if they want to launch a successful ART, they are going to have to find some! Many organisations are quick to offer up their existing Project Managers as Scrum Masters. While this might seem like the perfect solution, I have found that Project Managers tend to struggle to make the transition to Scrum Master. This means a simple mapping of existing Project Managers to Scrum Masters is just not going to cut it.

---

[132] To learn more about the Scrum Master role in SAFe check out: https://www.scaledagileframework.com/scrum-master/ (Accessed 16 July 2019).

If we are launching a new ART in an organisation with no Scrum Masters, we are probably on the hunt for 5 to 12 people (assuming one per team). In most job markets, sourcing experienced Scrum Masters is tough and sourcing 5 to 12 of them in one hit probably impossible. So, you are probably going to have to look inside your organisation.

When sourcing Scrum Masters the first thing I look for is a passion for Agile. The Scrum Master is supposed to be an Agile coach for the team, and, while you may not be able to find someone with deep experience, maybe you can source people who are interested in Agile and have the drive and self-discipline to learn. In the case of teams that are new to agility a Scrum Master that is one or two steps ahead of the team is not a bad place to start. In addition to passion, you are looking for people who like building teams. Servant leaders who enjoy supporting others. Oddly some of the best Scrum Masters I have worked with have been children's soccer coaches in their spare time, so I guess you could try sourcing some of them as well! Whatever you do, don't assume that Scrum Master is an admin job, this is almost certain to be a disaster.

Most organisations are quick to push back on the notion that Scrum Master is a full-time role. From a pure head count and funding perspective I get it. We have told you that you are not going to be able to repurpose your existing army of Project Managers, so you either need to hire 5 to 12 new people or repurpose 5 to 12 team members. I'm sure neither option is appealing. But here's the rub, you are betting the house on Agile and you have teams and Scrum Masters that are new to Agile. If the Scrum Master is only part time, they will be flat out getting the bare minimum done and their growth and consequently the team's growth will suffer. An investment in Scrum Masters is an investment in team agility and flow.[133]

---

[133] For many years the methodology team at Scaled Agile Inc. did not have a dedicated Scrum Master. When they eventually hired one, the team throughput went up.

If you just can't get the organisation to buy into full-time Scrum Masters my suggestion is that the Scrum Master also be a team member (e.g. part-time developer, tester, or business analyst) but this only works if their primary role is Scrum Master. I have seen the part-time Scrum Master approach used in organisations where the role of Scrum Master is not "allowed" to be used as a formal job title and the people in the role are more passionate about the primary skill than they are about being a Scrum Master where the end result is as disastrous as when an admin person is appointed Scrum Master.

The alternative part-time Scrum Master pattern is the shared Scrum Master approach; that is one Scrum Master to two teams. Personally, I just can't see how this works with SAFe. How can one person facilitate two teams through PI Planning simultaneously? Or facilitate concurrent sprint planning events or retrospectives?

> **Em's Anecdote**
> Having always been one to experiment, when a Scrum Master on one of my trains volunteered to Scrum Master two teams, we agreed to give it a shot. The Scrum Master in question was one of the best on the ART, so we all felt if anyone could do it, he could. It wasn't long before he was under time pressure and the team retrospectives were combined. Suffice to say it went downhill from there and we decided to source an additional Scrum Master, so we were back to one Scrum Master per team.

Adrienne's Anecdote

I tried this early in my transformation journey, too. I had joined an organisation as a full-time employee RTE and when we ran into this same problem, I chose the one Scrum Master to two team model. One Scrum Master resigned along the way and I didn't have a spare Scrum Master just lying about. By this time, I was the Solution Train Engineer (STE), leader of the LACE, and starting an Agile PMO. I also had 14 Scrum Masters and three RTEs reporting to me. I asked the best Scrum Master to take on that third team. Experiment? Well, yes, but it really was just a big disaster. That Scrum Master was set up to fail and so were those teams. Don't ever do this! That is the worst decision I ever made.

Sonya's Anecdote

One of the biggest challenges that face a new Scrum Master is their inexperience, especially if the organisation just sent them on a training without any support to develop them further. When the Scrum Master lacks experience and tries to survive by following a prescribed format, they do not grasp the importance of helping the Product Owner and the team create a relationship. They also do not understand how to help the team to be independent.

One of the things that I feel very passionately and strongly about any ART's capability to be successful is to have support for their Scrum Masters, Product Owners, and RTEs. This means making sure there are experienced practitioners on the train, providing ongoing coaching for all the skills required, and to foster communities of practice. So, to avoid this potential train wreck, especially when the Scrum Masters are not very experienced, find someone who has experience to provide coaching and mentoring.

> **Tips for Globally Distributed ARTs**
> Never keep the Scrum Master in one location, while the rest of the team is in another location. This is just plain crazy. The primary role of the Scrum Master is to facilitate the team. How can you do that if they are in another location and different time zone? I once had a client do this. When I asked them why, they explained to me the Scrum Master needs to be co-located with the RTE so that the RTE could understand the status of the team. This was one of those rare occasions on which I was left speechless.

Product Owners

The next role likely to seed lively debate is that of the Product Owner.[134] Just like with Scrum Masters, if you don't already have some sort of agility in place your organisation probably won't have Product Owners. But you will need them! The most common quick fix suggested by organisations desperate to repurpose their waterfall team members is to make their business analysts into Product Owners. This is normally not ideal; however, I do think it can work in some scenarios, for instance, when the business analyst is actually from the business. As opposed to what I have often experienced where the business analyst is actually part of the technology organisation.[135]

In my view, the ideal Product Owner is a business person that is trusted by the ART's Product Manager(s) and Business Owners. Ideally, they have subject matter expertise relating to how your business operates and the product/solution your ART is building.

---

[134] To learn more about the Product Owner role in SAFe check out: https://www.scaledagileframework.com/product-owner (Accessed 16 July 2019).

[135] In this respect my views do differ from the official SAFe guidance where the Product Owner is sourced from technology.

Now this is of course easier said than done, as I have yet to meet a business with half a dozen spare subject matter experts just waiting for an Agile team to adopt them, so they have something to do! But it doesn't hurt to ask!

> **Caution! Potential Train Wreck Ahead!**
> Of course, you should be careful what you ask for. I once worked with an organisation that had a policy whereby you were only allowed to run your project Agile if the business made a Product Owner 80% available to the project. Of course, the business wasn't silly, they knew how to get around this constraint. They had a simple choice—either find someone in their department who isn't adding a whole lot of value and allocate them to support the Agile team or hire a contractor off the street with no knowledge about the organisation or the product you are building and have them fill the role of Product Owner. Either way, problem solved!

If the business cannot provide dedicated Product Owners, then we will need to compromise. If I have to choose, I will always take less time from the right people over more time from the wrong people. This could manifest itself as a part-time Product Owner from the business or a Product Owner from the business split across multiple teams. If all else fails, then a business analyst from technology that is <u>trusted and empowered</u> by the business could work. Regardless of where they come from, Product Owners must have the necessary skills and knowledge to represent the business context for features and stories.

If you choose to have shared Product Owner the first and last day of the sprint it will be challenging for them to support sprint planning, sprint reviews, and sprint retrospective for multiple teams. In that case the Scrum Masters of the teams will need to collaborate and align on their teams' schedules so the Product Owner can attend all the teams' events. It will also be a good idea to have some working agreements between these teams for PI Planning so as to ensure the Product Owner doesn't run screaming from the building!

> **Caution! Potential Train Wreck Ahead!**
> Some of the worst advice I was ever given with respect to finding Product Owners was to use line managers. The Agile coach who gave me this advice took the perspective that both managers and Product Owners tell the team what to work on and set priorities therefore it was a natural fit. Instead it was disastrous.

What we had missed what that while the Product Owner defines what is to be done, they are not specifically directing the team. The Product Owners were so much more senior in the organisation than the Scrum Masters that it was impossible for the Scrum Masters to coach the Product Owners, therefore each team's success hinged on the inherent agility of the manager/Product Owner.

> **Tips for Globally Distributed ARTs**
> While a remote Product Owner is also less than ideal, I have generally found a Product Owner from and co-located with the business is a stronger pattern than a co-located offshore Product Owner from technology. Anytime I have experienced an offshore Product Owner from technology I have found the organisation's commitment to co-located teams to be admirable, but from an execution perspective the Product Owners' lack of organisational context and empowerment always negates the anticipated benefits.

Feature Owners

Another way I have addressed the availability of Product Owners has been by having Feature Owners. I know there is no such thing as a feature owner but bear with me while I explain.

Case Study:
There Is No Such Thing as a Feature Owner …
or Is There?

When an organisation introduces Agile, it is not uncommon for there to be a mass rollout of Agile Fundamentals training, where the role of the Product Owner is positioned as being an empowered business person who is co-located with and is 100% dedicated to working with the Agile team. This sounds wonderful in theory, but when we scale this begins to get tricky.

As we begin to scale Agile, the pressure on the business to provide more and more Product Owners exacerbates the situation. As much as we might want it to be the case, most businesses don't have a small army of people just waiting for a scrum team to come and adopt them. SAFe has historically attempted to address this capacity constraint by allocating members of the development organisation to the Product Owner role and adding the role of the Product Manager, who reports into the business and is effectively the Product Owner for the Agile Release Train. In SAFe the Product Manager is also empowered to ensure the dedicated ART budget is being invested in the right features.

As someone who has been the business sponsor of a large Agile program, I am very familiar with how challenging it can be to source enough business Product Owners to support multiple Agile teams. In the beginning, I opted for the "contractor off the street" solution. Well, that is a slight exaggeration—most of the contractors were not exactly off the street and were at least somewhat familiar with the solution context, but still not true business people. Regardless, the fact that these Product Owners reported to me as the business sponsor did give me a sense of comfort.

As ingenious as I felt my approach was, it was not the right solution. These proxy Product Owners caused all sorts of challenges for the delivery teams. They just didn't have the in-depth business knowledge required to support the Agile teams on a day-to-day basis. So, when I first came across SAFe's Product Owner model, Product Owners reporting into development felt like an even bigger compromise than the approach I already had in place.

I knew what we needed was real business people. I also knew the business units were never going to be willing to dedicate the right people to work with the Agile teams. So why not ask the business for something they can give—a Feature Owner. Rather than attaching the content authority to the ART in the form of a Product Manager or the team in the form of the Product Owner, why not have a content authority for each feature in the form of a Feature Owner?

Unlike a Product Owner, we didn't expect Feature Owners to be 80 - 100% dedicated to a single Agile team. Instead, we expected them to be available to the team(s) at least five hours a week, every week that their feature is being worked on. The idea was to ask the business for something that they have the ability to give. Almost anyone can find five hours a week for a month or two to contribute to getting a good quality outcome on an initiative that they care about. As a rule, I have found that once the Feature Owner and the Agile Team have established a relationship, a human connection, then the arrangement changes from a number of hours a week to all parties collaborating to contribute whatever time is necessary for successful delivery of the feature. From the team's perspective the Feature Owner is the ultimate authority and single voice of the customer on the scope and acceptance of the feature.

Over the years since I first used this model, I have found many other ARTs have faced similar challenges with respect to the availability of business Product Owners and the allocation of dedicated ART budgets. The feature owner model has often come in handy in these situations. Sometimes the Feature

Laying the Tracks

Owner is more like a Product Owner for a specific feature, co-located with the team and able to provide a large proportion of their time to the team while their feature is being developed. In other scenarios, the Feature Owner is supported by a Product Owner who is a member of the Agile team.

SAFe in Project Driven World
When working with ARTs in the digital domain, the role of Feature Owner has often been played by someone from the business unit funding the feature, while someone from the digital channel team plays Product Owner. This enables the commercial decisions regarding scope to be retained by the funding business unit while still enabling those responsible for the digital channel's customer experience to ensure consistency. In some cases, I have used this model to augment the technical Product Owner as advocated in SAFe.

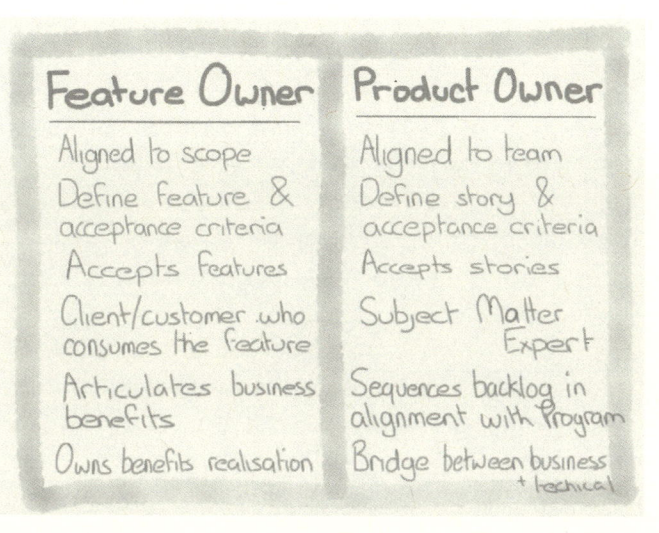

Feature Owner	Product Owner
Aligned to scope	Aligned to team
Define feature & acceptance criteria	Define story & acceptance criteria
Accepts features	Accepts stories
Client/customer who consumes the feature	Subject Matter Expert
Articulates business benefits	Sequences backlog in alignment with Program
Owns benefits realisation	Bridge between business + technical

Figure 13 - An example of the Feature Owner model as applied by one client

One of the most common concerns people raise about this model is the impact of multiple feature owners on the agile team. When applying the Feature Owner model within SAFe, we need to ensure that we have also provided the teams on the train with a force ranked, prioritised backlog, so there is never any doubt about the priorities of the features being delivered by each team.[136] Limiting feature WIP can also help minimise any confusion or competing priorities caused by multiple feature owners working with a single agile team.

So, while technically there is no such thing as a Feature Owner, perhaps there is a place for such a role in some circumstances. In my experience appointing a Feature Owner provides a pragmatic solution to some of the challenges we face when scaling Agile. In most cases, it does not replace the need for each team to have a Product Owner; instead, the addition of the Feature Owner augments the Product Owner and strengthens the connection between the business and the agile teams. I like to think of the Feature Owner model as prioritising access to the right people over more access to the wrong people.[137]

Epic Owners

Personally, I find the name Epic Owner[138] to be somewhat misleading. When people hear "owner" they think this role is like Product Owner or a Business Owner and therefore equate Epic Owner to that of an initiative sponsor, i.e. the person who is funding the endeavour. The primary responsibility of the Epic Owner role is coordinating the progress of epics through the system. Unlike a Business Owner or a traditional initiative sponsor, the Epic Owner

---

[136] Prioritising Features will be covered in Part 3, *Preparing the Cargo*.
[137] Adapted from http://blog.prettyagile.com.au/2015/12/feature-owner-scaled-agile-framework-safe.html (Accessed 16 July 2019).
[138] To learn more about the role of the Epic Owner in SAFe check out: https://www.scaledagileframework.com/epic-owner/ (Accessed 30 August 2019).

Laying the Tracks

is not necessarily commercially responsible for the epic achieving its economic outcome. In most cases it seems that Epic Owner Shepherd would be a more apt name for this role.

> **Protip**
> Project Managers often make good Epic Owners as they often have a good understanding of how things get done in the organisation. They know who to talk to, to get things moving and they have experience in building and presenting business cases. Business analysts are another good choice as they often have the facilitation skills needed to gather the information for the epic to progress. Sometimes the Epic Owner is even a Project Manager and business analyst pair.

Product Managers, Product Owners, UX Leads, and System Architects can also be Epic Owner. However, you will need to take care that they don't neglect their ART and team responsibilities while shepherding their epic though the system.

While I don't necessarily see Epic Owners as initiative sponsors, I can see the value in having an Epic Sponsor. After all, if the organisation is going to spend millions of dollars on a single idea then perhaps one of the Business Owners should care enough about it to sponsor it.

Sometimes we get asked if Epic Owner is a full-time role. This is unlikely, unless the Epic Owners have multiple epics to shepherd through the system. Remember the work involved in shepherding an epic is likely to be a lot less than the work involved in managing a traditional project. With any luck the world of nine months to write a business case and get it approved should be in the rear-view mirror.

Protip

Remember the ART will be WIP limited in how many features it can take into PI planning which means the number of epics to be refined should be in proportion to the size of the train. So, don't rush out to find 10 Epic Owners when the train can't progress than many epics at once. Even if you are on a path to launching a Solution Train that will likely happen incrementally. So, there is time to test and learn how best to balance the demand for epics in the context of the ART(s) capacity to deliver.

Caution! Potential Train Wreck Ahead!

Don't hand out Epic Owner roles to all the people you don't know what to do with during ART design. their time, most of which is likely to be waste.

SAFe in a Project Driven World

If you still have projects, then you will probably still have Project Managers. Sometimes we like to rename our projects epics as the first step in moving towards SAFe, in which case you might like to call your Project Managers Epic Owners or Epic Owners. As most projects have sponsors, I have used the term Epic Sponsor for these folks. We often ask Epic Sponsors to nominate Feature Owners to work as their empowered delegates to work with the teams. As the Epic Sponsors are commercially responsible for the work on the train, they are likely to be part of the Business Owner group.

Em's Anecdote

When I launched my first ART, I was working in development shop with 18 Project Managers each supporting approximately five projects each. When we moved to SAFe, we reduced this to four Project Managers each with a portfolio of around 15 projects. These Project Portfolio Managers were generally aligned to a specific line of business or program of work. They owned the relationship with this stakeholder group on behalf of the Agile Release Train.

The Project Portfolio Managers were expected to be servant leaders to the agile teams, protect them from bureaucracy and support them by removing blockers beyond their control. When new projects arrived, they would smooth the transition of the work to the teams by understanding the end-to-end project and the role the ART needed to play, establishing the priority and securing funding. They confirmed the stakeholders and inducted them into our delivery approach.

Most of our epics started with an analysis spike, which we call discovery. This is where our feature teams established the high-level design, estimated the effort involved in delivering the epic and worked out an indicative release plan based on their current backlog. The Project Portfolio Managers then overlayed the financial profile and packaged up the findings for inclusion in various enterprise gating processes.

During the delivery of their epics the Project Portfolio Managers participated in the ART Sync[139], escalated and resolved blockers, managed the project financials and co-ordinated epic level demos with stakeholders. Where necessary, these Project Portfolio Managers also negotiate changes in release

---

[139] To learn more about ART Sync in SAFe check out:https://scaledagileframework.com/program-increment/ (accessed 23 September 2019

> windows and commercial coverage for additional features. Post deployment, the Project Portfolio Managers arranged for the formal project closure, facilitated retrospective on the epic's delivery, and obtained a Net Promoter Score from the epic's sponsor.

Chapter Leads

You may recognise this term from the 2012 paper by Henrik Kniberg and Anders Ivarsson, *Scaling Agile @ Spotify with Tribes, Squads, Chapters & Guilds*.[140] For those who have not read the paper the definitions are as follows:

- A Chapter "is your small family of people having similar skills and working within the same general competency area, within the same Tribe."
- A Chapter Lead "is a line manager for his chapter members, with all the traditional responsibilities such as developing people, setting salaries, etc. However, the chapter lead is also part of a squad and is involved in the day-to-day work, which helps him stay in touch with reality."
- "A Guild is a more organic and wide-reaching 'community of interest', a group of people that want to share knowledge, tools, code, and practices."
- Where a Tribe is "a collection of squads that work in related areas" and a squad is "similar to a Scrum team". To me a Tribe is not unlike an Agile Release Train—a long lived team of agile teams.
- Noting that: "Chapters are always local to a Tribe, while a guild usually cuts across the whole organization."

---

[140] See: https://blog.crisp.se/wp-content/uploads/2012/11/SpotifyScaling.pdf (Accessed 9 August 2019).

Back before there was a Communities of Practice (CoP)[141] icon on the SAFe big picture, an RTE I was working with introduced me to this paper and we went about establishing Chapters and Chapter Leads for our ART (see case study below). Over the years since, I have established Chapters and Chapter Leads for almost every ART I have launched. When SAFe added the CoP icon to the big picture in 4.0, it did not talk specifically to the concept of Chapters; however, I think it would be fair to say the intent is for the most part the same.

---

[141] To learn more about Communities of Practice in SAFe check out: https://www.scaledagileframework.com/communities-of-practice/ (Accessed 16 July 2019).

Case Study:
Spotifying SAFe with Guilds, Chapters, and Squads

The first time I came across the Scaling Agile @ Spotify paper was when a Release Train Engineer I was working with decided that his train would benefit from creating a series of "Guilds." Despite his enthusiasm, I don't think he got past telling us his great idea was "Guilds" before the team laughed him out of the room having quickly reached the consensus that "Guilds" sounded like something from *The Lord of the Rings* and had no place on our Agile Release Train! I remember the RTE invoking the power of Wikipedia in his eagerness to help us understand his vision. *"According to Wikipedia, a Guild is a collection of artisans who are responsible for the practice of their craft,"* he argued. Resulting in only more laughter from the team. Not one to be easily deterred he took it on the chin and set about convincing me he was on to something ...

First let me give you some context. This train had been born in a world where the delivery team had a strong track record of failure to deliver on business outcomes. An endless parade of consultants had passed through the domain declaring the delivery problems to be the product of poor technical practices that had resulted in a lack of technical integrity in the platform. Prior to the launch of this train, management had created a new group called "Technical Governance" to define standards, oversee the technical integrity of the delivery, and provide an external "control" over solution design and build.

By the time the RTE pitched the idea of Guilds I had spent nine months trying to convince management that the train did not need an independent technical governance team as *"You cannot inspect quality in."*[142] His self-appointed mission was for the train to take ownership for the quality of what it delivered and more specifically to *"put the control and responsibility for core specialisations into the hands of the*

---

[142] W. Edwards Deming, Out of the Crisis, P.29.

people who are doing the work, in order to restore a sense of pride and satisfaction within their work." This mission was premised on the deeply held belief that *"to achieve true continuous improvement, the value stream needs to be owned, understood and improved upon by the people closest to it."* It was his hope that people with expertise in specific skill sets would meet regularly, as a Guild, in order to:

- Share knowledge
- Create tools
- Create training material and conduct training
- Set standards and practices
- Review changes in approach or technology
- Take an outside-in view of the system.

It has always puzzled me why he chose to start a discussion about Guilds rather than Chapters. For me, given we only had one train, it made sense that what we needed was Chapters. I'm not sure whether the RTE agreed with this logic or was just happy that I was bought in enough to argue the point, but in the end, we decide to form "Chapters."

For each specialisation a pair of Chapter Leads were nominated, and the cadence of regular Chapter meetings commenced. Every team on the train was represented by at least one person in each chapter. The Chapters quickly evolved to become a core part of how we operated, fully integrated into our end of sprint Bubble-Ups[143], taking ownership of train wide challenges, and setting the standards for the way we worked. As Taiichi Ohno noted, "without standards there can be no kaizen."[144]

I have continued to find the concept of Chapters to be useful when launching a New: Agile Release Train. In one case there

---

[143] For more information on Bubble-Ups check out http://blog.prettyagile.com.au/2013/06/bubble-up.html (Accessed 23 September 2019)
[144] James P. Womack, Daniel T Jones and Daniel Roos, The Machine that Changed the World: The Story of Lean Prodcution - Toyota Secret Weapon (New York: Free Press, 1990 pg.290.

was a large program team already in place when we started talking about launching a train. The existing structure essentially consisted of functionally aligned teams. There was a business analyst, functional analyst, Development and Test to all lower case. The leaders of each of these teams made up the membership of the Program Manager's leadership team. So, the first order of business in shaping this Agile Release Train was going to be helping the Program Manager shift her organisation from being made up of functional teams to cross-functional teams.

Given the Program Manager was also going to be the Release Train Engineer her world was about to change dramatically. In the new world, her lieutenants would be likely be the Scrum Masters, which at that point of time didn't even exist. Given their leadership and knowledge of the existing workforce, these functional team leads were going to be key to helping us getting to well-balanced, cross-functional teams. I think it was the memory of Anders Ivarsson and Joakim Sundén's talk at Agile 2013[145] that made me think of Chapters and in particular Chapter Leads as a mechanism to help with this shift. You see, at Spotify the Chapter Leads were the line managers of the chapters.[146]

We went on to work with the newly appointed Chapter Leads, to shape the agile teams. Scrum Masters were appointed and joined the Chapter Leads on the train's leadership team. The Chapter Leads facilitated regular chapter meetings and the Scrum Masters facilitated the sprints. My use of the Chapter Lead model with SAFe is continuously evolving. But one thing is constant it is never as simple as slapping a "chapter" badge on a group of people; these things take time.

---

[145] See: http://www.agileaustralia.com.au/2015/presentations/Agile-Australia-2015-Anders-Ivarsson.pdf (Accessed 9 August 2019).
[146] See: https://submissions.agilealliance.org/system/sessions/attachments/000/000/918/original/Scaling_Agile_-_Agile_2013.pdf (Accessed 9 August 2019).

> **Caution! Potential Train Wreck Ahead!**
> Don't overload the Chapter Lead role. Your Chapter Leads cannot be the person that reviews all the code, approves all the merge requests, triages all the bugs, etc. They are not superhuman and this is not respect for people. In the true spirit of lean leadership their purpose is to help the people in their chapter grow and excel in their chosen specialisation. As Deming said, *"Inspection does not improve quality, nor guarantee quality. Inspection is too late. The quality, good or bad, is already in the product. As Harold F Dodge said, 'You cannot inspect quality into a product.'"* [147]

> **Protip**
> Don't just create chapters for the technical skill sets. Have a Product Owner, a Scrum Master, and a Chapter Lead chapter too!

Technical Leads

If the teams are technology centric, we recommend that each team has a Technical Lead. This person should already be respected for their craftsmanship in the domain. Often these folks are the people who used to code and got "promoted" to a non-coding role. If they are to become a Technical Lead, they will need to knock some rust off their coding skills and contribute to burning down the team's backlog by writing code.

The Technical Lead is not the person who hands out individual tasks rather they are the trusted source of technical guidance within the team. Some organisations have people that explain to the offshore teams how something works and what to do next; these people might be good candidates for this role. Technical Leads are expected to help the system architect(s) solution features and epics

---

[147] Deming, W. Edwards, Out of the Crisis, p. 29.

and provide some early feedback on approaches. We usually have the Technical Lead form a Chapter with the System Architect(s).

When looking for Technical Leads, people who have the mindset and passion for XP[148] practices would be a good choice. It is okay if they are not awesome at XP practices now but if they are excited to learn and more importantly like to coach or mentor people then they will be a good fit. By way of contrast, a person who holds on to "their part" of the codebase and won't let anyone else touch it may not be the best choice.

The System Team

For some reason the role and make-up of the System Team[149] seems to cause no end of confusion. I see this team as having two core missions:

- Help the train go faster by building enablers such as automating as much of the continuous delivery pipeline as possible.[150]
- In the absence of a fully automated continuous delivery pipeline, start to build the infrastructure to help the ART integrate and deploy, thereby informing what needs to be automated next.

Perhaps put more simply, I see them as DevOps enablement for the ART.

Often this is the team that sets the development standards for the organisation. Often the skill sets needed for this team are not present in the organisation and need to be hired. If you can, staff it with rock stars. This should be the A-team, the ART's best and brightest. It can be difficult to source them, but it is well worth it. At Amazon, they put

---

[148] To learn more about Extreme Programming (XP) check out: http://www.extremeprogramming.org/ (Accessed 2 September 2019)
[149] To learn more about the System Team in SAFe check out: https://www.scaledagileframework.com/system-team/ (Accessed 16 July 2019).
[150] To learn more about the Continuous Delivery Pipeline in SAFe check out: https://www.scaledagileframework.com/continuous-delivery-pipeline (Accessed 30 August 2019).

their smartest people on infrastructure and enabling capabilities.[151] As they are an agile team, they also need a Scrum Master and Product Owner, with the latter often being the System Architect. Avoid this team becoming a silo by having them deliver their solutions back to the ART(s) and spreading their knowledge to upskill teams.

> **Protip**
> If you have the people with the skills to start working on automating the continuous delivery pipeline prior to the ART launch, start working on it today! It is never too early to start automating. As your organisation agile maturity evolves and you begin to deliver smaller and smaller batches of code, the cost of more frequent manual integration and regression testing is going to skyrocket! Of course, to be effective the System Team will need to understand the current system of work. We recommend they either undertake a study of the existing value stream and its tool chain before they start or participate in a *SAFe DevOps* class.[152]

---

[151] Thanks to Marc Rix for this tip!
[152] To learn more about the *SAFe DevOps* class check out: https://www.scaledagile.com/certification/courses/safe-devops/ (Accessed 16 July 2019).

> **Em's Anecdote**
> A problem I encountered with one of my early ARTs was justifying the funding for the System Team. Team as they were perceived as highly paid experts that were not directly working on "business priorities." One of our more lean-minded Scrum Masters took it upon himself to map the delivery process for the ART. This simple visualisation helped us identify the wealth of opportunity we had to improve cycle time and reduce cost through automation. We established that automating code promotion by building an automated deployment tool would take weeks out of our development process. Some quick, back-of-the-envelope math helped us establish that we would only need to achieve a 5% improvement in throughput to fund the System Team for six months and that was enough to sell our Business Owners on the investment.

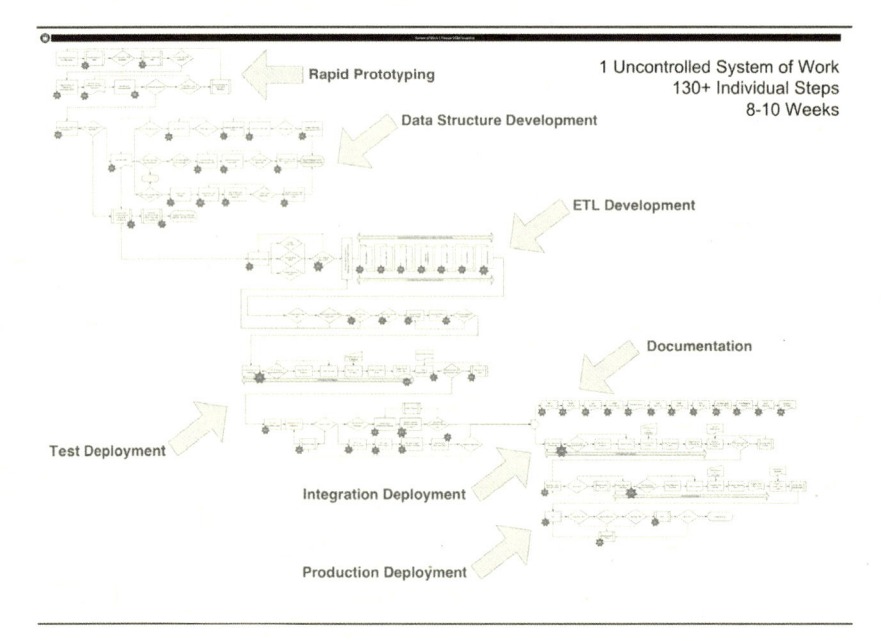

Figure 14 - Visualisation of the system of work. The stars in the bottom corner of each box indicates 1-2 days' worth of effort

Laying the Tracks

> **Caution! Potential Train Wreck Ahead!**
> The function of the System Team is not technical governance, well, at least not in the traditional sense. Remember quality has to be built in[153] or as Deming said, "you can't test quality in." The System Team is not a group of people who write standards and review code. Therefore, any technical governance being provided by the System Team should be in the form of automating as much as they can from coding standard rules through to deployments.

> **Protip**
> When building the backlog for your System Team don't forget about the database! Everyone's so focused on the code they forget about the data needing to promote, too. Do you know what happens when you promote code but not the associated data in the database? Nothing good!

While we are talking about data, you might consider building a golden data[154] set of known good records and maybe some known bad ones too. A good cadence-based activity for the train is to agree on the new data sets that should be added to the golden data set. That way, as new tests are created and data is added to the database you have a way to keep this important artefact healthy, too.

---

[153] To learn more about the SAFe Core Value Built-In Quality check out: https://www.scaledagileframework.com/safe-core-values/ (Accessed 16 July 2019).
[154] To learn more about test data management check out: https://www.ibmbigdatahub.com/blog/5-best-practices-test-data-management (Accessed 10 September 2019)

Case Study: Applying Organisational Management to Software Engineering

A number of years ago I worked with a System Team that was focusing on automating deployments. In theory they were working Agile. They were working in two-week sprints and demonstrating working software at the end of each sprint to their customers, the teams on the train. However, when it came time for the developers to start using the new tool, we couldn't get them to engage. We tried to send people from the system team to spend time with the developers to help them; it didn't work. We tried PowerPoint; it didn't work. Nothing worked. Not at all helped by the fact that the code was pretty buggy. In one instance, a team spent four hours trying to add a comment to a script and ended up deploying it manually.

The lead developer resigned before we got the teams using the new tool. His replacement turned out to be an eXtreme Programming (XP) guy.[155] He was horrified at the quality of what had been built, resulting in an almost complete rebuild, this time using TDD[156] and continuous integration! Despite this setback the end result was worth the wait. With the new automated deployment tool, the time taken to deploy something on the weekends went from a job that took three people all day to a job that one person could execute remotely from their iPad.

A few months later, the System Team had another change ready for implementation. With another change on the horizon I got thinking about a book a couple of us had been reading —*Switch:*

---

[155] To learn more about Extreme Programming (XP) check out: http://www.extremeprogramming.org/ (Accessed 2 September 2019)

[156] TDD stands for Test Drive Development. For more information see: https://en.wikipedia.org/wiki/Test-driven_development (Accessed 2 September 2019)

How to Change Things When Change Is Hard[157] by Chip Heath and Dan Heath.

Would we have been more successful last time if we had used the Switch Framework? Switch argues that for change to be effective you have to Direct the Rider (our rational side), Motivate the Elephant (our emotional side), and Shape the Path (clear the way).

This time we would be changing the source control repository from SVN[158] to Git. Given the experience with the automated deployment tool the System Team made a huge effort to get buy-in from the impacted teams. They spent countless hours at the whiteboard talking with teams about why version control is important and how version control will enable better data in development environments. There was some resistance, strangely enough because some engineers thought the proposal was to replace SVN with a bespoke in-house application called "GIT"! The conversation improved significantly once everyone got on the same page. To use the metaphor from *Switch* we had started by appealing to the developer's rational side, the Rider, by "pointing to the destination." Change is easier when you know where you're going and why it's worth it.

As the cut-over grew closer, the System Team scheduled a workshop to plan the change. They had learnt from the previous rollout that no amount of PowerPoint or documentation would make a difference. What worked last time was sitting with the engineers while they tried to execute the new process and helping them. If *Switch* was to be believed, we should: Follow the Bright Spots. Investigate what's working and clone it.

Replicating this approach was not as easy as it would seem at face value. With automated deployment tool the change was

---

[157] Chip Heath and Dan Heath, *Switch: How to Change Things When Change is Hard,* (London: Random House, 2010).

[158] For more information on Subversion check out https://en.wikipedia.org/wiki/Apache_Subversion (Accessed 23 September 2019)

less invasive, only impacting the engineers executing a given deployment. A member of the System Team could sit with the engineer each time they needed to use the new deployment tool until they were comfortable. With Git, we needed all six teams to make the change at once. After coming to the realisation, the System Team were not Gremlins and could not be multiplied by adding water, a different approach was required.

In the days leading up to the planning meeting, the RTE had been giving a lot of thought to the rollout approach. His original instinct was to include all the things that "we just had to do" in the scope of the change. The theory being that the engineers were going to have to use a new tool anyway, so they wouldn't know the difference. Thankfully his train of thought eventually led him to refer back to *Switch*. He knew his instincts were wrong, we needed to: Shrink the Change. Break down the change until it no longer spooks the Elephant. He talked to the System Team Product Owner about the magnitude of the change. They discussed their hopes and fears for the upcoming deployment and decided to defer the major change to the current branching strategy, continuing with a branch by project rather than moving to branch by feature.

Even with a smaller change we were still going to need more support than the three System Team developers could provide if we were going to be successful. Again, using the advice from *Switch*, the RTE suggested we look to increase the pool of subject matter experts by growing our people: Cultivate a sense of identity and instil the growth mindset. Each team was asked to nominate a Git Champion that was passionate about the change and respected by their peers. The System Team then partnered with the "volunteers" to define the process that would be used to migrate the non-production code from SVN to Git.

When the change was deployed, to quote the System Team Lead Developer, "It went scarily well." That is not to say we have not had some hiccups since. Such as the time someone accidentally deleted the master branch in order to overcome a merge conflict, by using an SVN technique as opposed to a Git technique. Thankfully these types of errors are easy to back out with Git!

All things considered, the concepts we used from *Switch* lived up to their promise. I do think we missed a trick when it came to the third component of the Switch Framework— "Shape the Path." While the hiccups we experienced have not been catastrophic, with more focus on ideas like "building habits" they might have been avoided completely. So next time you are looking to change the behaviour of your software engineering team don't forget: For things to change, somebody somewhere has to start acting differently. Maybe it's you, maybe it's your team. Each has an emotional Elephant side and a rational Rider side. You've got to reach both. And you've also got to clear the way for them to succeed.[159]

Shared Services

SAFe guidance considers Shared Services to be folks needed by the ART but unable to be dedicated to the ART.[160] From my perspective there are two types of shared services: 1) those who can be dedicated to the ART and 2) those who cannot be dedicated to the ART.

For the first group I like to have them as a team on the train with a Scrum Master. If there are only two or three of these folks, I have sometimes chosen to have them join with the Trifecta to create what we call the Program Team. My primary concern is that every person on the ART belongs to a team; after all, it is no fun and pretty lonely being an island!

---

[159] Adapted from: http://blog.prettyagile.com.au/2013/11/switch-in-action-business-change.html (Accessed 16 July 2019).

[160] To learn more about Shared Services in SAFe check out: https://www.scaledagileframework.com/shared-services/ (Accessed 16 July 2019).

If the intent of the ART is to accelerate value delivery, then you will need to be cognizant of the skills the ART is dependent on. Where there is significant demand for a specific skill, attempt to get someone with that skill set dedicated to the ART Shared Services team. One of the most common roles we find the need to have in the ART Shared Services team is Information Security but over the years I have seen all sorts of roles from Business Change Management to Legal being dedicated to an ART.

While the second group is not dedicated to the ART, they still need to attend PI Planning and to plot their dependencies on their own swim lane on the Program Board[161]. We often refer to these folks as Subject Matter Experts rather than Shared Services to avoid confusion.

User Experience (UX)

We are often asked where UX fits on the ART. As with most things—it depends![162] If the solution being delivered by your ART has a heavy user interface component, you are probably going to want a UX person on every feature team. As Jeff Gothelf says in his book *Lean UX,* "*For Lean UX to work in Agile, the entire team must participate in all activities ...*"[163]

Even if you don't have quite enough people to have a UX person in every team you might still want to use this approach and hire to fill the gaps. If this is not feasible, you can always have UX shared services team on the ART to support all the teams. If the solution is less user centric, a single UX person as part of Shared Services might suffice.

As with the other disciplines we recommend forming a UX Chapter. The Chapter Lead or UX Lead is responsible for developing,

---

[161] For more information on the SAFe Program Board check out: https://scaledagileframework.com/pi-planning/ (Accessed 23 September 2019)

[162] To learn more about UX in SAFe check out: https://www.scaledagileframework.com/lean-ux/ (Accessed 30 August 2019).

[163] Jeff Gothelf, *Lean UX: Applying Lean Principles to Improve User Experience,* (O'Reilly Media, 2013), Kindle Edition, Location 1749.

communicating and maintaining the UX vision and UX runway.[164] In trains with a heavy UX (or CX focus) the UX Lead may also be part of the Trifecta.[165]

> **Em's Anecdote**
> One ART we launched chose to have a UX as a component team. During day one of PI Planning it became clear that every team was going to be dependent on the UX team creating a mass of interdependencies. In the Management Review and Problem-Solving[166] meeting at the end of day one, it was suggested that the UX team be split up so that there was a UX person in every team. At the end of the first PI, the feedback from both the teams and the UX folks was overwhelmingly positive. The experiment had been a success!

Organisational Change Management[167]

Another frequently asked question is where does "business readiness" fit on the Agile Release Train—again, it depends. This time it depends on the frequency, complexity, and impact of

---

[164] To learn more about the UX vision and runway in SAFE check out: https://www.scaledagileframework.com/lean-ux-and-the-safe-program-increment-life-cycle/ Accessed 30 August 2019).

[165] If there can be four people in the Three Musketeers then surely there can be four people in a Trifecta!

[166] For more information on the SAFe Management Review and Problem-Solving check out: https://scaledagileframework.com/pi-planning/ (Accessed 23 September 2019)

[167] "Organisational Change Management (also known as Business Change Management) is the process, tools and techniques to manage the people side of change to achieve the required business outcome. Change management incorporates the organizational tools that can be utilized to help individuals make successful personal transitions resulting in the adoption and realization of change." https://www.prosci.com/resources/articles/change-management-definition (accessed 25 August 2019).

releases to the user base and the magnitude of the changes. I have worked on ARTs where teams have released new functionality to external customers every week and there were dedicated business readiness analysts on the feature teams. I have also worked with trains where the frequency of release is far less, and business change management has been a small component team on the ART.

> **Claire's Anecdote**
> Ironically my first brush with formal change management was just prior to the launch of our ART. We were upgrading an ERP (enterprise wide software) after years of neglect. I represented my chapter at excruciating and confusing change management requirement sessions which wanted to map every single minor change into a change management strategy. I spent the majority of the sessions trying to educate the Change Manager on Agile and how we'd be better working with the business directly on these vendor-driven updates, and in fact, we already were! The Change Manager eventually decided her time was better spent elsewhere. When we launched the ART, we had a dedicated Communications/Change manager from the business embedded with the teams and working side by side with us every day. She wasn't interested in mapping changes to strategies (or if she was, she didn't inflict it upon us). This was a much-improved model!

What About Me?[168]

The move to form an Agile Release Train is likely to be disruptive to the current organisational structure and hierarchy. While SAFe is clear in its guidance that the ART is a virtual organisation and

---

[168] "What about me?" by Australian rock band Moving Pictures was the number one single in Australia in 1982. This song tends to get stuck in my head every time I start to talk about the people whose roles are being impacted by the ART formation.

therefore no HR restructure is required, there are still enumerable changes to people's roles that are very real and cannot be ignored. The three most prevalent "what about me" conversations we encounter relate to Managers, Project Managers, and business analysts.

What Happens to Managers?

In the SAFe guidance article, *The Evolving Role of Managers in Lean-Agile Development*,[169] it is clear that the role of management will change as the organisation adopts SAFe. For managers that are somewhat removed from the day-to-day activities of their direct reports this change should not be too painful. For some, the shift will be primarily one of mindset as they start exemplifying SAFe core values.

For frontline managers that are used to allocating tasks to team members the shift to agile may well be more confronting. In this scenario, I have tended to use the Chapter Lead model as described earlier. While this is not specifically a SAFe pattern, I think it is congruent with the SAFe concept of Communities of Practice.[170]

> **Protip**
> Whatever approach you take to addressing the role of managers you must make sure everyone has something to do once the train is launched. For example, if you have managers that are used to allocating work to team members and that is no longer required because the agile team will self-organise, the manager in question needs to have new responsibilities to replace the ones that are no longer required. If you don't do this the managers will do what they have always done and give work to their teams, thereby undermining the new operating model.

---

[169] See: https://www.scaledagileframework.com/the-evolving-role-of-managers/ (Accessed 16 July 2019).
[170] https://www.scaledagileframework.com/communities-of-practice/ (Accessed 16 July 2019).

What Happens to Project Managers?

Most Project Managers are quick to recognise that there isn't a Project Manager role in the SAFe big picture.[171] I suspect that is because there are no projects in SAFe and therefore nothing to project manage! Many organisations "fix" this by repurposing all their Project Managers as Scrum Masters. I have never seen anything good come of this approach. Not to say some Project Managers can't become Scrum Masters if this is something they aspire to do.

A more measured approach would be to focus on the skills of the individual and where they can add the most value. There are numerous things Project Managers excel at, e.g. long-range planning, tracking empirical data, understanding performance, stakeholder communication, risk management, and finances, to name a few. We can still get huge value from their skill set and need to find where some might make good Product Owners, others make good Scrum Masters, and others go on to be Epic Owners (or Shepherds!).

> **SAFe in a Project Driven World**
> While there are no projects in textbook SAFe, that may not always hold true in the real world. Let's face it; if you still have projects as your source of funding you will probably still need Project Managers, but chances are their role will change. For example, if your Project Managers are used to producing plans and allocating work these responsibilities will sit with the agile teams going forward, while finances and potentially some risks, issues, or external dependencies may still be part of the Project Manager's role.

---

[171] See: https://www.scaledagileframework.com/ (Accessed 16 July 2019).

What Happens to Business Analysts?

Business Analyst is another role that does not appear on the SAFe big picture resulting in many questions about the role in SAFe. I have seen organisations "fix" this by either making all the business analysts Product Owners or Scrum Masters. Realistically, some Business Analysts will be a good fit for either the Product Owner or Scrum Master role, but it is unlikely that it will work in every instance and therefore a blanket remapping of roles is probably not a great choice.

Over the years I have observed four common patterns:

Business Analyst as Product Owner—This works best when the Business Analyst is part of the business, ideally the same business unit as the Product Manager. This is a good fit for Business Analysts that are subject matter experts that are both trusted and empowered by Product Management. The Scrum Masters may need to provide coaching to ensure their team does not start to work in mini waterfalls, where the POs sit by themselves and write reams of stories that they then hand over to teams at sprint planning.

Business Analyst as Team Member—This is the most common outcome I see come out of ART design workshops. Teams need these skills, but there is always the inherent danger that the team will start to waterfall. Watch out for teams getting into a pattern where the business analyst where the Business Analyst team essentially becomes a go-between. The team member approach works best when the Business Analyst is able to contribute to the team in additional ways such as coding or testing.

Business Analyst as Scrum Master—This works best when the Business Analyst is part of the delivery organisation and has strong facilitation skills. With this approach you'll need to watch out for the Business Analyst that is used to telling the team what to build, turning into telling the team what to do. Business Analysts tend to be very detail oriented and can sometimes need to be reminded that the role of the Scrum Master is to facilitate the team to outcomes, not take over and do the analysis work for them.

Business Analyst as Epic Owner—This works best when the Business Analyst has experience with business case development and strong facilitation skills. In this model I often create Epic Owner pairs by pairing the Business Analyst with a Project Manager. The risk inherent in this model is that the Business Analyst starts to produce documents rather than facilitate the right conversations.

Who's on First?

Once you have waded through the multitude of ART design decisions, it is time to determine who belongs in each role. For most organisations the managers end up deciding which people should be in which team. Ideally this is done collaboratively with index cards as described above. However, there is an alternative, where people decide for themselves which team they can best contribute to. I first learned of this concept from Sandy Mamoli, who later wrote a book with David Mole about their approach: *Creating Great Teams: How Self Selection Lets People Excel.*[172]

If you go with the managers and index cards approach you will want to have an indicative structure in place by the time you get to epic prioritisation. After epic prioritisation, you can make any final tweaks and communicate the change to the ART. If you are planning on self-selection, I have tended to do this as part of the Seven-Day Quick-Start.[173] Using either approach you will need to think about Product Owners upfront as delivering the Product Owner class will be the next thing you do in the journey to launch your train.

---

[172] Sandy Mamoli and David Mole, *Creating Great Teams: How Self-Selection Lets People Excel.* (Pragmatic Bookshelf, 2015). PDF Edition.

[173] The details of how to go about running a self-selection event in the context of SAFe (and our Seven-Day Quick-Start) is covered in Part 5 All Aboard!

Case Study:
Self-Selecting Teams for an Agile Release Train

A few years ago, I was invited to work with an organisation that was structured in functional teams, to help them launch an Agile Release Train. When I facilitated *Leading SAFe* training for the department's leadership team, I took the liberty of highlighting the opportunity to form interchangeable feature teams, with Chapters to maintain communication and collaboration within specialisations. While I was at it, I threw into the mix the concept of using Sandy Mamoli's self-selection approach to create the teams.

Self-selection is something I had always wanted to try but I had struggled to find a willing victim to experiment on. In my view, letting the people who actually do the work decide how best to organise themselves to deliver was the ultimate application of "those who do the work know the most about it." A handful of the leaders in the training expressed an interest in this rather radical approach in which people decide for themselves which team they should be a part of, but overall the consensus was that it would not work in this organisation.

The very next week fate intervened, and the entire ART launch plan was rendered null and void by the announcement of an impending organisational change. We couldn't form teams and launch the ART if we didn't know who would be in the department in eight weeks' time! So, we rescheduled the ART launch. Never one to be discouraged, I again put forward the idea of using self-selection to form teams. This time my approach was to suggest self-selection as a way to boost morale given the changing organisational landscape. I am fairly sure the department head thought I was completely delusional when I was adamant that we could trust people to make the right choices, but in the end he agreed.

The first thing I did once there was agreement to use self-selection as the approach to forming teams was buy and read Sandy Mamoli's book: *Creating Great Teams: How Self-Selection Lets People Excel*. My experiences with watching people bastardising SAFe made me want to try and stick as closely to Sandy's guidance as possible. Specifically, we chose to keep the number of constraints placed on the teams to the absolute minimum.

Our first order of business was to determine what shape the teams should be, and what mission each team should have. There were two notable exceptions: the Pipeline Team[174] and the System Team. In both cases the Teams members were allocated to team and were not given the opportunity to participate in self-selection. Initially this made me uncomfortable, but after checking in with some of the impacted parties, it seemed that they were expecting this and were comfortable with the approach. We decided to form six evenly matched feature teams. This meant we could have six teams of eight or nine people, with a Scrum Master, a Product Owner, and two team members from each discipline. The final step in our preparations was marrying up Product Owners with features.

With one week to go until the self-selection event, things were feeling somewhat under control. We had a copy of Sandy and Dave's book and we had downloaded their Self-Selection Pocket Guide[175] to use as a checklist. We had a venue booked, we had agreed on the constraints for the squads, we had written up the FAQs, and we had a plan to ensure there were photographs of everyone who would be on the train to use in the event. All we needed to do was get the newly anointed Product Owners up

---

[174] The pipeline team consisted of relationship managers which were similar to the Project Portfolio Managers discussed earlier.

[175] See: https://nomad8.com/articles/self-selection-pocket-guide/ (Accessed 30 August 2019).

Laying the Tracks

to speed on their features and prepared to talk to them at the self-selection event and we would be all systems go.

On the day of the self-selection event flip charts were drawn up for each squad and a Product Owner's photo added. Everyone else's photos were laid out on a trestle table at the front of the room. By 9:15 a.m. we had almost full house, so we decided to kick off. I opened with a quick run-through of the agenda for the day, followed by the RTE who set the scene for why they had chosen to use self-selection as the approach to form teams. Then it was back to me to run through the logistics for the morning.

First everyone needed to collect their photo from the front of the room. Next we heard from each of the Product Owners about their features and why people should choose their squad. Then it was time for the self-selection to begin.

Some people moved quickly, almost running to the squad they wanted to join. Others were more cautious. At the end of the 10-minute time box for Round One we were faced with a few unexpected outcomes. First, no one had remembered to brief the interns, so they formed their own team! Secondly, no one was without a home. Thirdly, adherence to the "rules" was sketchy at best.

One of the recommendations in *Creating Great Teams* is to minimise the constraints. For this self-selection we had come up with three rules: (1) do what is best for the company, (2) teams needed to be made up of eight or nine people and (3) each team should have a least one person from each of the functional groups. At the end of Round One we had a number of teams of nine and some teams of five or six. We also had teams that were completely lacking in some skill sets.

Round Two was marginally better. There was some movement but also some very stubborn participants and the teams still varied greatly in size. Each team played back to the room their overs and unders and then we took a morning tea break, during which we reminded everyone of the number one rule—do what is best for the company.

At the end of Round Three, we introduced confidence voting. Using a "fist of five"[176] we asked each team their confidence that their team could deliver on its mission. Where squads responded with a one or a two, we asked what they needed in order to increase their level of confidence. This helped the teams get far more specific about what skill sets they were missing. We also asked the RTE and the department head to vote, which helped maintain focus on the big picture and doing what is best for the company.

In the final round, a couple of people were nudged by management to move teams, in the best interests of the company and the ART. This felt a little uncomfortable; however, it also seemed like it was the only way we were going to get to an outcome on the day. Despite the "management interference," when it came to the final confidence vote all the squads voted confidence of three or above. It was a wrap.

Reflecting on the self-selection event there were a few lessons learned:

Don't assume everyone knows everyone

One of the things I discovered after the self-selection event was that there were not a lot of existing relationships between the functional teams. Given they were a co-located team of teams, I had just assumed they all knew each other. Seriously, I surprise myself sometimes! I have told the story of the beginnings of the EDW Agile Release Train countless times, always explaining that there were circa one hundred people that had worked

---

[176] To learn more on the 'fist of five' check out:https://scaledagileframework.com/pi-planning/ (accessed 24 September 2019)

together for years, mostly co-located over a couple of floors in the same building, that did not know each other's names. Why did I think this team would be any different?!

Be crystal clear on your expectations

In *Creating Great Teams* Sandy and David recommend minimising constraints. I completely agree with this; however, I would temper this advice by suggesting you also need to be clear about your expectations. If the constraints and your expectations aren't aligned, you are sure to end up disappointed. In this case we wanted evenly matched feature teams—ideally with two people from each competency, but we didn't tell anyone that!

Don't seed the teams with missions

As you already know we chose to follow Sandy and David's guidance and seed each team with a mission. We did this by pre-allocating features to Product Owners and using these features as a proxy for the team mission when seeding the teams. Unlike the patterns that Sandy and David have observed where people tended to choose a team based on who they want to work with, on this train people tended to choose teams based on the work! The weird part of this was that teams were not going to be changed for at least six months, but the features only represented 10 weeks' worth of work. I think if I had it over, I would try and structure the event so that the newly formed teams pulled down the features that they wanted after the self-selection event!

Communicate earlier

This was simply a miss. There were lots of good reasons why we did not communicate earlier but I do think it hurt us on the day. At a minimum I would like to have communicated the problem we were trying to solve and the constraints before the event. This provides an opportunity to flush out any flaws with the thought process and gives people more time to make considered choices.

> In the end none of these challenges had a catastrophic impact on the ART. In fact, these challenges paled into the background as the ART hit the ground running, with a momentum that had the whole company talking about the marked changed in the department since the train launched.[177]

W.R.A.P.

ART design is definitely more art than science, no pun intended! You will not get every decision right the first time—no one ever does. In their book *Decisive*, Chip and Dan Heath provide the following advice to help us make better decisions:

- **W**iden your options
- **R**eality-test your assumptions
- **A**ttain distance before deciding
- **P**repare to be wrong.[178]

While all four elements of the W.R.A.P process are valuable, I always like to bring focus to the last one. Given we know we are going to make mistakes, how do we execute each decision in a manner whereby it will be okay if we need to revisit it again later? Even though I am a huge fan of persistent teams and ARTs, you should know that almost every train changes shape in some way over time as you inspect and adapt your SAFe implementation.

---

[177] Adapted from: http://blog.prettyagile.com.au/2016/11/6-Day-SAFe-Quick-Start-Pitching-Self-Selection.html, http://www.prettyagile.com/2016/12/6-day-quick-start-prepare-safe-squadification.html, and http://www.prettyagile.com/2017/01/facilitating-team-self-selection-safe-art.html (Accessed 30 August 2019).
To learn what happened when the this ART ran their second and third self-selection events check out: http://blog.prettyagile.com.au/2017/08/re-squadification.html (Accessed 30 August 2019).

[178] Chip Heath and Dan Heath, *Decisive: How to Make Better Choices in Life and Work*, (New York: Crown Publishing, 2013) p. 23.

Planning the ART Launch

Now you have a train design it is time to work with the Trifecta and the Business Owners to create the launch plan. We think of this as PI Planning for your first PI Planning!

Choose a Launch Date

The first step is to agree on a date for the Quick-Start.[179] This is often easier said than done. When it comes to setting a date, our approach is to target approximately 8 to 12 weeks after the ART Leadership has taken *Leading SAFe*. From there we start eliminating dates by avoiding:

- Any date prior to the next committed release or any committed milestone that cannot be missed. The Quick-Start will take the entire train offline for a week, so any committed outcome is likely to be impacted
- Public holidays for regions represented on the train (and if distributed don't forget to check the public holidays in all countries and regions as these often differ)
- School holidays in countries where annual leave or PTO[180] is commonly taken in line with school holidays
- External or internal conferences or offsites that will make key executives unavailable to support the event.

Then cross-check the remaining dates with the availability of your Scaled Agile Partner or SPCs and I promise you there won't be many options left.

---

[179] If you are not familiar with the SAFe Quick-Start approach check out: https://www.scaledagileframework.com/train-teams-and-launch-the-art/ (Accessed 26 August 2019).
If you are not yet convinced of the value of a Quick-Start then sit tight we will cover this in Part 5 All Aboard!
[180] For those not based in North American PTO stands for Paid Time Off or Personal Time Off.

> **Protip**
> If your ART is part of a Solution Train, you will need to fall in line with the existing cadence. If some of the factors mentioned above make this challenging, you might like to do a shorter PI so that you can sync up with your Solution Train at the end of the PI.

Visualise the Schedule

Now you have chosen a date, it is time to plan. The first thing we put in is the Quick-Start window at the end of the schedule. We prefer to run a Seven-Day Quick-Start as follows:

- Days 1 and 2: SAFe Scrum Master training with SSM certification[181]
- Day 3: Team Formation/Self-Selection workshop
- Days 4 and 5: SAFe for Teams with SAFe Practitioner certification[182]
- Days 6 and 7: Program Increment Planning

It is useful to visualise the calendar from today, to the Quick-Start, and through first PI including Inspect and Adapt and PI2 planning, blocking out dates where there are holidays or other events that will prevent ART launch preparation work occurring. Then working backwards, we start to plot the training and workshops that we recommend occur before the launch, including:

- Leading SAFe for the ART leadership

---

[181] To learn more about the *SAFe Scrum Master* class check out: https://www.scaledagile.com/certification/courses/safe-scrum-master/ (Accessed 10 September 2019)

[182] To learn more about the *SAFe for Teams* class check out: https://www.scaledagile.com/certification/courses/safe-for-teams/ (Accessed 21 July 2019)

Laying the Tracks

- SAFe Product Owner/Product Manager training with POPM certification[183]
- Epic Writing Workshops
- Epic Prioritisation
- Writing and Solutioning
- Impact Mapping Workshops
- Feature Definition Workshops
- Feature Prioritisation

We also plan out communications, stakeholder briefings, and any other readiness activity that makes sense in the organisational context.

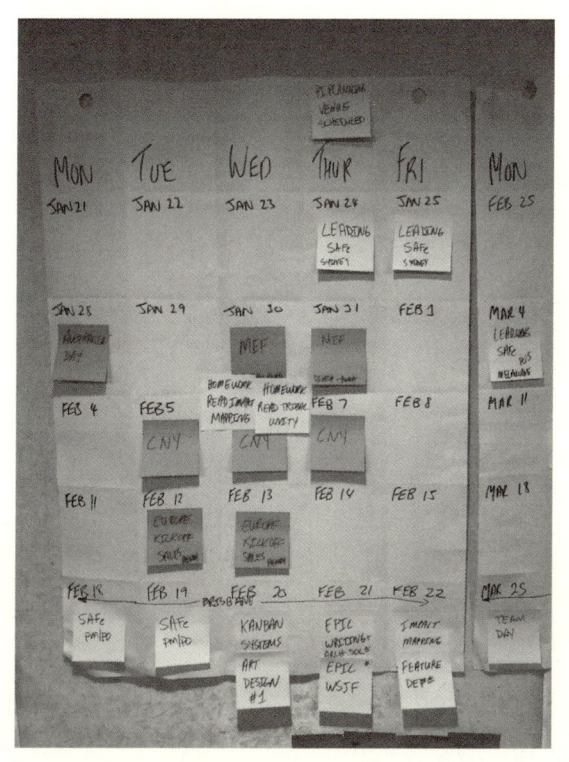

Figure 15 - Example of an ART Launch Plan

---

[183] To learn more about the *SAFe Product Owner/Product Manager* class check out: https://www.scaledagile.com/certification/courses/safe-product-owner-product-manager/ (Accessed 10 September 2019)

As many of these events require commitment from senior leaders either to attend sessions or free their people up to attend sessions, bringing the Business Owners to the gemba,[184] sharing the plan, and asking them to accept it is generally a good choice.

Figure 16 - Pebbles Sy, SVP & Chief Information Officer (left) and Martha Sazon, SVP & Broadband Business Head accepting the ART Launch plan shown behind them, Globe Telecom; printed with permission

> **Protip**
> Once your ART launch schedule is agreed be sure to share it with the folks who are impacted. Randomly scheduling events with little notice diminishes the importance of them and results in people opting out or turning up ill-prepared.

Visualise the Plan

Just like a team in PI Planning, the Trifecta should build a plan to get to launch, with one sheet of flip chart paper per sprint. To help maintain focus, I like the Trifecta to work in one-week sprints. Using the milestones/events on the launch schedule, the Trifecta will brainstorm the work they need to do to prepare for each event, decide when it needs to be done, who is going to own it, and plot it on the plan.

---

[184] Gemba is a Japanese term meaning "the real place" where the work is done.

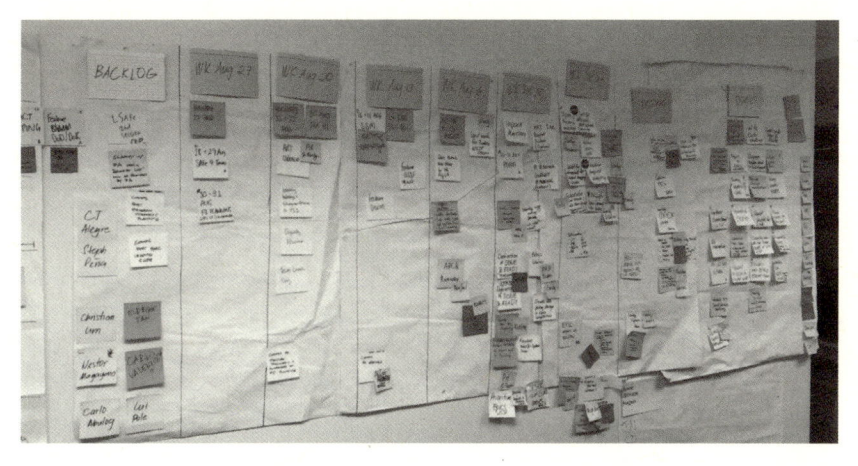

Figure 17 - A PI plan to get to PI Planning

At the end of the session, take a confidence vote and agree on the cadences. The RTE gets to start practising their marshalling skills right away as they facilitate this team toward the ART launch. What better way to that than have the Trifecta start to behave like a scrum team and do what scrum teams do? Sprint planning, daily stand-ups, backlog refinement, the sprint demo, and retrospectives should suffice. Use the sprint demo as an opportunity to bring the Business Owners to the Gemba. Create a ROAM "Kanban Board" to visualise the risks and issues. When the Business Owners come to the Gemba have them ROAM the risks and get them to start practising removing impediments.[185]

---

[185] To learn more about ROAM check out the content under Program Risks: https://www.scaledagileframework.com/pi-planning/ (Accessed 26 August 2019).

Figure 18 - Risk "Kanban Board"

Training the Product Organisation

We like to deliver the *SAFe Product Owner/Product Manager*[186] (POPM) class within a couple of weeks of the *ART Leading SAFe*. While there are no mandatory prerequisites for this class *Leading SAFe* is recommended. For our clients we insist attendees take *Leading SAFe* before the POPM class. The way the POPM class (and the exam) is structured it assumes knowledge of *Leading SAFe*. In our view this makes it difficult content to teach to an audience that does not have this knowledge. This can be made even more challenging when part of the class has taken *Leading SAFe* and the other hasn't.

---

[186] To learn more about SAFe Product Owner/Product Manager check out: https://www.scaledagile.com/certification/courses/safe-product-owner-product-manager/ (Accessed 26 August 2019).

> **Protip**
> Occasionally we get asked to deliver a POPM class to an audience that has not been through *Leading SAFe*. The potential client is quick to tell us that it will all be okay, all the attendees are familiar with SAFe. Unfortunately, this is often not the case, and the audience is so curious about SAFe that the class gets derailed while you cover content that is in *Leading SAFe* but not in POPM. If you find yourself in this bind, consider teaching *Leading SAFe* instead of POPM. You can always draw attention to the role of the Product Owner and Product Manager in SAFe as you teach *Leading SAFe*.

Who should attend?

Obviously, the ART's Product Owners and Product Managers need to attend the class. We also insist that the RTE and System Architect join. If you have an architecture team, they would also benefit. The UX folks, Epic Owners, and Business Owners are also musts. Many of your shared services team members will also benefit from this class, especially if their relationship with the ART means that they provide requirements. Information Security is a good example of this.

Even though there is no Project Manager or business analyst role specified in SAFe, as we have already discussed you may well have people in these roles currently. If they have knowledge of the work that is likely to be prioritised for this ART, including them in this class will both help them learn about the new way of working and enable them to contribute to shaping the backlog. If you still have spare seats, inviting Scrum Masters and Technical Leads would be a good choice.

> **Em's Anecdote**
> When attending classroom training, people often choose to sit with their peers. We recently taught a class with four tables of four people. The attendees had gone and found their functional group friends—architecture, UX, Product Owners, and the Agile PMO. Our first order of business for that class was to suggest we get a bit more Agile and form cross-functional tables teams. Time to start working in a new way!

> **Protip**
> This class allows the participants to walk the lifecycle of an epic starting with the epic Hypothesis Statement.[187] We always ask our classes to collaborate as a table group to write up an epic from their real-world context. We also warn them that the epic they choose they will work with for the remainder of the class, so to choose something that at least one person on the table is knowledgeable about. Through this exercise we start to illustrate the benefit of cross-functional teams working together in a transparent manner. Those who knew nothing about the initiative before gain context and those who did know about it gain clarity of thought, the end result being shared understanding and alignment.

---

[187] To learn more about Epics in SAFe check out: https://www.scaledagileframework.com/epic/ (Accessed 16 July 2019).

Laying the Tracks

Chapter Summary

In this chapter we explored:

- The role of Leading SAFe in helping managers start their change journey
- How to set up your Leading SAFe classes for success
- Identifying the people to fill the key ART roles of Business Owner, Release Train Engineer, Product Manager, and System Architect
- Recommended design principles for creating the Agile Teams for your ART
- Approaches for working with vendors on an ART
- Identifying the people to fill the right candidates for the specialist roles of Scrum Masters, Product Owners, Epic Owners, and UX
- Introducing additional specialist roles such as Feature Owners, Chapter Leads, and Business Change Management
- Forming the System Team
- Approaches to Shared Services
- Guidance on creating the System Team
- How to address roles that are not on the SAFe Big Picture like Line Managers, Project Managers, and Business Analyst
- Using Self-Selection to form teams
- Preparing to be wrong with your initial ART design
- Setting the date to launch and visualising the plan to get to launch
- Training the Product Organisation to load the cargo on the train

PART 3
PREPARING THE CARGO

I always say there are four key ingredients to a successful ART launch:

1. Leadership mindset
2. Agile Release Trains and Agile Teams
3. A prioritised backlog of Features that meet the definition of ready
4. The education to plan and execute a Program Increment.

The focus of this section is getting to a prioritised backlog of Features that meet the definition of ready for PI Planning.

Understanding the SAFe® Requirements Model

For those who like to read UML[1] data models, SAFe provides a comprehensive scalable requirements model on the Scaled Agile Framework website.[2] For everyone else, including me, below is a crash course in the SAFe Requirements Model.[3]

---

[1] UML is the Unified Modelling Language.
[2] See: https://www.scaledagileframework.com/safe-requirements-model/ (Accessed 16 July 2019).
[3] Thanks to Claire Sanders for the image.

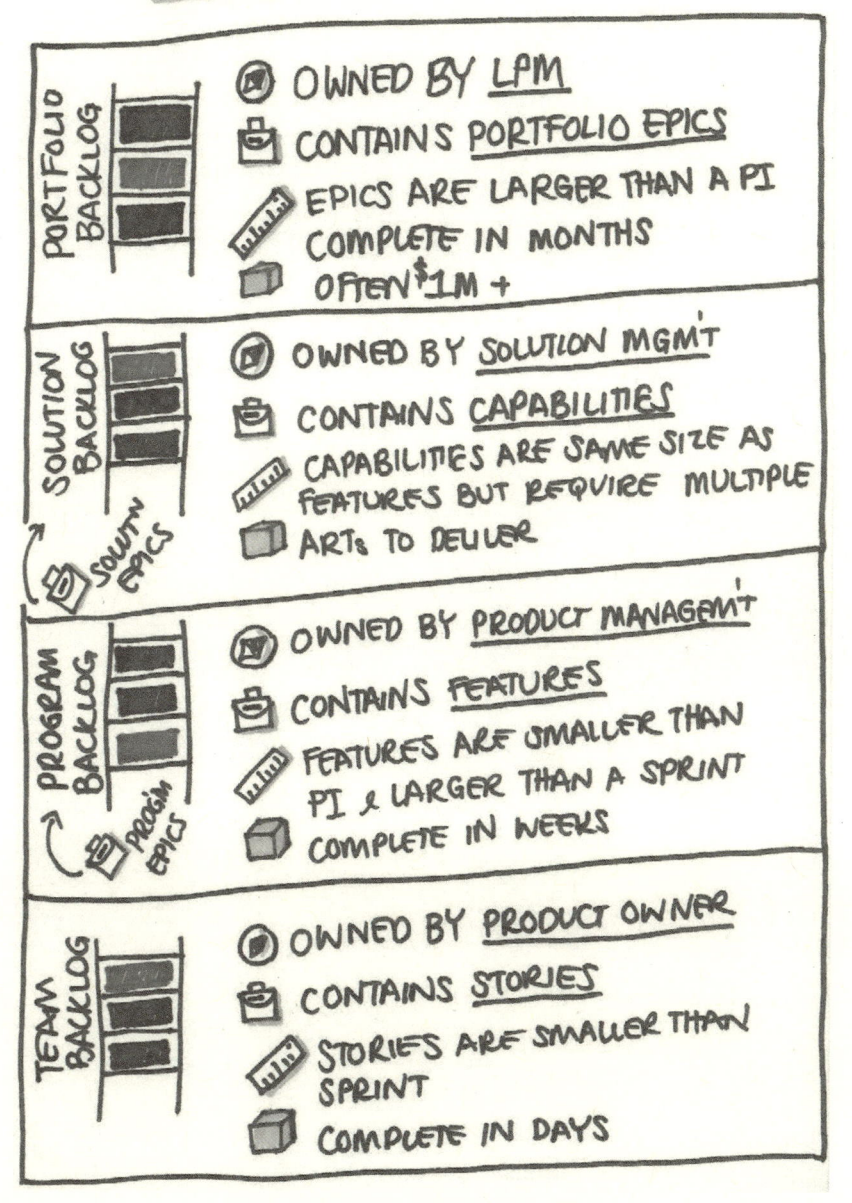

Figure 19 - The SAFe Requirements Model

Identifying the Program Epics

Many organisations transitioning to SAFe live in the world of projects. When this is the case, we find the easiest way to start building the epic backlog is to use the existing projects. We ask the organisation for a list of projects they have in mind for delivery by the ART, including whatever is in flight. Of course, if they don't have projects you can just ask them for their list of big ideas. This list almost always completely dwarfs the delivery capability of the ART. When this occurs, we ask the Business Owners to actively cull all the epics that do not align with the organisation's strategy. (Sometimes this results in the organisation realising they don't have an aligned strategy, which might be an indication that the organisation would benefit from SAFe's *Lean Portfolio Management* course.)[4]

Even if the Business Owners are able to cull the list you will probably still get to the point where you need to ask them to identify the top four or five epics to be considered for the upcoming PI. While you could work on defining more, much of this will likely end up being waste as priorities shift and the maturity of the ART evolves over time. Given the context for this book is a single ART we are specifically interested in Program Epics.[5]

---

[4] To learn more about SAFE's Lean Portfolio Management class check out: https://www.scaledagile.com/certification/courses/lean-portfolio-management/ (accessed 19 August 2019).

[5] If your ART is part of a Solution Train or Portfolio, we would expect that the portion of the Solution or Portfolio Epics that relates to this train would have been identified as Program Epics or Features and passed to this ART. For more information check out: https://www.scaledagileframework.com/implementation-strategies-for-business-epics/ (Accessed 2 September 2019).

> **Protip**
> There is no rule that states that every ART has epics. While epics are almost inevitable in large enterprises, smaller businesses with one or two trains sometimes don't have epics. Whatever you do, don't force them to create epics because there are epics in SAFe or your agile tool says you need them. There is nothing wrong with a train that only has features, just remember to make sure those features fit in a program increment! If this is your context you can now jump ahead to the section on **Defining Features**.

Defining the Program Epics

It is important to have the organisation complete Epic Hypothesis Statements[6] for each project or initiative, including anything in flight that won't be completed before the ART launch. We like to do this in an Epic Writing Workshop. Sometimes organisations will resist this, explaining that "we already understand this project, we have been working on it for months." "No problem," I say, "this won't take long then." ;-)

> **Em's Anecdote**
> A number of years ago, I started working with a new client. As part of onboarding me they showed me the backlog they had prepared for the year ahead, on a very neat slide. They explained that we would not need to spend a lot of time on backlog refinement as the program of work was already defined for the entire year. In our first meeting to review the backlog, I made the mistake of asking them to tell me about one of the line items. As it turned out there was no detail behind that line item,

---

[6] For more information on the Epic Hypothesis Statement check out: https://scaledagileframework.com/epic/ (accessed 24 September 2019)

> or in fact most of the line items on their one-year plan. We were going to have to have some conversations if we were going to have a backlog to take into PI Planning!

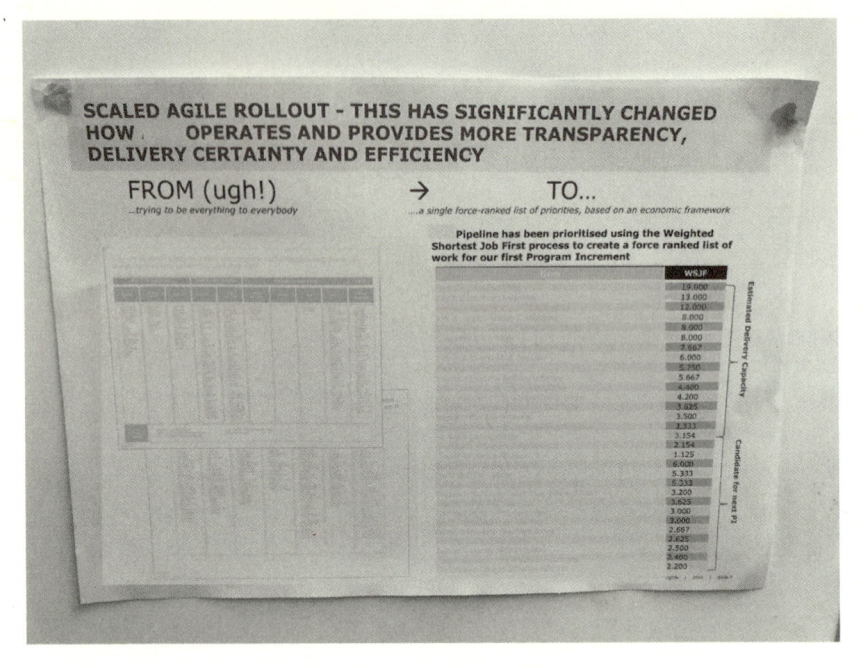

Figure 20 – Refining the backlog

Good epic writing is a collaborative process. It requires participation from the person who came up with the idea and knows the most about it along with appropriate folks from the business, product, the customer facing channels, back of house, UX/CX, and technology that will play a role in bringing the idea to life. Without fail it takes the organisation a couple of hours to agree on the Epic Hypothesis Statement for the first epic and even then, there are usually several items to be clarified after the session. No matter how well known the project or idea is, we have never found the process of writing good Epic Hypothesis

Statements to be quick or easy. Really, no kidding; not once has this gone "fast." It is fascinating to me that an organisation might have been working on a particular initiative for a year but when we ask them what the business outcome hypothesis is, they have absolutely no idea!

> **Caution! Potential Train Wreck Ahead!**
> Whatever you do, do not let someone sit by themselves and type up a series of Epic Hypothesis Statements on a wiki page and declare their job done! Organisations that are used to traditional project management will often make this rookie mistake in their eagerness to get started. Another way people get themselves into trouble is not having a balanced community of technology and business people in the room. We use the Epic Hypothesis Statements later to develop the solution so creating a shared understanding of the desired outcome is going to be key to success.

> **Protip**
> We have groups work together on a flip chart or a whiteboard to define epics, so that they are big and visible, and everyone can contribute. If we are working with a large group, we will split the attendees into smaller groups of five or six then at periodic moments we have the groups play back their epic to the rest of the room and get some feedback. There is often a number of "ah-ha" moments as people start saying *"Oh, I didn't know that"* or *"Are you sure that's right? Because we aren't building that."* By writing epics collaboratively in workshops, we are building a common understanding of the work in all of the very smart heads (not just the Epic Owners).

> **Maarit's Anecdote**
> In one client organisation it was hard to come up with good descriptive epics, so they created a "ten second rule." You have to, in ten seconds, explain in plain English what your epic is and what it does. If you cannot do this, go and practise and come back next time. The result was that the client was able to abandon complex language and focus more on the value of each epic.

> **Tips for Globally Distributed ARTs**
> When you are first launching the train try to bring the participants for the Epic Writing Workshops together in one location for a few days. We find that many of the people who need to work together to bring these big ideas to life have never met each other. Providing an opportunity for these folks to meet early in the life of an initiative will accelerate building a foundation of trust that the players can then rely on as they move forward together.
>
> Over time this may not always be practical in which case I recommend creating an even playing field for all the participants. If one workshop participant is going to be remote, move the entire workshop to an online setting and instead of a white try sharing a Google Doc.

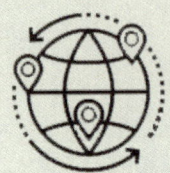

Warming Up With the Pixar Pitch

A good warm-up activity for an Epic Writing Workshop is writing a Pixar Pitch. I came to learn of this from Daniel Pink's book *To Sell is Human*,[7] where he outlines "six promising successors to the

---

[7] Daniel H. Pink, *To Sell Is Human: The Surprising Truth About Persuading, Convincing and Influencing Others*, (Melbourne: The Text Publishing Company, 2012). Kindle Edition pp. 170-173.

Preparing the Cargo

elevator pitch" including the Pixar Pitch which he adapted from Kenn Adams' Story Spine:[8]

THE STORY SPINE

THE STORY SPINE	STRUCTURE	FUNCTION
Once upon a time...	Beginning	The world of the story is introduced and the main character's routine is established.
Every day...		
But, one day...	The Event	The main character breaks the routine.
Because of that...	Middle	There are dire consequences for having broken the routine. It is unclear if the main character will come out alright in the end.
Because of that...		
Because of that...		
Until finally...	The Climax	The main character embarks upon success or failure
And, ever since then...	End	The main character succeeds or fails, and a new routine is established.

Published at aerogrammestudio.com, ©Kenn Adams

Figure 21 - The Story Spine

When introducing the Pixar Pitch, I explain that this is an approach used by Pixar to pitch their films and share with them the *Finding Nemo* example from *To Sell is Human*.[9]

Once upon a time there was a widowed fish named Marlin who was extremely protective of his only son, Nemo.
Every day, Marlin warned Nemo of the ocean's dangers and implored him not to swim far away.
One day in an act of defiance, Nemo ignores his father's warnings and swims into the open water.
Because of that, he is captured by a diver and ends up as a pet in the fish tank of a dentist in Sydney.

---

[8] See: http://aerogrammestudio.com/wp-content/uploads/2013/05/The-Story-Spine-via-aerogrammestudio.png (Accessed 9 April 2019).
[9] Daniel H. Pink, *To Sell Is Human*, p. 171.

Because of that, Marlin sets off on a journey to recover Nemo, enlisting the help of other sea creatures along the way.
Until finally Marlin and Nemo find each other, reunite, and learn that love depends on trust.

At this point it is possible that your audience will start to snigger. Don't panic! It is okay for them to laugh. We want them to relax and have some fun. The first time I ran this exercise I was working with the Academic Registrar at a major Australian university and the result was just awesome.[10]

Business Outcome Hypothesis

The most critical aspect of the Epic Hypothesis Statement is the Business Outcome Hypothesis. Unlike a project, an epic is done when "*its anticipated business outcome has been achieved*"[11] therefore I like the Business Outcome Hypothesis to be a clearly measurable goal. This helps shift the focus from requirements to outcomes, i.e. "success from a business perspective, even if the delivered scope ends up being different from what was originally envisaged."[12]

In Gojko Adzic's book *Impact Mapping* he suggests a good goal (which for me is the same as a Business Outcome Hypothesis) will enable "*the delivery organisation and business sponsors to re-evaluate the plan as new information becomes available. For this reason, good goals tend to be SMART: Specific, Measurable, Action-oriented, Realistic and Timely.*" He goes on to suggest "*defining a model for business value first, and then defining goals as increments of business value, explaining how the situation should change in the future. This is particularly effective when you have a set of key performance indicators for product performance. For commercial products and organisations, try to define goals that have an obvious link to money.*"

---

[10] Adapted from: http://blog.prettyagile.com.au/2014/06/pitching-pixar-pitch.html (Accessed 9 April 2019).
[11] Knaster, Richard Knaster, SAFe Distilled p. 207
[12] Gojko Adzic, *Impact Mapping: Making a big impact with software products and projects*, (Provoking Thoughts, 2012), Kindle Edition, Location 155.

Examples:

- Starting to trade in Brazil by March next year
- Increasing user conversion by 20% in three months"[13]

> **Pro-Tip**
> When an organisation starts writing epics, you'll be amazed at how much fluffy marketing language appears. For example:
>
> - The user interface will be easy and intuitive to use
> - The customer experience will be industry leading
> - We are building the best thing since sliced bread. Okay, not that one but you get where I'm going.
>
> Epics need to be specific and measurable; however, this does not mean thirty pages of "the system shall" statements. For example, instead of easy and intuitive maybe the user flow needs to take less than five minutes to complete a straightforward registration.

If you find the epic has multiple Business Outcome Hypotheses split the epic so that each Business Outcome Hypothesis has its own unique epic.

> **Robin's Anecdote**
> On one occasion I was asked to take over an initiative to complete an automated delivery pipeline that continued to flounder. The first thing I found was that there was not any definition of what completion looked like and the stakeholders kept asking the team to bring them another rock. Once I was able to get the organisation to identify the minimal acceptable product they would take, the pipeline team was magically able to deliver.

---

[13] Gojko Adzic, *Impact Mapping*, Location 163.

Epic Splitting Patterns

We know that smaller batches move through the system faster[14] and smaller jobs receive higher Weighted Shortest Job First (WSJF) values[15] therefore it follows that smaller epics are going to be a better choice. It is with this lens that we will encourage clients to split epics early and often. In addition to the approach of splitting by goals outlined above, splitting by customer segment and channel are other common patterns we use.

Some folks get concerned that if we start splitting the epics not everything will get delivered. This is of course quite possible, and some leaders are going to have a hard time with this. You may need to remind them to "take an economic view"[16] and that "Simplicity—the art of maximizing the amount of work not done is essential."[17] If delivering all of the original epic is the right economic decision then it will be prioritised, and if not we have avoided unnecessary work.

> **Adrienne's Anecdote**
> We were working with a client that was on a path to hire more people to fill out their train, but at the time we were developing their epics they only had three teams. (We referred to this train as a tram![18]) SAFe is great at helping organisations see their real

---

[14] To learn more about the advantages of small batches check out SAFe Principle #6: https://www.scaledagileframework.com/visualize-and-limit-wip-reduce-batch-sizes-and-manage-queue-lengths/ (Accessed 16 July 2019).
[15] To learn more about WSJF check out: https://www.scaledagileframework.com/wsjf/ (Accessed 16 July 2019).
[16] To learn more about the SAFe Principle #1 Take an Economic View check out: https://www.scaledagileframework.com/take-an-economic-view/ (Accessed 31 August 2019).
[17] This is principle #10 of the Agile Manifesto: http://agilemanifesto.org/principles.html (Accessed 31 August 2019).
[18] See: https://en.wikipedia.org/wiki/Trams_in_Melbourne (Accessed 11 August 2019).

> capacity. Refining a dozen epics for a baby train (or team) is simply a waste of time as there is no way the train can meaningfully progress more than one or two epics.

Leading Indicators

Often organisations struggle to identify leading indicators as they are not used to using a test and learn mindset to validate their ideas. When making a financial investment in an epic it is important know what early indicators would make us want to "pivot or persevere."[19] after delivering on the Minimal Viable Product (MVP).[20] To help leaders identify possible leading indicators we share Dave McClure's Pirate Metrics model,[21] named for the acronym **A.A.R.R.R.**—the sound that pirates make.

The Pirate Metrics are:

> **A**cquisition—gain new customers
> **A**ctivation—new customers use your product or service
> **R**etention—customers return and use your product or service again
> **R**eferral—customers refer their friends to your product or services
> **R**evenue—generate revenue from customers using your product or service.

Using the Pirate Metrics as a frame of reference we then ask the person who came up with the idea for the epic: *"What would you need*

---

[19] Eric Ries, *The Lean Startup: How Today's Entrepreneurs Use Continuous Innovation to Create Radically Successful Businesses,* (New York: Crown, 2011).
[20] According to the Scaled Agile Framework "The MVP is the smallest thing that can be built to evaluate whether the hypothesis is valid." https://www.scaledagileframework.com/continuous-exploration/ (Accessed 25 August 2019).
[21] See: https://www.slideshare.net/dmc500hats/startup-metrics-for-pirates-long-version (accessed 9th April 2019).

to see in the first three months of this idea being in market to make the decision to keep investing?"

> **Protip**
> Just like with the Business Outcome Hypotheses Leading Indicators need to be specific. If you use fluffy marketing language not only will you not know what you are trying to achieve but you won't know when to stop investing in the idea or when to keep going. An "unprecedented increase in user registrations" isn't specific enough to be able to measure. Something like acquiring one thousand user registrations in the first ninety days would be more suitable.

Enabler Epics

SAFe makes a distinction between Business Epics and Enabler Epics,[22] where the latter is often more technical in nature and likely part of the Architectural Runway.[23] These are often sponsored by technology and scoped by the System Architect. If you do have Enabler Epics, it is important that Epic Hypothesis Statements are written for these too. This is something that is often missed.

> **Caution! Potential Train Wreck Ahead!**
> The most commonly forgotten-about enablers seem to be the backlog for the System Team. If you don't yet have a mature Continuous Integration or Continuous Delivery (CI/CD)[24] implementation where

---

[22] To learn more about the role of Enablers in SAFe check out: https://www.scaledagileframework.com/enablers/ (Accessed 18 July 2019).

[23] To learn more about Architectural Runway in SAFe check out: https://www.scaledagileframework.com/architectural-runway/ (Accessed 31 August 2019).

[24] To learn more about CI/CD check out:https://scaledagileframework.com/continuous-delivery-pipeline (Accessed 24 September 2019)

> you can integrate and deploy many times a day then there is definitely going to be an epic or two in bringing that to life. It is important that the work of the System Team is transparent and visible in the same way as the rest of the train.

> **Protip**
> When building out your CI/CD capability don't forget about creating test infrastructure for NFRs. You will also need a golden data set/data store and have a cadence to refresh it with more test points with known good and bad records.[25]

A common enabler epic we come across is the re-platforming or migration epic. This is often the project that the technology team has been trying to do for years but has been deprioritised in favour of delivering business features. Here even the most seasoned Lean-Agile thinker can fall back into some old habits. These initiatives are generally large and often our instinct is to build out the entire new platform and then migrate to it.

The problem with this approach is twofold. A large upfront build effort is likely to consume a significant portion of your ART(s) capacity leaving very limited capacity to deliver new business features. Secondly, there is no easy way to cut over to the new platform because the business, understandably, won't stop wanting to add new features to the legacy system while we are building the new one. Our approach is to look for a win-win where the business gets new functionality on a refreshed platform.

We start by holding an Epic Writing Workshop for the enabler epic. If the epic is large you will want to split it. As with a regular business epic start by identifying the MVP, the work you need to do to prove the re-platform or migration hypothesis. This is likely to be getting

---

[25] Thanks to Felix Rüssel for reminder on the Protip.

the bare minimum foundational pieces (e.g. install and configuration) of the platform or technology working.

Next, look at the product vision and roadmap with a view to identifying epics or features that could be delivered off the new platform. Carve off the parts of the enabler epic needed to support this business functionality and deliver that. Rinse and repeat this pattern until you have implemented enough business functionality to migrate the business to the new platform.

At this point, you may still have a portion of the enabler that has yet to be delivered as it was thought to be required to deliver on the business vision. Don't just blindly proceed with this, pressure test the remaining features first as perhaps we don't actually need them. You may also find there are parts of the legacy system that don't need to be migrated.

As Mik Kersten says in *Project to Product*, "the only technical debt work that should be prioritised is the work that increases future flow through the value stream. Tech debt would never be done for the sake of software architecture alone. [26]

Most enterprises start to realise that they are in a constant state of evaluating new technologies, deprecating older ones, and moving to new systems continuously. The architectural runway is key to seeing how this will happen and how it will change over time so that we don't end up with 10 single sign on solutions.

Identifying the Minimal Viable Product (MVP)

I sometimes wonder if Minimal Viable Product is the most misused term in agile. It is often confused with the smallest, crappiest thing you can deliver with the time and budget available to you. This, however, is not the definition of MVP! *"The MVP is the smallest thing that can be built to evaluate whether the hypothesis is valid."*[27]

---

26 Mik Kersten, *Project to Product*. Location 1512
[27] See: https://www.scaledagileframework.com/continuous-exploration/ (Accessed 9 April 2019).

> **Adrienne's Anecdote**
> Organisations used to project based thinking, where all the scope has to be delivered, sometimes struggle to see delivering less as a good thing. They are conditioned to thinking big. One US based client thought that a new fully featured insurance product offering in three states was an MVP. It was after all only three states and not all fifty! The more achievable MVP was a single small feature in a single state, even a single county, that would be fast to implement and fast to get feedback on to enable a fast decision to pivot or persevere.

> **Protip**
> Depending on the outcome hypothesis building a "steel thread" might be a good choice for an MVP. The "steel thread" is the shortest, skinniest path through the architecture that demonstrates a working functional path for the MVP. The mindset here is to get something working fast to mitigate risk, to get feedback and enable the teams to learn fast. It is amazing how much teams can learn about how integrations will or won't or how components will or won't work together when they build out a "steel thread."

Epic Solutioning

The other part of defining an epic is creating a high-level solution. This often makes the architects very nervous, especially if they are used to spending weeks or even months documenting solutions. It will be important to remind them to breathe and reassure them that mistakes and oversights will not result in beatings. Get them to start by writing a list of assumptions first (e.g. what already exists, environments, etc.). All anyone expects is that they do the best they can with the information they have. However, we do expect that they have actively participated in the Epic Definition Workshop as this is where the epic content should come from!

> **Em's Anecdote**
> One group of architects we worked with were forever complaining about having to attend Epic Writing Workshops as it was "a business thing" and they weren't needed. Then we asked them to whiteboard the solution, at which point they had many questions for "the business" who of course were not at the epic solutioning workshop because that was "a technology thing"! It only took this scenario playing out a handful of times before this train's Trifecta recognised that having full attendance by both business and technology people at epic workshops leads to shared understanding, saving time and rework!

To make epic solutioning as quick and as simple as possible we ask the System Architect to produce an Architecture on a Page. This is a view of the architecture stack on a page that shows the big components and deployment patterns. Most of the time the System Architect knows what to do and a diagram appears within a few days of the request being made, but occasionally getting an architecture on a page has been akin to pulling teeth! When this happens, we go to the whiteboard and get on with it. If all else fails Adrienne starts to brush off her old system engineering hat and shares an example like the one below or try suggesting they use the OSI model,[28] TOGAF application architecture diagrams, or some UML diagrams to guide their approach. Anything is going to help.

---

[28] See: https://www.geeksforgeeks.org/layers-osi-model/ (Accessed 9 April 2019).

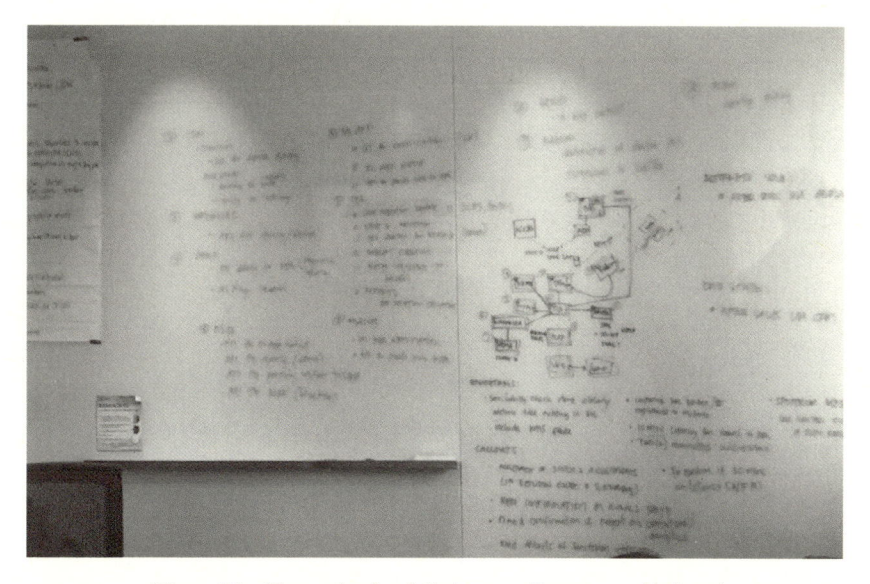

Figure 22 - Example of a Solution on a Page on a whiteboard

With the diagram in hand we ask the System Architect(s) to mark up what needs to be created, extended or deprecated on the Architecture on a Page. We also ask them to tell us the level of impact to the architecture. Is this a small, medium or big change? This shared context is built based on the organisations understanding of the change will be good enough for now. We call the marked-up architecture a Solution on a Page. Our goal is to understand enough about the nature of the changes to be able to provide a ballpark estimate on the effort to implement the epic.

Program Epic Prioritisation

In SAFe we prioritise using Weighted Shortest Job First (WSJF)[29] which requires us to know both the Cost of Delay and the approximate effort required to deliver the epic. The goal of program epic prioritisation is to identify which epics we should break into

---

[29] To learn more on WSJF check out:https://scaledagileframework.com/wsjf/ (Accessed 24 September 2019)

Features first. Epic prioritisation is the role of the Business Owners (we refer to them as the "voters") and is often facilitated by the Product Manager(s) or RTE. This session is also attended by the Epic Owners whose role it is to pitch their epic to the Business Owners using the Epic Hypothesis Statement. Remembering that the Business Owners are a cross-section of business and technology stakeholders who have a vested interest in the outcomes the ART.

> **SAFe in a Project Driven World**
> If your epics are in fact projects, with funding tied to them, they probably have a business sponsor. We referred to this person as the Epic Sponsor in our exploration of the Epic Owner role in Part 2 Laying the Tracks. In this scenario, we would expect the Epic Sponsors to be pitching their epic(s) to their peer group being the other Epic Sponsors and the Business Owners. Noting that the Epic Sponsors and Business Owners could be one and the same.

> **Adrienne's Anecdote**
> Some Business Owners will want to delegate this meeting to someone on their staff. This generally doesn't go well. The delegate rarely has the same richness of understanding of the needed outcomes. With one client a sudden and unexpected resignation resulted in the Business Owner having to delegate the session. I quizzed the delegate if he felt comfortable participating on behalf of the Business Owner and he was sure they we in full alignment. So, we went ahead and facilitated the session with the delegate only to have the Business Owner join the next session and completely reprioritise the list! With 20-20 hindsight on our side we would now say if a Business Owner can't make it to a WSJF session then they have to live with the decisions made by their delegate or we postpone the session.

We time box the prioritisation meeting relative to the number of epics. The first time you do this allow around thirty minutes per epic, e.g. for four epics you would need two hours and for ten epics you would need five hours. Remember to right size the number of epics you take into the session the size of the ART. We recommend keeping the number of "voting" participants to a reasonable size; remember, as we talked about with teams every additional person in a group makes an exponential difference to the complexity of communication within the group.

Start the session by giving each Epic Owner three minutes to pitch each of their epics and take questions. In an ideal world these would have been socialised before the session, but experience teaches us even if the Epic Hypothesis Statements are distributed before the session they are rarely read by all participants in advance of the session.

Once everyone has seen the epics, it is time to calculate the cost of delay. In most cases we use the three levers recommended by SAFe:

- User/Business Value
- Time Criticality
- Risk Reduction/Opportunity Enablement

Occasionally, I have a client that wants to add a lever or separate user value from business value. For example, a client I worked with in the higher education sector added a lever for Student Experience. Another client took a similar approach by adding Customer Experience.

> **Caution! Potential Train Wreck Ahead!**
> While it is okay to add a lever to the cost of delay formula take care you don't break it! Model out how the new data will impact the answers before you commit. I once had a client spend many, many hours pouring over Don Reinertsen's *The Principles of Product Development Flow*[30]

---

[30] Donald G. Reinertsen, *The Principles of Product Development Flow*, p. 31

> trying to work out the perfect mathematical model to calculate cost of delay. They decided on nine metrics that they then tried to extract from the various project managers via a spreadsheet. This did not go well. If you can easily produce the data for a more robust cost of delay then go for it! But if you make it all too hard no one will participate and then you will have nothing.

Before the prioritisation session we create an index card for each epic, including enabler epics. We use blue cards for business epics and pink cards for enabler epics. This is where we zipper our backlog together into one cohesive backlog of work for the train. We write the SAFe Cost of Delay levers on a whiteboard or a sheet of flip chart paper and put this somewhere the voters can see it. We also set up a wall or whiteboard with rows labelled with the modified Fibonacci estimating numbers.

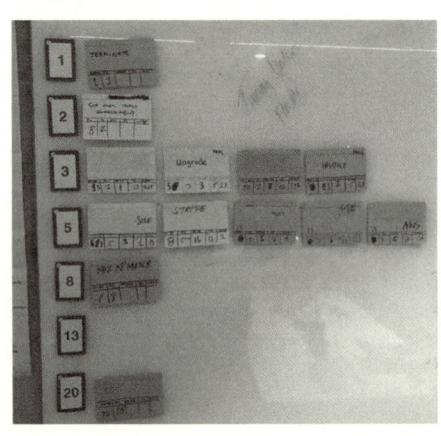

Figure 23 - Prioritisation Setup - Fibonacci sequence poker cards in a column to facilitate relative sizing; in this case for timing criticality and our template for WSJF

To calculate the Cost of Delay we like the Business Owners to use relative sizing with estimating poker.[31] It never ceases to amaze me

---

[31] See: https://en.wikipedia.org/wiki/Planning_poker (Accessed 10 September)

Preparing the Cargo

how powerful it is to have a group of executives debate the relative value and urgency of their pet projects over a game of estimation poker. Witnessing an executive walk into a WSJF session adamant their epic needs to be the number one priority only to willingly defer it once they can see their epic in the context of all the business demand for the train certainly makes a nice change from the LVD (Loudest Voice Decides) or HiPPO (Highest Paid Person's Opinion) prioritisation often seen in large organisations.

We give each Business Owner a set of estimating poker cards with the numbers 1, 2, 3, 5, 8, 13, and 20 from the modified Fibonacci sequence (deliberately excluding 40 and 100 as they skew the data). In the same way that a Scrum Master facilitates a team through an estimation session, we then facilitate the Business Owners estimating User/Business Value, Timing Criticality, and Risk Reduction/Opportunity Enablement using estimation poker.

Starting with User/Business Value we ask the voters to find the epic with the smallest User/Business Value and call it one. Then place it on the board in the row marked 1. If you have more than one smallest and the voters all agree they are exactly the same, then you could call both of them 1. Now pick another epic at random, have the epic owner provide a two-minute reminder of the epic and allow a three-minute time box for questions.

When this time box expires, we ask the voters to select their cards. From here we follow the standard facilitation rules to get a unanimous result. We continue relative sizing it until all the epics have been given a User/Business Value number and placed in the right row. Before we move on to the next lever, we ask the room to sense check the relativity between the epics and make changes as agreed by the group. We then write the values on the epic cards and rinse and repeat for the Time Criticality and Risk Reduction/Opportunity Enablement.

> **Protip**
> As the epics are being discussed annotate the SAFe cost of delay definitions with context from the room creating a reminder of how they interpreted the levers for next time they do this. Often some data points emerge as key to decision making. This also serves as a reminder to the participants to "bring data" next time.

To complete our WSJF calculation we also need to know Job Size. Ideally the job size estimates should come from the people who will do the work; however, when we first launch an ART, we generally don't have the full ART available to support the readiness activity in the same way we do once the ART is operational. Specifically, you are unlikely to have fully formed agile teams available to provide the job size for the features.

In this case we will, as a one-off, ask the Chapter Leaders and/or Technical Leads to do this with the System Architect. They usually observe the first part of the session to learn about the epics. Then once the cost of delay is completed, we move our focus to job size. Here we ask the technical folks to do the voting and the Business Owners to observe and learn. As you have not yet established normalised estimation for your train, this sizing is usually done by finding the smallest epic, calling it one point and then relatively estimating the others.

> **Protip**
> Estimates from the people who do the work will always be stronger than any other estimation. So, once your ART is launched you need to make space in your system of work to allow teams to provide estimates in story points as an input to WSJF sessions. Our preferred approach for this is to set aside capacity as part of PI Planning. We will cover this in more detail in the PI Planning in Part 5 *All Aboard!*

Preparing the Cargo

Once the relative job sizing estimation is complete, we can calculate WSJF. We then select between two and five epics, depending on the size of the epics and the ART, to progress to the next stage. Often the result is unexpected and there may be some discussion about overriding the findings. Be careful how you handle this. The value of the result you have just achieved is more than just the numbers, it is the alignment amongst the stakeholders.

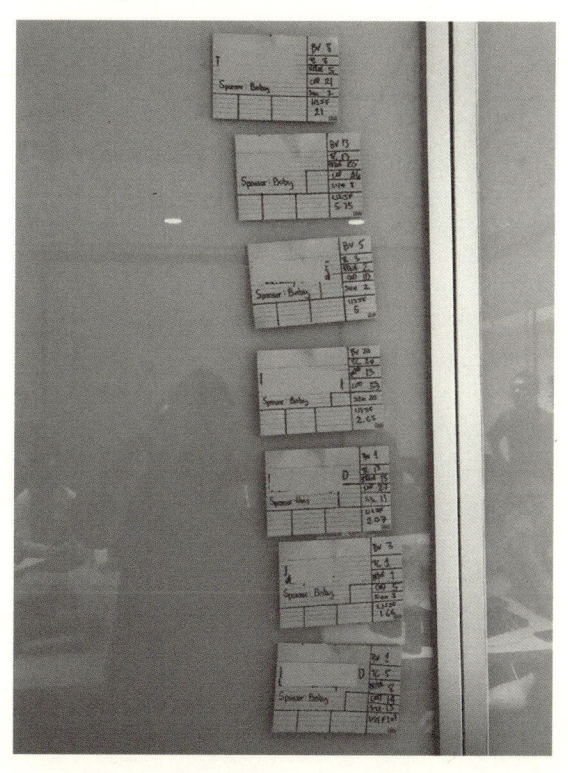

Figure 24 - Final prioritization order from WSJF

If someone is particularly concerned that a particular epic "fell below the cut line" I ask them to talk to the group about their concerns. Often new information appears that was missed in the earlier discussion, meaning that the value of a particular lever was understated. In these scenarios I ask the group to revote given the new information and in most cases the problem is resolved.

> **Protip**
> If all your enablers sink to the bottom of the prioritisation list, consider applying capacity allocation[32] to the ART's backlog, so that some portion of capacity is reserved for enablers. This can also be useful if the trains backlog consists of items from different customer segments and the organisations wants to create a balance investment between them.

One of the realisations that often comes after the first WSJF session is that size does matter. Even though the voters were introduced to WSJF in *Leading SAFe* the reality that small, valuable epics float to the top doesn't hit them until they see it play out in the real world. You can see it beginning to dawn on them during the session. The Business Owners start to get this incredulous look on their faces and then finally say what is on their mind. "This is a game! If I want my epic to make it through prioritisation, I just need to make it smaller!" Well, it won't be the only thing you need to do but this will surely help.

Once the organisation starts to understand how WSJF works it starts to behave differently. Instead of epics (or projects) being feature magnets, collecting every possible requirement and bundling them together into the "perfect" initiative, the organisation starts to identity the nuggets of value inside their big initiatives and break them out into small, separate epics. Is this gaming the system? Perhaps yes, but the best systems give you the result you want when they are gamed and, in this instance, we are getting more flow efficient decisions which is exactly what we want.

Epic prioritisation is not a one-and-done exercise. You will need to establish a cadence for this going forward. Remembering the value of

---

[32] To learn more about how capacity allocation works in SAFe check out the section on *Optimizing Value and Solution Integrity with Capacity Allocation* in the "Program and Solution Backlogs" article: https://www.scaledagileframework.com/program-and-solution-backlogs/ (Accessed 18 July 2019).

Preparing the Cargo

small batches and fast feedback, my preference is to have this group meet once a sprint during PI Execution. This could even be tacked on to the end of the System Demo,[33] so all steering conversations happen at once. We recommend agreeing to this cadence while you have the group together for the first WSJF session and getting the calendar invite sent so there is one less thing to worry about arranging post PI Planning.

ART Design Validation

Once you can see the priority epics and their high-level solutions, take a moment to validate your ART design. This is particularly important if you have formed a value stream aligned ART, with people from multiple different business units and departments. A simple way to do this check is to take the Solution on a Page for each of the epics and highlight or mark up in some way what changes your ART has the skill sets to action.

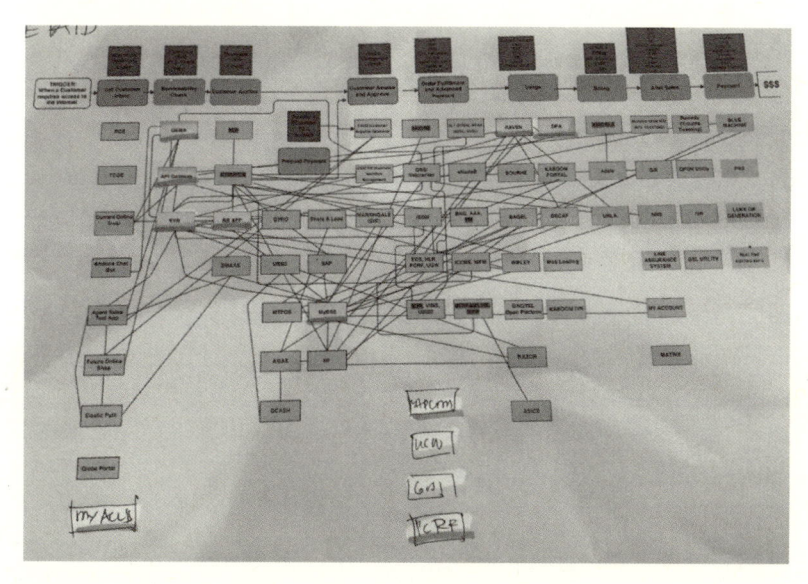

Figure 25 - An epic is being overlaid on an ART. Note the hand drawn boxes added for skills and systems not on the ART.

---

[33] To learn more about the System Demo on SAFe go to: https://www.scaledagileframework.com/system-demo/ (Accessed 18 July 2019).

It is possible that not all the skills are on ART. There will be some instances where a skill is required infrequently or as a one-off, for example inputs from legal or establishing a new data centre. This part of the build can be treated as an external dependency. You will need to make sure that the team that needs to deliver the dependency is present at PI Planning, so that the delivery approach can be discussed and agreed. An Epic Owner can also help with coordination before, during, and after PI Planning.

Should you find out that a skill is needed for many epics but is missing on the train then you have a problem; but better to find out now than in PI Planning. Epics are often with an ART for multiple Program Increments, so you might like to look at adding these skill sets to the train, building up these skills through mentoring or pairing, or if this is not possible at least have people with these skill sets represented at PI Planning. If the missing skill sets really are key to delivering on the PI Objectives, I would expect to see this issue surface during day one of PI Planning, providing an opportunity for the issue to be addressed in the Management Review and Problem-Solving session.[34]

Impact Mapping Epics Into Features

When it comes to writing features, I have often been asked how do I get the Product Managers to put pen to paper and write features? My answer is I don't! My go-to approach to breaking down epics into features is Gojko Adzic's *Impact Mapping*.[35] This is one of the reasons I am so particular about getting to a single SMART Business Outcome Hypothesis for an epic, so that I can then use it as the Goal when creating an Impact Map.

---

[34] To learn more about the Management Review and Problem Solving Session in PI Planning check out: https://scaledagileframework.com/pi-planning/ (Accessed 10 September 2019)

[35] To find out "How I fell in Love with Impact Mapping" check out: http://blog.prettyagile.com.au/2014/02/how-i-fell-in-love-with-impact-mapping.html (Accessed 9 April 2019).

What Is an Impact Map?

"An impact map is a visualisation of scope and underlying assumptions, created collaboratively by senior technical and business people."[36] Essentially it is a mind-map developed via a facilitated discussion of why, who, how, and what as follows:

- **Why** are we doing this? The **Goal**.[37]
- **Who** can produce the desired effect? **Who** can obstruct it? **Who** are the consumers or users of our product? **Who** will be impacted by it?[38] The **Actors**.
- **How** should our actors' behaviour change? How can they help us to achieve the goal? **How** can they obstruct or prevent us from succeeding?[39] The **Impacts**.
- **What** can we do, as an organisation or a delivery team, to support the required impacts?[40] The **Deliverables**.

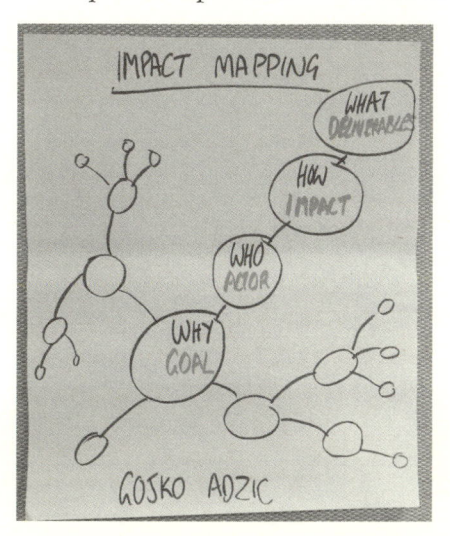

Figure 26 - Impact Mapping explanation

---

[36] See: https://www.impactmapping.org/drawing.html (Accessed 9 April 2019).
[37] Gojko Adzic, *Impact Mapping*, Location 149
[38] Gojko Adzic, *Impact Mapping*, Location 163.
[39] Gojko Adzic, *Impact Mapping*, Location 187.
[40] Gojko Adzic, *Impact Mapping*, Location 206.

Facilitating an Impact Mapping Workshop

For an Impact Mapping Workshop to be effective you need the people who know the most about the idea in the room, this likely includes the person who is sponsoring the epic. You will also need the Trifecta, UX, some Product Owners, Chapter Leads, and Technical Leads. Depending on the scope of your ART representation from Information Security, Customer Support, and other Shared Services folks should also be considered.

We open the session by sharing the Epic Hypothesis Statement and validating the Business Outcome Hypothesis is the Goal. Then we brainstorm the actors often ending up with a large number that we have to prioritise. Next, we brainstorm the possible impacts prioritise the ones we hypothesize will move us the furthest distance towards our goal. Finally, we brainstorm the deliverables which end up becoming our initial feature set for the epic.

Using Impact Mapping to get to features is a great fit for SAFe as features derived from an Impact Map have the benefit hypothesis built in. Our hypothesis will always be that the *deliverable* will have an *impact* on an *actor* that will help achieve the *goal*. The example below from Gojko Adzic's book *Impact Mapping* illustrates:

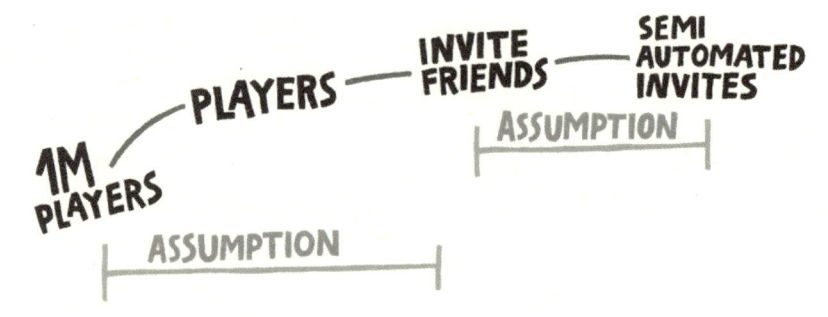

Figure 27 - In this example from Impact Mapping the hypothesis is that delivering "semi-automated invites" will impact the "players" who will then "invite friends" to play helping achieve the goal of having "1 million players"[41]

---

[41] Image used with permission from Gojko Adzic

Preparing the Cargo

As you work through the Impact Map be cognisant that you will rarely need to deliver every feature for an epic. The work needs only to continue until the Business Outcome Hypothesis is achieved or the optimal economic benefit is realised. Therefore, it is also not necessary to surface every possible feature in your first Impact Mapping session. Impact Mapping is best used iteratively. Define the first half a dozen features or so, deliver them, and measure the outcomes. Then if further features are required to achieve the business outcome you can revisit the Impact Map with the knowledge you have already gained and identify more.

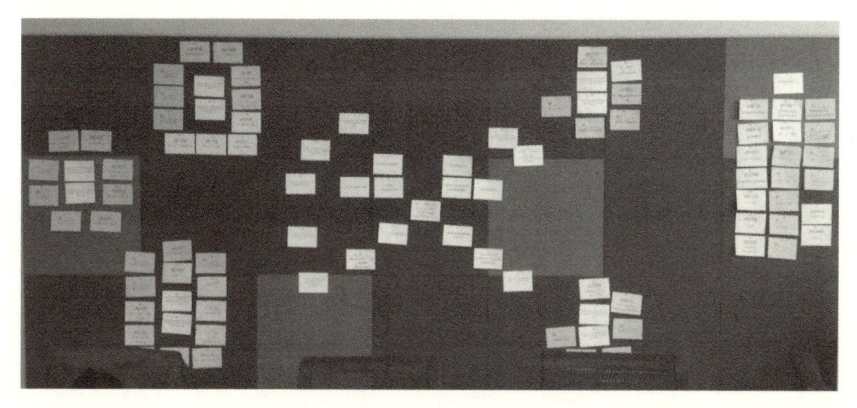

Figure 28 - Example Impact Map

Defining Features

If your organisation does not have epics, then you start defining the cargo for your ART here. SAFe advocates the Feature and Benefits (FAB) Matrix[42]; however, we prefer using User Voice for features.[43]

---

[42] For more information on SAFe's Feature and Benefits matrix check out: https://scaledagileframework.com/features-and-capabilities (Accessed 9th September 2019)

[43] Some folks prefer not to use User Voice for features; we tend to anchor our definition of feature and story on size, whereby a feature is smaller than a PI but bigger than a sprint and a story is smaller than a sprint. We think this helps avoid any such confusion.

This is because Impact Mapping provides us with Features that can be written in this way as per the illustration below. However, getting a feature ready for prioritisation and PI Planning takes more than writing a description using either the FAB or User Voice approach.

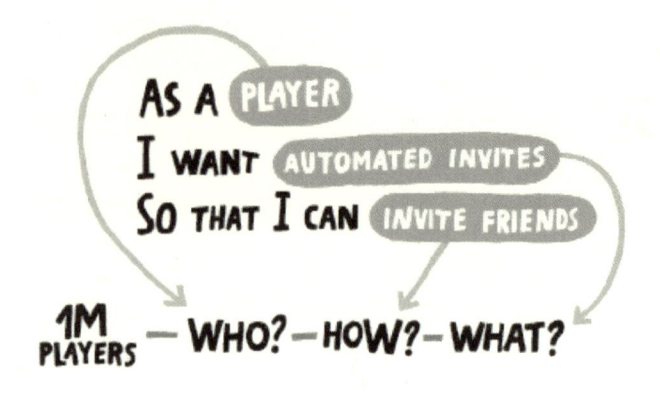

> AS A (PLAYER)
> I WANT (AUTOMATED INVITES)
> SO THAT I CAN (INVITE FRIENDS)
>
> 1M PLAYERS — WHO? — HOW? — WHAT?

Figure 29 - An example of a User Voice feature derived from an Impact Map.

> ⚠️ **Caution! Potential Train Wreck Ahead!**
> Don't go overboard with writing business features (or enabler features). As was the case with epics, your ART is naturally WIP limited by the number and type of teams. SAFe suggests you take your Top 10 features (including enablers) into PI Planning. Depending on the ART's mix of feature and component teams this may or may not be enough work. While the right number might be more than ten it probably won't be forty either! While we know smaller things go through the system faster[44] if we have too many large features on a small train it can be overwhelming.

---

[44] To learn more about the benefits of small batch check out SAFe principle #6: https://www.scaledagileframework.com/visualize-and-limit-wip-reduce-batch-sizes-and-manage-queue-lengths/ (Accessed 11th August 2019).

> **Em's Anecdote**
> I once had a client prepare 110 Features for PI Planning! The Chapter Leads had spent weeks working with an SPC filling out the FAB matrix and sizing all 110 features. When it came time for PI Planning the ART was only able to deliver 15 and the work that had been done on the remaining 95 was never used.

As with epics, we recommend cross-functional groups with representation from the customer facing business units, product management, architecture, UX, and technology work together to define features on flip chart paper or a whiteboard to enable better collaboration. In addition to the features you identify via your Impact Maps you will need to surface any inflight works that are unlikely to be completed before PI Planning and include it in your backlog for prioritisation.

> **Protip**
> If you have a large group in your feature definition workshop break it into smaller groups to create the first draft of the features. Each group works for a twenty-minute time box and then shares their progress with the rest of the group, receives some feedback, and then adjusts their feature definition accordingly.

It is likely that there will be more potential features than the ART will be able to consume in its first couple of PIs. When this happens, it can be helpful to split the epic so that the MVP set of features and enablers progresses while the remaining features are aligned to a newly created epic that is put into the epic backlog for prioritisation.

Definition of Ready

One of the significant challenges a lot of ARTs face in their first program increments is having a backlog of ready features for PI Planning. There are two ways in which we recommend ARTs address this. The first is creating a program Kanban system[45] for getting features to ready (which we will explore in Part 6 - Staying on the Tracks) and the second is being clear on the entry criteria for PI Planning, which we call the Definition of Ready. Just as every program Kanban system should reflect the unique circumstance of the ART it supports, the definition of ready for your ART will be context specific. We expect features to meet the definition of ready prior to prioritisation as this detail helps inform the prioritisation discussion.

Here is an example of definition of ready for Features that we use with our ARTs:

- Name (short phrase)
- Description (As a _____, I want _____, So that _____)
- Acceptance Criteria (Given_____, When_____, Then_____)
- Assumptions
- Dependencies external to the ART
- Dependencies on other Epics or Features
- Meets the I.N.V.E.S.T[46] criteria
- Smaller than a PI[47]
- Out of scope items listed
- Subject Matter Experts specified
- Wireframes complete

---

[45] To learn more about the Program Kanban in SAFe check out: https://www.scaledagileframework.com/program-and-solution-kanbans/ (Accessed 2 September 2019).

[46] The acronym I.N.V.E.S.T. was originally suggested by Bill Wake as a way to remind folks of the characteristics of a good user story. See: https://xp123.com/articles/invest-in-good-stories-and-smart-tasks/ (Accessed 28 July 2019). We like to use I.N.V.E.S.T for features as well, as stories, with the main difference being that while features should be small, so they most likely take more than a sprint and less than a PI to deliver.

[47] If the feature turns out to be bigger than a PI split it.

Preparing the Cargo

- Size in Story Points[48]
- Non-Functional Requirements defined
- Solution on a Page complete.

Protip
While perhaps not all of the above criteria will apply to your ART, in our experience this is a good place to start. As your ART matures, so should your definition of ready. Be sure to take the time to get feedback from all the players involved in feature readiness and PI Planning (including the agile teams) and refine your definition of ready as necessary.

Caution! Potential Train Wreck Ahead!
The wireframes completed as part of Feature Readiness are not supposed to be the final product. The key information the team needs is the workflow and what data will be displayed and captured on the screens. It is a good idea to think about what GUI[49] elements are envisioned to work on the screen, too. Is there a pick list, radio buttons, tables, etc? This should be just enough information for the team to understand whilst still having room for the final design to emerge from the team.

There GUI elements can form the beginning of a UX architecture runway and a configuration-controlled repository of coded elements, too. What elements have already been created and can

---

[48] Ideally, the feature size would be provided by the teams on the train. This is rarely, if ever, practical for a new ART that has yet to be launched so we skip this criteria for the first PI only. Once the train is launched you will need to allow time for teams to contribute to feature readiness. Here we expect the entire team to participate.

[49] GUI stands for Graphical User Interface: https://en.wikipedia.org/wiki/Graphical_user_interface (Accessed 27 August 2019).

> be reused in that wireframe? What new elements will be created for this feature? Once the gaps are known, the UX team can create the enablers to fill out the runway. If there aren't enough UX people on the train to do that then the teams will needs to build the elements as a part of the feature and will contribute that element back into the shared repository.

Feature Solutioning

The last item on our Feature Definition of Ready is the Solution on a Page. Again, using the ART's Architecture on a Page, the System Architect creates a Solution on Page by annotating what needs to be created, extended/modified, or deprecated for this feature to be delivered. Sometimes this will surface missing components of the epic solution or even the Architecture on a Page, in which case, don't panic, just update as appropriate.

Next thing to do is to start thinking about creating some sequence diagrams, data models, and any or all of the other modelling diagrams that make sense to communicate the changes. We do this with the System Architect and the Technical Leads on whiteboards so it can be changed on the fly. Use colour to indicate anticipated size of changes for the components, what components are tightly coupled and opportunities for refactoring.

> **Caution! Potential Train Wreck Ahead**
> By highlighting opportunities to refactor the intent is not to replace the XP practice of refactoring[50] incrementally, but to acknowledge where there is known significant technical debt that could be refactored as part of delivering the feature(s).

---

[50] See: http://www.extremeprogramming.org/rules/refactor.html (Accessed 24 September 2019)

If the entire refactor is bigger than you can reasonably include the feature, there are a couple of choices. You can try to refactor what you need for your feature and leave the rest for another time. (Just write an enabler for the rest of it so you don't lose sight of it.) Or you just write the enabler for the entire refactor and add it to the feature backlog for prioritisation. We bias to the first approach as we believe refactoring as you go is an awesome discipline for technology organisations to practise.

Protip

Ask the System Architect(s) to pay special attention to identifying enablers. Impact Mapping is unlikely to have uncovered all of them as it is very user centric. It can also be useful to ask the Architects to check for completeness against the original epic and highlight any gaps they uncover. Enabler features will also need to meet the definition of ready prior to prioritisation.

Definition of Done

SAFe has multiple levels of Definition of Done (DoD): Team Increment, System Increment, Solution Increment, and Release.[51] These are provided as an example, but you will need to review and adjust these to your context. We find it simpler to think about the DoD for stories (team increment), features (system increment), and release. It is important to define, agree, and communicate the DoD for Stories and Features for the train ideally before starting to size the work and certainly before this first PI Planning event.

---

[51] To learn more about the SAFe Definition of Done check out: https://www.scaledagileframework.com/built-in-quality/ (Accessed 28 August 2019).

The ART's DoD should speak to:

- The DevOps and development practices the train is expected to use
- The build pedigree and data set quality
- What environments that work should be accepted and demonstrated from?

The DoD must be anchored in the reality of what the ART is currently capable of achieving. The train should be able to achieve this from day one. So, if you don't write unit tests today don't put that in, unless you have a plan to upskill the ART before launch. If one team has more skills than the broader train, then by all means they can (and should) alter their team DoD to reflect this, but no team is allowed to deliver less than the train's DoD.

The DoD should be revisited every PI with a view to strengthening it. For example, as the System Team burns down their backlog the level of automation of the Continuous Delivery Pipeline[52] should improve and this should subsequently be reflected in the ART's DoD.

Completing the Lean Business Case for an Epic

For those working with epics, you should now have enough information to complete the Lean Business Case template.[53] If your ART has been provided with value stream funding there should also be guardrails in place[54] including a specific dollar value threshold that triggers the need for an epic to complete the Lean Business Case and be tabled at the

---

[52] To learn more about the SAFe Continuous Delivery Pipeline check out: https://scaledagileframework.com/continuous-delivery-pipeline (Accessed 28 August 2019)

[53] You can download a copy of the SAFe Lean Business Case template from: https://www.scaledagileframework.com/epic/ (Accessed 22 July 2019).

[54] To learn more about Lean Budgeting Guardrails in SAFe, check out: https://www.scaledagileframework.com/guardrails/ (2 September 2019).

Portfolio Sync for approval.[55] If this does not exist you might want to consider running the SAFe Lean Portfolio Management course to get this closed out. In the short term, seek guidance from one of the other guardrails, the Business Owners, as to their expectations.

If you know the threshold, it is time to add up the estimates for the MVP feature set and if the threshold has been reached, then complete the Lean Business Case template. Don't over engineer this. It is supposed to be lightweight, perhaps, five to ten pages when complete. Anyone who has experienced the massive ordeal to get a traditional business case approved will find this a pleasant change. Don't be too concerned if the organisation is not ready for this approach yet. Once we visualise the flow of epics through your system with the Program Kanban challenges with your business case process will likely appear as a bottleneck to flow which will hopefully result in the organisation moving to a Lean Business Case approach.

To complete the Lean Business Case, you will need to be able to estimate the cost to implement. If you work in a place where many of the products you build are similar to something you have built in the past you could use past actuals from a similar size and scope epic to estimate the cost of the new epic. If this is not your world then you will want these estimates to come from the people who do the work. As we know, this won't be practical for PI1 so you may have to live with your traditional estimating approach for the epics targeting PI1.[56]

Post PI1 Planning you should be able to leverage the teams on the train to provide estimates and then leverage your cost per story point model to translate these estimates into dollars.[57]

---

[55] To learn more about the Portfolio Sync in SAFe check out: https://www.scaledagileframework.com/lean-portfolio-management/ (2 September 2019).

[56] Sometimes this step is unnecessary as the epics targeting PI have already been "approved" for implementation. The features from the "approved" epics will be included in prioritisation for PI Planning.

[57] You can access our white paper on Cost per Story Point here: http://bit.ly/CostPerPointWP

Prioritising Features

We use WSJF to prioritise features as we did with the epics. For this session you should include the MVP feature set(s) identified in the Impact Mapping sessions. Depending on your context the participants in the session may be different. If you had the Business Owners prioritise the epics, then it may make sense for someone closer to the work to prioritise the features, along with Product Management and the System Architect. Features are often pitched by the epic owner or members of the Product Management team. If you are in a world without epics, then the Business Owners would be the participants and the features would be pitched by Product Management and the System Architect(s). As was the case for epic sizing prior to PI1, you will need to leverage Chapter Leads, Technical Leads, and the System Architect(s) to vote on this. From a process perspective feature prioritisation is a rinse and repeat of **program epic prioritisation covered earlier.**

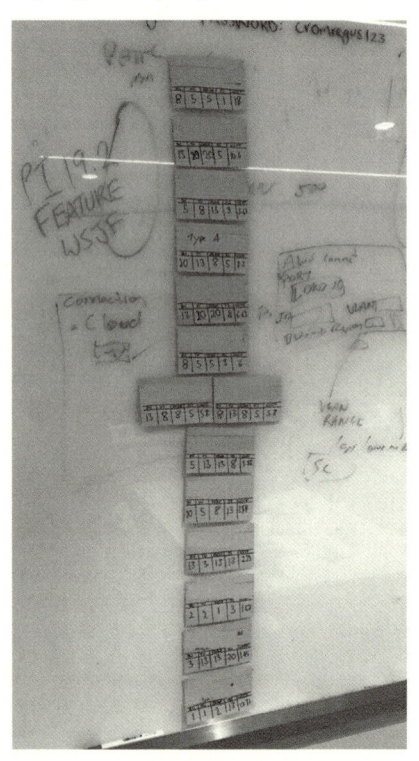

Figure 30 - Completed Feature WSJF Prioritisation

Preparing the Cargo

Protip
As was the case with the epics you will want to be conservative about how many features you attempt to prioritise. My rule of thumb for an ART of mainly feature teams is to have two features per team ready for PI Planning plus a couple of additional features in case there is a need to swap something out if a feature is smaller than anticipated. For ARTs of component teams, you may want to be even more conservative. And don't forget to include enablers!

Em's Anecdote
One Product Manager I worked with used the definition of ready as a blunt instrument to reduce the list of features to be prioritised. In the previous PI the train had really struggled to deliver on its commitments, as so many of the features had been under baked at PI Planning. I suggested to him prioritising features that did not meet the definition of ready would result in history repeating itself and it was not at all fair on the teams. He agreed and decided that going forward only features that meet the agreed definition of ready would be included in prioritisation sessions.

One of our Product Managers was faced with the problem that too many features were immature at PI planning. So, he started to use a matrix to raise awareness with the business. It is a simple 4 quadrants with one axis on the business importance and the other axis on the readiness. It very quickly shows which important features are not ready yet and helps to focus the business on those ones.

Consignes préparation PIPL
Le carré magique Valeur Métier / Maturité du besoin

- A partir des valeurs Métier et de la Maturité du besoin
  - Distribution des FT dans 4 carrés
  - Permet de partager rapidement avec le métier

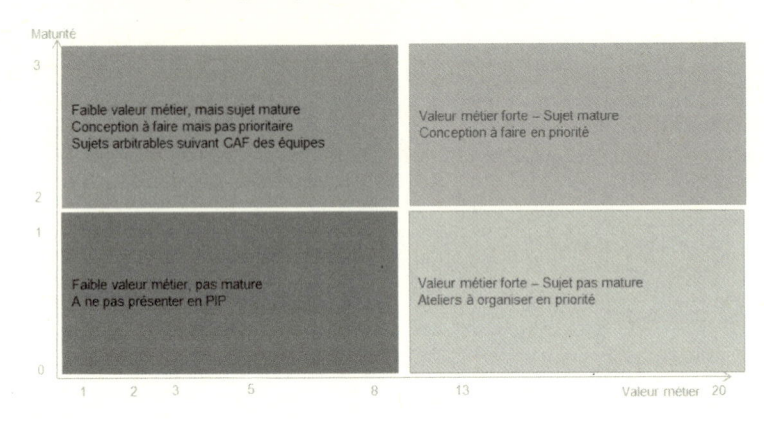

	Maturité	
	Faible valeur métier, mais sujet mature Conception à faire mais pas prioritaire Sujets arbitrables suivant CAF des équipes	Valeur métier forte – Sujet mature Conception à faire en priorité
	Faible valeur métier, pas mature A ne pas présenter en PIP	Valeur métier forte – Sujet pas mature Ateliers à organiser en priorité

Figure 31 - Example of Feature Readiness Matrix (in French!) from Cécile.

At the end of the prioritisation session, the features should be forced ranked 1 to n and everyone will probably be very pleased with themselves and a little tired. But before you let them go, take a minute with Product Management and the Business Owners to plot some of the leftover features on the Product Roadmap so you can share this with the ART at PI Planning. Two birds with one prioritisation meeting! Sharing the Product Roadmap also informs the Architectural Runway,[58] allowing the System Architect to surface any enablers that will be required for features targeting future PIs.

---

[58] To learn more about the Architectural Runway in SAFe check out: https://www.scaledagileframework.com/architectural-runway/ (Accessed 20 July 2019).

Em's Anecdote

I once worked with a Product Manager who had to step out of class during the WSJF lesson in Leading SAFe. When he returned to the classroom, he disagreed with the outcome for the feature prioritisation his table had done in his absence. They were quick to tell him that if you don't turn up you don't get a vote!

When it came time to prioritise the features for his first PI, he very diligently sat down and calculated the WSJF for each feature all by himself! He then proceeded to very proudly hand over the prioritised list to the train without socialising it with the ART's stakeholders. Adding insult to injury he had also failed to invite them to PI Planning. However, the ART's stakeholders, who also happened to be the Product Manager's peers, tracked him down. They arrived at PI Planning at midday on day one each with a list of priorities that they wanted the ART to deliver this PI. Sadly, this resulted in the RTE and Product Manager spending most of the PI Planning event playing politics rather than supporting the teams.

As with epics, you will want to put this session on a cadence once your ART is launched. If your ART is going to have enough ready features for next PI Planning, you would expect to be adding features each week. The new features will need to be prioritised relative to the features already in the backlog. If this meeting has to be cancelled due to there being no features available to prioritise then this is an early warning sign that you will have under baked features for your next PI!

> **Caution! Potential Train Wreck Ahead!**
> Do not let the priorities get arbitrarily overruled after the prioritisation sessions. This tends to happen in one of two scenarios: 1) When the participants in the WSJF session were unhappy with the outcome but did not raise their concerns in the session; 2) When a more senior executive that was not in the session overrules the prioritisation. Regardless of how this comes about, it will undermine the organisation's confidence in the process. If you let this happen once, it is likely to keep happening PI after PI. So, nip it in the bud fast.
>
> My best advice is to reconvene the WSJF session with the same attendees and have the debate play out there. Try and understand what information was missed in the first session and use that to inform any changes to the prioritisation. By bringing the group back together you get shared understanding of the reason for the change and the entire group has the same learnings to apply next time, thereby preserving the integrity of the process.

Allocating Feature to Teams

Wherever possible we prefer teams to choose for themselves what features they work on. I've found teams like to have a say in what they work on. Sometimes they want to work in an area that is familiar to them so that they can fine tune their agile mastery, other times they want to learn something new. Both seem worth encouraging to me. We recommend the RTE to facilitates a cross train conversation about feature allocation so that teams that have been working in a specific area for a long time can call this out and ask the other teams to step in and help. This pattern is of course more practical with an ART of feature teams than with an ART of component teams, where often the nature of the feature determines which team(s) works on it.

> **Protip**
> A fun approach I have used to get cross train collaboration on feature allocation I call the Feature Auction. This activity was inspired by the auctions on the reality TV show *Survivor*[59] and Luke Hohmann's Buy a Feature Game.[60] The set-up involved each feature being given a price tag that was relative to its job size. For instance, a 1-point feature could cost $10 and a 13-point feature might cost $130. (Or once you are using story points a 30-point feature might get a $30 price tag!) Each feature team is given an equal amount of cash, divided equally among the team members. Each team is given an hour to review the full feature set and allocate their cash to the features they want to work on. At the end of the hour the team needs to have a bidding strategy for the auction. Starting with the highest priority features teams "bid" for the feature they want until they run out of cash.

In some organisations the leadership won't be ready for this. They will be keen for certain features to go to certain teams due to their experience with the given subject area, often with the lens that this will be the more "cost effective" approach. In the spirit of choosing my battles, I have tended not to fight this one prior to the ART launch; there will be plenty of time to do that once the train has left the station and the feature auction is added to the cadence of the ART!

---

[59] For those not familiar with *Survivor*, the premise is a group of people are "stranded" in some remote location and have to fend for themselves for about six weeks. Each week there are a number of challenges where contestants can win rewards. One such contest is an auction, where survivors are all given a set amount of cash and can bid against each other to "win" rewards.

[60] See: https://www.innovationgames.com/buy-a-feature/ (Accessed 9 April 2019).

Where a feature will be delivered by multiple teams, we have found it helps to have one team take the lead. The lead team needs to ensure the end-to-end feature gets delivered and hangs together. It often also makes sense for the lead team's Product Owner to be the lead Product Owner for the feature.

Socialising Features with Teams

Whatever approach you use to allocate feature to teams, make sure you make time to brief the teams on the features prior to PI Planning. For the first PI, I would plan for a two-hour session per feature with the team(s) that will work on the features led by the Product Management and System Architect(s). Ideally, this will not be the socialisation approach you use once the ART is operational, but hopefully it is good enough to get you through the launch.

> **Case Study:**
> **How to be Agile With a Fixed Scope Business Case**
>
> How do you embrace change when your hands are tied by corporate red tape?
>
> Many organisations I work with have existing business cases with fixed scope, time and cost expectations when they first decide to "go agile". The early conversations about "going agile" are generally prompted by either some misstep with a previous project or delivery issues with an inflight project. Agile is the magic answer that is going to radically improve the way Information Technology delivers projects. As the technology teams begin to "embrace change" and deliver "clean code", pressure begins to mount on the business processes that govern the project. Cries of "that's not very agile" are heard at every turn and the tension between the business and technology that had started to relax begins to increase again.
>
> If you're in middle management, you begin to feel trapped. You don't make the rules. Changing the corporate business

case process is beyond your scope of influence. The project's governance board is holding you accountable for delivery of the project exactly as it is laid out in the business case and supporting business requirements document. So how do you escape the locked box and enable true business agility?

Start by understanding what is truly within your control. Often, we have more control over our circumstances than we think. Even though the box is locked we already have some keys that might work. For many this may be the traditional change control process. Yes, really. It might actually be friend and not foe if used in the right way for the right reasons. Please bear with me while I explain...

One of the first times I was appointed the Business Sponsor of a major strategic program of work, the appointment came with a completed Business Requirements Document (BRD). This document had been tirelessly compiled by a small project team over a period of about 12 months after which it had been endorsed by the program's executive stakeholders. This document was also the artefact on which the business case and associated time and cost estimates were based. When I first inherited the program, I actually felt pretty good about the situation as I knew a lot of work by a lot of good people had gone into getting us to this point. Unfortunately, as is so often the case, all the good will and detailed requirements were not enough to stop this program rapidly heading south.

As it became clear to me that the project was struggling, I found that as the business owner of the project I had surprisingly little control over how the program's funds were being spent. I learnt that the "normal process", which had been followed in this instance, allocated the entire IT component of the business case approved funds to IT at the beginning of the financial year. Week after week I attended program status meetings where I would hear about all the reasons things weren't going to plan and what was going to be done to try and solve these challenges. I could, and did, challenge the delivery team but in hindsight my impact was minimal. To add insult to injury, I also had the "privilege" of providing a monthly status update to the governance board, where I got to explain why the project was spending to plan but not delivering to plan!

The next time I found myself in the role of business sponsor, I had also found agile. Two days of Agile Fundamentals training had taught me that that you can stop an agile project at any time, just ship what you have and don't fund the next sprint. That was great in theory but what do you do if you have already handed over a year's worth of funding to the delivery organisation? As it turns out the process of transferring all the funds for a given program to IT at the beginning of the financial year was a tradition but not actually a rule. With this new-found knowledge in hand, it was time to enlist the support of Finance.

The Finance folk seemed particularly interested in making sure the project adhered to the time/cost/scope in the business case and to put it bluntly, I think Agile scared them. Luckily Agile was flavour of the month and Finance were looking for a way to at least be seen to be supportive. With this in mind we pitched a change of approach. We, that is the business team, would govern the distribution of the program's funds to IT, one project and one release at a time. More specifically, we established a local change control board. Individual projects (subcomponents of the broader program), were given seed funding to "discover" the first release and would then be funded on a release by release basis.

The term "change control board" might not feel very agile, but in this case it was definitely a step forward. Through this process we achieved transparency. I could see how the money was being spent - not just in terms of "labour" but in actual outputs and outcomes. At one point I learned that every deployment was accompanied by tens of thousands of dollars of documentation, a pretty scary finding when you are striving for more frequent deployments! This new level of transparency helped me, as a business person, better understand the challenges faced by the delivery team. It enabled a new level of dialogue, whereby both groups started to constructively debate and challenge the status quo. As time went by, we delved into topics such as the makeup of the agile teams, the viability of offshoring, the cost of deployment, and what was the best place to invest our limited funds. Eventually I even began to feel I had some control over my destiny and the ability to help make the changes needed for the program to succeed.

If you are the business sponsor of a project, both you and your governance group are likely to feel very nervous as you take your first steps into the world of Agile. You share a responsibility to make the right fiscal decisions on behalf the organisation. You are used to having these decisions informed by formal documentation and the traditional stage gate processes. This approach may well be flawed but it is what you know and are used to working with. It may feel uncomfortable at first, but by moving to small batch funds release and achieving transparency, your sense of comfort will in due course exceed what you have experienced in the past. Even more importantly you will start to have true insight into what has historically been a black-box process that the IT people told you "you're not technical enough to understand."

In the words of Bjarte Bogsnes, author of Beyond Budgeting: *"Traditional management fears transparency because it threatens control. But as Jeremy Hope, cofounder of the Beyond Budgeting Round Table, puts it, 'Transparency is the new control system.' There is a reason why thieves and crooks prefer to operate at night. Maybe Enron would have been in existence today if there had been more transparency. When everybody can see what everybody spends and how everybody performs, it does something no formal control system is able to deliver."*[61]

---

[61] Bjarte Bogsnes, *Implementing Beyond Budgeting: Unlocking the Performance Potential*, (Hoboken: Wiley, 2009), Kindle Edition, Location 462.

With this more flexible but also more tightly controlled funding process in place, it is time to turn our attention to navigating the "signed off", "locked down", "fixed scope" requirements contained in the Business Requirements Document (BRD) that underpins the business case.

Software developers working in traditional software development shops have been conditioned to expect their work to arrive in the form of requirements documents. Many organisations new to Agile have fallen into the trap of transposing hundreds of pages of requirements documentation into thousands of "user stories" in a misguided attempt to provide "Agile requirements" to the dev teams. As logical as this may seem to some this is not the answer. To quote Mary & Tom Poppendieck:[62] *"A detailed list of requirements is not the starting point for good engineering. The Wright brothers did not start with requirements; they started out with an idea: build a glider and learn to fly it and then add power (and don't get killed in the process)."* So, our challenge is clear, we need to make a shift from requirements to ideas.

Some Agilists might recommend throwing the requirements document in the bin and starting over with a blank piece of paper. Do not do this! I have been on the receiving end of this approach and it is not much fun. While I am sure it was well intentioned at the time, it was immensely frustrating for the people who had already invested many hours in workshops providing the original requirements, followed by many more hours reviewing reams of documentation. On the other extreme, this does not mean you should try locking the technology team in a room with the BRD and none of the stakeholders that contributed to it. I have seen this done too and it is equally as disastrous.

In the spirit of focusing on ideas whilst staying grounded in commercial realities, I advocate moving the spotlight from

---

[62] Mary Poppendieck and Tom Poppendieck, *The Lean Mindset: Ask the Right Questions*, (New Jersey: Addison-Wesley, 2013), p. 76.

the individual line items contained in the BRD to the business benefits embedded in the project's business case. With your business benefits in hand, you still need to get to features that are deliverable by an agile team in a number of weeks. What's more, you want to move mindset from "progress against scope items" to "progress against projected benefits", so you want those features to have measurable benefits.

My preferred approach is to use Gojko Adzic's Impact Mapping. Taking one business benefit at a time, create an impact map for each. The measurable business benefit becomes the S.M.A.R.T. "goal" and through the process of impact mapping you can discover the features (the "deliverables") that are likely to change the behaviour of the people who contribute to the "goal." As Jeff Patton says, *"at the end of the day, your job isn't to get the requirements right—your job is to change the world."*[63] By using Impact Mapping to identify features, you will be forced to consider how each deliverable contributes to the benefits baked into your business case

Now coming back to the BRD; the trick is to think of it as a head start rather than a ball and chain. Find the middle ground. Include the people who provided the original requirements in the impact mapping sessions and use the existing requirements as a starting point for the conversation. Of course, there is a risk that the impact mapping workshops uncover new ideas/features that weren't included in the original documentation or, perhaps even worse, requirements that cannot be mapped to the business case benefits. As the intergalactic hitchhikers say - DON'T PANIC! Remember that change control process we talked about? What if you used change control to discuss the deltas? i.e. scope that is no longer relevant as it does not map to the benefits and scope that should be added in order to achieve the benefits. "Embrace change" and shape the delivery scope so that it aligns with the intended benefits.

---

[63] Jeff Patton, *User Story Mapping: Discover The Whole Story, Build The Right Product,* (Sebastopol: O'Reilly, 2014), p. xliii.

> As BDD expert James Ferguson Smart says, *"At the end of the day, business people want the software being built to help them achieve their business goals. If the software is delivered in this regard, the business will consider it a success, even if the scope and the implementation vary considerably from what was originally imagined." .*[64]
>
> However, in the enterprise context sometimes this won't be enough. Introducing "change control processes" to create a paper-trail for significant scope decisions might feel anti-agile, but if you have a BRD to manage too, odds are you're attempting to be agile while standing in a waterfall. Why not borrow some waterfall tools, and put them to a higher purpose?[65]

> **Robin's Anecdote**
>
> Many of our products are incredibly large such as the next vehicle to take man to Mars, combat systems to deter violence, or aircraft. In all of these cases having a lightweight change control process enables all of the teams to understand the current state of play and why decisions have been made, which actually allows them more agility. I think this all depends on the context. If I am building small mobile apps, I do not need the overhead. But a complex system of systems with emergent behaviour needs some additional support.

---

[64] John Ferguson Smart, *BDD in Action: Behavior-Driven Development for the Whole Software Lifecycle,* (New York: Manning Publications, 2015), p. 71.

[65] Adapted from: http://blog.prettyagile.com.au/2015/05/how-to-be-agile-with-fixed-scope.html and http://blog.prettyagile.com.au/2015/05/how-to-be-agile-with-fixed-scope_27.html (Accessed 10 April 2019).

Chapter Summary

In this chapter we explored:

- The SAFe Requirements Model
- Defining, refining, solutioning, and prioritising Business and Enabler Program Epics
- Identifying the Minimal Viable Product and the value of building out a "steel thread"
- Validating the ART Deign based on the priority epics
- Using Impact Mapping to decompose epics into features
- Defining, refining, solutioning, and prioritising Business and Enabler Features
- Agreeing the definition of ready for feature for prioritisation and PI Planning
- Creating a Definition of Done (DoD) for the ART
- When and how to use a Lean Business Case for an epic
- How to match features with delivery teams
- What to do if your epics are really projects with fixed time, cost, and scope business cases.

PART 4

SETTING THE TIMETABLE FOR THE TRAIN

We are almost ready to launch, we have a train design, cargo (features) and now we just need the timetable (cadence). The ART's cadence is its heartbeat. It is helpful to agree on the ART's cadences and get the calendar invitations out before PI Planning. This section provides an introduction to all the events you need to schedule; however, the details of how to facilitate the events not already covered by "Preparing the Cargo" can be found in "All Aboard!" and "Staying on the Tracks."

> **Em's Anecdote**
>
> Sometimes I am invited into organisations to review their SAFe implementation. On one occasion I arrived at the client site after the program increment had completed. My first question was "When is PI Planning?" The RTE's response was "We haven't decided yet …" followed by "I'm not sure if we will be allowed to spend two days on PI Planning …" Yes, this was another of those rare occasions in which I was left speechless. Establishing a cadence and socialising the calendar as part of your ART launch is a sure-fire way to avoid this particular train wreck!

Program Increments

The SAFe guidance recommends 8-, 10-, or 12-week Program Increments.[66] Organisations with long delivery cycles will tend to gravitate to 12 weeks as they will perceive this as a very short period of time. Once they are up and running, they often realise that 12 weeks is a very long time! One way to know if 12 weeks is too long for your organisation is the existence of a mid-PI review where there is a significant reshuffling of priorities.

We prefer 10-week PIs in most cases as this gives the organisation five learning cycles a year, one more than you get on a 12-week cadence.

---

[66] To learn more about Program Increments in SAFe, check out: https://www.scaledagileframework.com/program-increment/ (Accessed 20 July 2019).

Setting the Timetable for the Train

Most clients like this logic and run with this pattern, unless they have highly distributed teams, in which case travel costs will tend to result in them choosing four PI Planning events a year rather than five.

> **Maarit's Anecdote**
> Some organisations are overly worried about the cost of PI planning. Imagine my surprise when one Business Owner stated to me that the planning cost is peanuts compared to his opportunity to change the course of the company more frequently! His point was that having Business Agility brings monetary benefits!

As we know everyone attends, either in person or virtually as part of distributed teams. Getting the time zones right so that one group of people aren't up half the night is key. If you have to go off-site to get a venue knowing the scheduling a year in advance helps you reserve room(s) on the dates you need.

> **Caution! Potential Train Wreck Ahead!**
> One client for which I launch a couple of ARTs decided to align their Program Increments with the enterprise release calendar, which was not on a fixed cadence. This meant every PI was a different length, with some PI being 16 weeks long! Some PIs would even change length after planning due to delays with the enterprise release. These ARTs also had a pattern of waterfalling their Program Increments with a number of sprints dedicated to development, then the last couple of sprints of each PI being dedicated to testing and integration! They just could not fathom that it was possible to decouple the PI planning cadence from the enterprise release schedule and therefore they never found smarter ways of delivering value outside the enterprise release calendar.

> **Em's Anecdote**
> Another ART I worked with faced similar challenges with alignment to the enterprise release calendar; however, their approach was almost the complete opposite. They entirely decoupled the planning cadence from the enterprise release calendar. Every feature that was prioritised for delivery by the train was assessed to see if it needed to be included in the enterprise release, and only those that were tightly coupled to tier one applications went through the enterprise release process. This ART started to dramatically reduce time to value as two-thirds of its features were able to be independently deployed and released outside the enterprise process.

> **Adrienne's Anecdote**
> I was working at an organisation that was distributed across three locations in the continental US. We had enough people to have three trains and were working to launch the Solution Train. Two of the locations were in the Eastern time zone and one in the Mountain time zone. This organisation did a great thing by budgeting travel for two of the locations to travel to the third. The bulk of staff were in the Eastern time zone so the folks in the Mountain time zone were always travelling. It also meant that we had to plan on two travel days for every IP Sprint[67] and one day for the I&A. While a ten-week PI would be great it would mean the travel budget would be that much bigger again. Given the business was willing to fund four rounds of travel (which was really cool) I didn't want to push it. So, we planned on a thirteen-week cadence.

---

[67] To learn more about the IP Sprint in SAFe, check out: https://www.scaledagileframework.com/innovation-and-planning-iteration/ (Accessed 2 September 2019).

The thirteen-week cadence had some nice benefits. For starters a fifty-two-week year can be nicely divided into four PIs which gives the business a pretty consistent budget to plan with. It also allows a week for the trains to co-locate, get better together, and plan together without having to sacrifice innovation time or training.

I remember the first time we had the Solution Train assembled together. People who had worked together for ten years actually got to meet in person for the first time ever! One executive suggested we have some games on site for people to play. Enter casino night, cornhole games,[68] etc.! Some of the executive leaders took advantage of having their teams together to have some key strategy meetings while planning was happening. Many an executive told me that this was one of their most productive weeks as they could have in-person meetings and make some key decisions.

Finally, we knew that on or about January, April, July, and October 20/21st would be PI Planning. I can schedule offsite facilities and people can plan their vacation time accordingly. There is a flip side to this coin. You do have a thirteen-week PI. Some would say thirteen weeks is pretty slow to refresh the backlog for the train. So, smaller features are key. But I think the value of people getting to form the culture of the trains was pretty fantastic.

Another benefit of thirteen-week increments is that finance typically understand the concept of quarterly planning. If we want to get them used to something different it is a good starting point for them to get their feet wet before we incrementally move to shorter PIs.

---

[68] For those not familiar with a cornhole game please refer to: https://en.wikipedia.org/wiki/Cornhole (accessed 28 August 2019).

> **Protip**
> No matter what your cadence avoid PI Planning during major holiday periods. For Australia that is mid-December through to after Australia Day, for Europe that is most of July and August. Also be aware of regional holidays like Chinese New Year in Asia and Diwali in India, etc. You may need to add a sprint or shorten your PI to avoid some of these issues. For example, we often add an extra sprint to the PI that runs over Christmas as almost no one is in the office between Christmas Eve and New Year's Day. If you do have people in the office during times when many people are on leave, make sure this is reflected in the PI Plans.

Sprints

In line with SAFe guidance we default to two-week sprints.[69] Occasionally a client will want to work in three- or four-week sprints. They will have 101 reasons why this is necessary in their context, but no one has ever managed to convince me it is a good idea. In fact, it's usually an indicator that their batch sizes are too big. In my experience, the best thing to do with an ART that wants longer sprints is stick to two weeks. The shortened time box drives creativity and will in due course help the ART find ways to deliver working products and services in smaller time boxes. A two-week sprint also means the system demo occurs every two weeks which acts as a forcing function for frequent integration which exposes assumptions sooner and contributes to better overall quality.

---

[69] See: https://www.scaledagileframework.com/scrumxp/ (Accessed 21 July 2019).

> **Em's Anecdote**
> In my life as a business sponsor, the first "agile" projects I experienced used four-week or one-month sprints. Progress was slow. Projects didn't deliver working product until two or three sprints had passed. The "showcase" at the end of each month left me baffled as to what the teams had been working on rather than wowed by progress, so I requested the shift to two-week sprints. Between us, my logic was they can only screw up so much in a two-week time box! An unexpected but wonderful side effect of this shift was that the teams started to think differently about how they worked as they strove to deliver value in a two-week time box.

> **Adrienne's Anecdote**
> If you think about how people work and ask yourself honestly if you have a deadline for something due on Monday when do you start? Most people in the training room laugh and say Sunday night! This is Parkinson's Law in action.[70]
>
> I recently had an exchange with a person in *Leading SAFe* who was sure there was a good reason a team would want to have three-week sprints. There may be a reason, but it won't be one that will support faster flow and feedback. Along those lines I had a team ask me about going to three-week sprints because they had a really low completion rate of stories in the backlog. I explained Parkinson's Law to them and said let's run an experiment. Let's run a one-week sprint and see what happens.

---

[70] Parkinson's law says that "work expands so as to fill the time available for its completion." See: https://en.wikipedia.org/wiki/Parkinson%27s_law (Accessed 3 September 2019).

> They agreed to the experiment. The first thing we learnt was that their stories were way too big; they had started to break stories down in layers of cake because they were used to do working that way in the past and they hadn't learned to pair program so they weren't cross skilled. All of these things were making it hard to deliver their stories in a two-week sprint. In a one-week sprint, it was impossible. But before we ran this experiment it was hard for the team to see that it wasn't the length of the sprint that was the problem, it was how they were working. Anytime a system is struggling to deliver, if you reduce the WIP the bottlenecks will surface.

> **Protip**
> When choosing the sprint cadence, it can be wise to avoid choosing the Monday-to-Friday sprint pattern. Public holidays and long weekends often make Mondays and Fridays non-workdays which is disruptive to your ART's cadence. Plus, statistically Monday has the highest incidence of sick days. The most common approach is to use Wednesday to Tuesday sprint cadence, and this is what we default to. When coupling the Thursday/Friday PI Planning pattern above, this creates space for the teams to do some backlog refinement for Sprint 1 on the Monday and Tuesday post PI Planning.

ART Sync

SAFe offers the option to combine the twice weekly Scrum of Scrums and Product Owner Syncs into an ART sync. This is certainly my preferred pattern. In *Tribal Unity*, I suggest going a step further and holding a daily Cocktail Hour which includes a daily ART Sync we call Tribe Sync.[71]

---

[71] Em Campbell-Pretty, *Tribal Unity*, p. 50.

Case Study: Cocktail Hour—The Heartbeat of the Agile Release Train

In my life as a business sponsor of software development programs I spent innumerable hours in program meetings—project status meetings, RAID[72] meetings, Steering Committees, Governance meetings, "Come to Jesus meetings," you name it. When I was appointed to my first role on the delivery side of the fence, I thought running these meetings was essential. After all, every IT General Manager I had ever worked with followed this practice.

Everybody hated these meetings, particularly the three-hour Monday morning Program Review. Twenty-five people and a hundred-page status report made for a long start to the week. The morning's discussion would revolve around the true status of the Watermelon Projects (green on the outside and red on the inside) and the lack of progress from one week to the next on the seemingly endless list of actions. From the day I inherited this meeting, my team was on at me about getting rid of it.

My RTE was a lean enthusiast and was quick to suggest I could forgo these meetings in favour of daily stand-ups. My first response was to tell him he was an idiot (not for the first time, I may add!), but I went on to say that I was open to the concept. He would just need to prove it before I discontinued the weekly program meeting. The result was "Cocktail Hour," inspired by the "Daily Cocktail Party" in Henrik Kniberg's *Lean from the Trenches*.[73]

---

[72] A RAID meeting is where the RAID log is reviewed. RAID stands for Risks, Assumptions, Issues and Dependencies.
[73] Henrik Kniberg, *Lean From the Trenches: Managing Large Scale Projects with Kanban.* (Pragmatic Bookshelf, 2011), Pages 13-18.

9:00 a.m. The Trifecta Stand-Up
This is a fairly informal operationally focused session, used to let the Trifecta understand each other's priorities for the day ahead.

9 :15 a.m. Team Stand-Ups
Facilitated by the Scrum Masters these sessions generally follow the traditional scrum format, and all need to happen concurrently for the ART Sync to work.

9:30 a.m. ART Sync
Some days it felt like every man and his dog came to this stand-up. Held in front of the Program Feature Kanban,[74] it is attended by all the Scrum Masters, Product Owners, Technical Leads, Chapter Leads, Epic Owner, Shared Services, Product Support, the Trifecta, and any other interested party.

9:45 a.m. Pipeline Stand-Up
Taking inputs from the ART Sync the Epic Owners and the Trifecta meet at the Program Epic Kanban[75] wall to align on priorities with respect to readiness for the next PI Planning event.

10:00 a.m. System Team Stand-Up
The System Team hold their stand-up after ART Sync so that they can factor the needs of the teams on the train into their planning for the day ahead.[76]

---

[74] We will cover how to build the Program Feature Kanban in Part 6 - Staying on the Tracks.
[75] We will cover how to build the Program Epic Kanban in Part 6 - Staying on the Tracks.
[76] Adapted from: http://blog.prettyagile.com.au/2014/03/communication-cadence-heartbeat-of.html (Accessed 21 July 2019).

System Demo

SAFe's System Demo is like a Sprint Review for the entire ART in a one-hour time box.[77] Depending on the mix of feature and component teams on your ART, the complexity of your technology stack, and the maturity of your DevOps infrastructure, the ease of preparing this event can vary greatly.

ART Show

At the simpler end of the spectrum is an ART of feature teams that is fully integrating its code base daily or more frequently. In this scenario, I have tended to merge the Team Sprint Demo with the ART System Demo creating an ART Show.[78] Each team gets a twenty- or thirty-minute time box, with the sessions being held back to back on the last day of the sprint and attended by the entire ART and its stakeholders. In this world I would expect that the Product Owner has been progressively accepting stories throughout the sprint, so the purpose of this demo is to get feedback from the broader stakeholder base.

In more complicated scenarios such as the ART I worked with that had teams from sales, software, hardware, and firmware, an integrated system demo every two weeks just wasn't practical. When I asked them during training how often they fully integrated everything in their ecosystem the answer was "only when we have to" which I eventually established was probably about once a year. So, for their first PI, their target was to integrate and demo after six weeks.

---

[77] To learn more about the System Demo in SAFe check out: https://www.scaledagileframework.com/system-demo/ (Accessed 21 July 2019).

[78] Thanks to Garth Andrews for the clever name.

> **SAFe in a Project Driven World**
> If your ART is funded by projects, it is possible that you do not have a homogenous set of stakeholders to attend your System Demo or ART Show. In this case you may like to sequence the demos one epic/project at a time so the stakeholders can choose to only attend the session(s) they are interested in. Each session would still be attended by the entire ART and the teams working on features relating to the specific epic demo the PI Objectives relating to the epic that have been completed during the sprint.

Load the Cargo on Cadence

The processes we used to prepare the Program Backlog for PI1 should be operationalised as part of PI Execution. It can be helpful to put Epic Writing Workshops on cadence so that you have a regular time booked with the Trifecta, Shared Services, and Chapter Leads to work on incoming epics. Two hours once a sprint is probably a good place to start and you can always adjust this as you learn more about your system of work.

We also recommend putting the WSJF sessions on cadence. Depending on your context you might need a meeting for epics and features or a single session for both. As mentioned in *Loading the Cargo*, after System Demo may be a good time for this.

Finally, don't forget to schedule a **Feature Auction** (or some event where features gets matched to teams) every sprint. I like to do this on day seven of the sprint.

Tribal Unity Events

In *Tribal Unity* I suggest adding some events to your ART's PI and Sprint cadence with a view to helping your ART evolve a "one-team culture." One of those events is Cocktail Hour as mentioned in the ART Sync section above. Some of the others are outlined below.

Setting the Timetable for the Train

Unity Hour

Unity Hour is *"An all-hands gathering, first thing in the morning on the first day of every two-week sprint."* [79] However, this is not your average all-hands meeting! For starters, it is fun, and its sole purpose is to strengthen the social fabric of your ART. While the agenda for you Unity Hour will always be evolving, you should look to include the following elements:

- Shout outs (Thank yous to train members from train members)
- Adds, moves, and changes (who is coming and going)
- A snack
- A learning activity[80]
- A sharing activity
- Train and/or Company announcements (keep this short and sweet).

> **Caution! Potential Train Wreck Ahead!**
> One well-intended RTE decided to ask his Scrum Masters if they wanted to do Unity Hour. The Scrum Masters were quick to respond that there were too many meetings already. While it may seem counter to my strong stance on servant leadership this is one of those times it is okay for the leader to just make the decision. It will take some time for the train to see the value in spending time together having fun, but over time they will feel the difference it creates.
>
> When I first started this practice, I used to have my Scrum Masters round up some of their team members who were too busy writing very important code to come and play with the rest of us. In my view, if you are going to do Unity Hour make attendance mandatory. No one has to participate in an activity that makes them uncomfortable, but everyone needs to be there.

---

[79] Campbell-Pretty, Em, *Tribal Unity,* pages 32-42.
[80] Make sure the teams are mixed up for these activities to help build new connections across the train.

> **Tips for Globally Distributed ARTs**
> If your ART is distributed this will be logistically more challenging, but don't let that stop you. Try rotating the host location of the event from sprint to sprint.

> **Claire's Anecdote**
> Of course, since there are no second-class citizens on our trains, Unity Hour for globally distributed trains require more preparation. At one of our distributed clients, we found success in having an informal host at each site. We'd have a video call the day before and run through the plan, sharing anything that needed printing or organising ahead of time. We often played games which would require some kind of set-up. We even played "celebrity head"[81] as a distributed team. Finding that cross-cultural sweet spot was interesting!

Reunification

Bookend day one of your sprint with a thirty-minute reunification event towards the end of the day. Have the teams bring their sprint goals (from sprint planning) and share them with the ART. Ask the teams to call out any changes from PI Planning that other teams need to be aware of and highlight dependencies they have from or on other teams.

---

[81] Celebrity Heads is a game where celebrities' names are written on index cards and then attached to the player's head (often using a headband). Players take turns asking questions to determine what famous person's name is stuck on their forehead. For every "yes" answer you gain, you are permitted in asking another question. The first person to guess who they are wins. Adapted from: https://somerandomstuff1.wordpress.com/2017/03/28/how-to-win-at-celebrity-heads/ (Accessed 25 August 2019).

Bubble-Up

Referred to as Tribal Kaizen in *Tribal Unity* this event is held on the last day of each sprint after all the teams have completed their retrospectives where "we *ask the teams to "bubble up" the challenges identified in their retrospectives that are outside their sphere of influence.*"[82] In the same way that an ART Sync is the scaled-up version of a team stand-up, the bubble-up is a scaled-up version of the team retrospective.

To make this work we align all the team retrospectives so are held around 3:00 p.m. on the last day of the sprint. We then schedule the "bubble-up" for 4:30 p.m. We ask each team as part of their retrospective to capture systemic impediments to flow that are outside their control. Then each team sends a delegate (this does not need to be the Scrum Master) to the "bubble-up" where they share the impediments. Sharing this around the team members provides transparency into problems and problem solving, as well as reinforcing that leadership are there to support and enable the teams.

In *Tribal Unity*, we suggest that it is the role of the leadership to improve the system of work for the teams.[83] When applied to SAFe, we see this as the role of the Trifecta, supported by the Chapter Leads (if you have adopted this model). These challenges can also be used as inputs to Inspect and Adapt Problem Solving Workshop[84] in place of holding another retrospective.

---

[82] Em Campbell-Pretty, *Tribal Unity*, p. 50.
[83] Em Campbell-Pretty, *Tribal Unity*, p. 60.
[84] To learn more about the SAFe Inspect and Adapt event, check out: https://www.scaledagileframework.com/inspect-and-adapt/ (Accessed 24 August 2019).

Time	Day 1	Day 2	Day 3	Day 4	Day 5
9 am	Unity Hour	Cocktail Hour	Cocktail Hour	Cocktail Hour	Cocktail Hour
10 am	Sprint Planning				
11 am					
Noon					
1 pm					Epic Workshop
2 pm			Chapter Meeting		
3 pm					WSJF
4 pm	Re-unification				

Time	Day 6	Day 7	Day 8	Day 9	Day 10
9 am	Cocktail Hour	Cocktail Hour	Cocktail Hour	Cocktail Hour	Cocktail Hour
10 am	B/log Refinement				
11 am					
Noon					
1 pm					ART Show
2 pm		Feature Auction	Chapter Meeting		
3 pm					Retrospective
4 pm					Bubble-Up

Figure 32 - An example of a sprint calendar for a co-located ART including Tribal Unity events

Innovation and Planning (IP) Sprint

SAFe recommends the last sprint of each Program Increment is reserved for Innovation and Planning, the IP Sprint.[85] For some organisations this is a really hard sell. Business Owners, Product Management, and Epic Owners can be quick to express their displeasure at the idea of "no new work" getting done for two whole weeks! It is important to remember that SAFe without the IP Sprint is not SAFe or safe!

Many ARTs we work with choose to run PI Planning on the second Thursday and Friday in the IP Sprint. This leaves Monday and Tuesday open to train new team members in *SAFe for Teams*[86] or run another two-day SAFe class to support the ART's continuous

---

[85] To learn more about the IP Sprint in SAFe, check out: https://www.scaledagileframework.com/innovation-and-planning-iteration/ (Accessed 20 July 2019).
[86] To learn more about the SAFe for Teams class check out: https://www.scaledagile.com/certification/courses/safe-for-teams/ (Accessed 21 July 2019).

learning journey with the Inspect and Adapt being scheduled for Wednesday. For a distributed ART this means those who need to travel can come in Sunday night and leave Friday night.

	Wednesday	Thursday	Friday	Monday	Tuesday
Week 1				Training	Training
Week 2	I&A	PI Planning	PI Planning		

Figure 33 - Example of an IP Sprint calendar with PI Planning on the second Thursday and Friday

Em's Anecdote

One ex-Program Manager turned RTE I worked with was horrified at the idea of two weeks of "no work" at the end of the PI. After explaining that we would at a minimum need a week, so we had time for Inspect and Adapt and PI Planning, she reluctantly agreed to a one-week IP Sprint. The one-week IP Sprint was a nightmare. Between closing off their first PI, getting ready for the next PI, Inspect and Adapt and PI Planning was an extremely high stress week. Interestingly they went with a two-week IP Sprint in PI2!

The next time I came across a client that was reluctant to invest in a two-week IP Sprint, I suggested they go with a one-week IP Sprint. Of course, at the end of PI1, they told me, "We are NEVER doing that again!"

Inspect and Adapt

Generally, the Inspect and Adapt (I&A) is the day before PI Planning. This pattern is particularly prevalent when people need to travel to get to the PI Planning location as it reduces the number of days they need to be away from home. For co-located trains you may prefer to have some breathing room between I&A and PI Planning so that you have time to add the improvement items to the PI Planning backlog.

According to the Scaled Agile Framework there are three parts to the I&A event: the PI System Demo, Quantitative measurement, and the Retrospective and Problem-Solving Workshop, and the whole thing should take less than four hours.[87] In my experience you are better off allocating an entire day to this. While you probably won't need the whole day, giving people a couple of hours down time leading into PI Planning might actually be a good choice.

The same people who assigned the Business Value in PI Planning must attend the Inspect and Adapt to assign the Actual Value. This seems to be a challenge for some organisations so you will want to set this expectation early.

> **Em's Anecdote**
> I once had a client that would forget to schedule their I&A every single PI. Then as the IP Sprint got close, they would suddenly remember and try and schedule it only to find out that Business Owners (who were C-level execs) were unavailable. So, they would end up having to have the System Demo portion of the I&A after the IP Sprint had completed and the new PI had commenced.

With the ART design compete, the cargo loaded and the time table set, it is finally time for the train to leave the station. All Aboard!!!

---

[87] To learn more about the SAFe Inspect and Adapt event, check out: https://www.scaledagileframework.com/inspect-and-adapt/ (Accessed 24 August 2019).

Chapter Summary

Cadences are a key part of becoming predictable and getting the train from one PI Planning to the next. In this chapter we explored:

- Deciding on the length of the ART's Program Increment
- Setting the sprint ceremony cadence
- Establishing the cadence-based events to keep the train on the tracks.
- Incorporating *Tribal Unity* into the ART timetable.
- Scheduling the Innovation and Planning Sprint events, including PI Planning and Inspect and Adapt.

PART 5
ALL ABOARD!

According to the Scaled Agile Framework, *"the easiest and fastest way to launch an ART is through the ART Quick-Start approach."*[88]

A textbook Quick-Start goes something like this:

- In the weeks prior to the Quick-Start:
    - The feature backlog is refined and prioritised (using WSJF)
    - The people who will be doing the work are grouped in teams with a Scrum Master and Product Owner
- Days one and two of the Quick-Start all the teams attend the two-day *SAFe for Teams*[89] training, sitting at team tables. During the training they work with real features from the program backlog
- Days three and four the train holds its first PI Planning event
- Day five is reserved for other set-up activities
- And then you start sprinting!

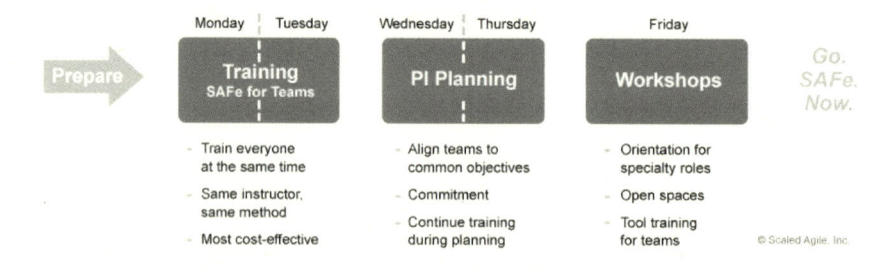

Figure 34 - The one-week, all-in ART Quick-Start approach[90]

---

[88] To learn more about the SAFE Quick-Start check out: https://www.scaledagileframework.com/train-teams-and-launch-the-art/ (Accessed 21 July 2019).

[89] To learn more about the SAFe for Teams class check out: https://www.scaledagile.com/certification/courses/safe-for-teams/ (Accessed 21 July 2019).

[90] Image source: https://www.scaledagileframework.com/train-teams-and-launch-the-art/ (Accessed 10 September 2019)

Despite Quick-Start having always been the recommended approach to launching ARTs, my sense is that it is the exception rather than the rule when most folks launch trains. My guess is that most people think it sounds like utter madness. I know I thought it was madness too until I tried it and realised it was truly amazing. It is my hope that from this chapter you will gain some insights as to why this approach is such a powerful way to launch an Agile Release Train.

> **Em's Anecdote**
> The first time I quick-started an Agile Release Train it was rather circumstantial. My client had a multiyear waterfall program of work that was coming to a close and wanted to move to agile for "business as usual" development. His challenge was that after the final "drop" of the inflight program was complete there was a very small time box before the next release of features was expected. We were going to need to move quickly. So, I suggested to my client we try a one-week launch, the SAFe Quick-Start.
>
> While the Quick-Start was not without its challenges I was completely sold. At the end of the week, the teams on the train were not the world's most amazing agile teams, but they were agile. Perhaps the most convincing testimonial was from the Business Analyst Team Leader turned Scrum Master who told me two sprints after the Quick-Start that the train had delivered more in the last month than they had in the last two years of the waterfall program. While I'm sure that was an exaggeration, I think it speaks volumes as to the power of the Quick-Start.

Our Quick-Start Pattern

While the textbook Quick-Start is only five days, we have been running a seven-day pattern for the past couple of years.

- Day one and two is the SAFe Scrum Master class[91]
- Day three is Team Day
- Days four and five all the teams attend the two-day SAFe for Teams training
- Days six and seven the train holds its first PI Planning event
- Then you start sprinting!

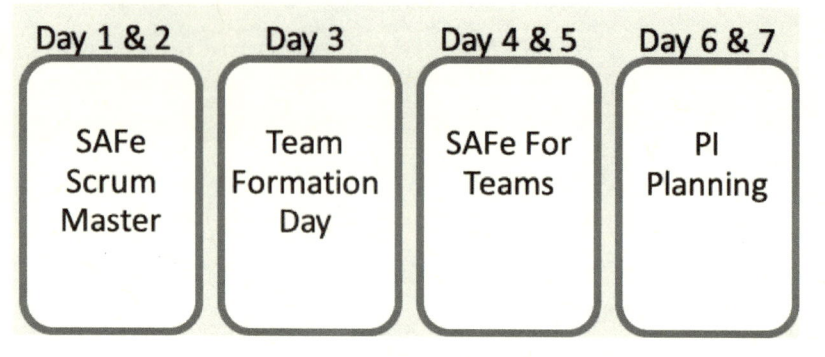

```
┌─────────────┐  ┌─────────────┐  ┌─────────────┐  ┌─────────────┐
│ Day 1 & 2   │  │   Day 3     │  │ Day 4 & 5   │  │ Day 6 & 7   │
│    SAFe     │  │    Team     │  │  SAFe For   │  │     PI      │
│    Scrum    │  │  Formation  │  │    Teams    │  │  Planning   │
│   Master    │  │    Day      │  │             │  │             │
└─────────────┘  └─────────────┘  └─────────────┘  └─────────────┘
```

Figure 35 - The Seven-Day Quick-Start

This is an evolution of the six-day Quick-Start approach that emerged out of a unique set of circumstances and a super tight schedule in 2016.[92] It is this pattern we will explore in detail in this chapter.

> **Tips for Globally Distributed ARTs**
> If your ART is not co-located, you are going to have some big decisions to make. Ideally you will co-locate everyone for the Quick-Start. If you choose this option, I promise you won't regret it. The value of people meeting face to face and getting to know one another as people, rather than faceless names on the other end of a phone call or email, is priceless.

---

[91] To learn more about the SAFe Scrum Master class check out: https://www.scaledagile.com/certification/courses/safe-scrum-master/ (Accessed 10 September 2019)

[92] See: http://blog.prettyagile.com.au/2016/11/6-Day-SAFe-Quick-Start-Pitching-Self-Selection.html (Accessed 30 August 2019).

If you choose not to co-locate everyone, we recommend at least trying to minimise the number of locations involved. Can you have one site per continent? Per region? Per country? Or at least per city?

Caution! Potential Train Wreck Ahead!

I once participated in a PI Planning event as a last minute "ring in"[93] to support one location in a multiple location PI Planning event. While the organisation had five or six office locations along the eastern seaboard of Australia, they had decided to semi co-locate by using two locations for PI Planning.

In theory this sounds okay. The time difference was only half an hour; everyone would be on a corporate site, therefore inside the firewall, reducing connectivity challenges, and everyone spoke the same language. The reality was horrible. We had no end of connectivity issues and the majority of the senior leaders were at one site, leaving my site in the dark when challenges were encountered. The best thing to come out of that PI Planning event was a decision to co-locate the entire ART in one location for all future PI Planning events!

Em's Anecdote

Another ART I worked with took a dramatically different approach to addressing the distributed nature of their ART. They flew out four teams from China to join the rest of the train in Australia; for the first two PIs. On each visit, the Chinese teams stayed in Australia for a week after PI Planning so that they would have more face-time with their Australia-based colleagues and stakeholders. This gave people across the country time to get to know one

---

[93] A "ring in" is Australian for a person that is not a regular member of a group that is added late to fill a gap.

another better, share meals and share stories. This built the all-important social fabric upon which they could rely as they worked together to solve issues and deliver solutions during PI execution.

Logistics

It is easy to underestimate the effort required to pull together an event of this nature. It can be 100+ people, seven days, and often many locations. If you have a program coordinator or you can borrow an executive assistant to help you get organised this will be a good choice.

Venue considerations

- ❏ Try to book the same space for Team Day, *SAFe for Teams*, and PI Planning and ensure the venue understands you will be leaving materials in the room overnight. This should be one big room that can comfortably seat the entire train and its stakeholders.
- ❏ Confirm availability of the venue for the Management Review and Problem-Solving Session on the evening of PI Planning day one.
- ❏ Find out if you are allowed to use Blu-Tack and/or painter's tape on the walls and if not source foam board or cork board to use for team spaces and all program boards.
- ❏ If possible, book a space with natural light.

Darren's Anecdote

My client had found and booked the location. They showed me the picture; it's a wonderful wedding venue. It looked perfect! I asked can I check it out. They said, "No need, we have done it. Look at the pictures." I really should. They said, "Honestly, it will be fine". I got there on the morning of PI Planning and I asked can I put Blu Tack on the walls? NO! They have all just been painted! And there was no Wi-Fi!

> **Tips for Globally Distributed ARTs**
>
> You will need the venues at all locations to have access to compatible high-quality video conferencing facilities. Ideally you will want a movable camera so that you can zoom in on people speaking and information they are sharing on boards or sheets of flip chart paper. You will need a dedicated video conferencing room at each location for any team that has team members at multiple sites. You will also need a video conferencing room at each location (in addition to the main planning room) to enable team-to-team conversations across the various sites.

Of course, if you are choosing to collate, the biggest logistics hurdle is going to be travel and accommodation. You may want to factor this in when you choose a venue. Perhaps look at venues that can also offer group rates on accommodation, and that will be easy for the out-of-town folks to get to. If you are going to have folks travel internationally start planning early. It is not uncommon for it to take weeks or months for visas to be arranged depending on the countries you need to arrange travel to and from.

In addition to the above, the SAFe Program Increment Toolkit[94] contains an ART Readiness Workbook which includes a checklist for facilities and supplies.

There is also an opportunity to engage people who are interested in helping or who want to know more about the logistics of the event. A common pattern we see is the Scrum Master community working as a team to support the RTE preparing for the event.

---

[94] The SAFe Program Increment Toolkit is available for download from the SAFe Community Portal by SPCs in good standing.

PI Planning Room Set-Up

We recommend pre-allocating teams and other stakeholders to tables. The RTE should talk to the teams about who they think they need to work closely with. It is likely that the teams with dependencies will want to be near each other. Teams like the System Team and Shared Services that interact with all of the other teams are probably best seated centrally. Observers and other non-team members often end up with seating in the middle of the room, as tables with wall space are prioritised for the teams.

> **Protip**
> An ART's first PI Planning event tends to generate a lot of buzz in the organisation. While this can be awesome in how it creates visibility of the change you are making it can also result in dozens of people wanting to come and "observe." If you have ever been in a PI Planning event, you know it's loud. Every extra person in the room will add noise. So, make sure these folks have a place to go to work quietly.

Stationery

The ART Readiness Workbook [95] also includes a supplies tab for stationery. Personally, I like to be a little more generous when providing supplies to the teams. My thinking is that you buy stationery at the beginning of each PI to support the teams through the PI. This can be particularly useful in organisations where stationery costs are controlled, or your train is in a country that can't easily access good-quality Post-it Notes! We have included our recommended supply list in the Appendix.

---

[95] The ART Readiness Workbook is part of the SAFe Program Increment Toolkit.

Scrum Master Training

The addition of the SAFe Scrum Master class to the suite of certified SAFe classes created the perfect bridge to help the train's Scrum Masters prepare for PI Planning.[96] Some clients are quick to tell me they don't need the SAFe Scrum Master class as their Scrum Masters already have experience with Scrum and/or are Certified Scrum Masters (CSMs) or Professional Scrum Masters (PSMs). However, it is likely that they all come with different mental models and assumption. No matter how well they have been trained previously, having a common training, language, and understanding is priceless. In short, experience with Scrum and Scrum Master certifications can provide a good grounding for SAFe Scrum Masters, but it is not a good substitute for the SAFe Scrum Master class.

The SAFe Scrum Master class prepares the Scrum Master for their role on an Agile Release Train, paying particular attention to how you go about facilitating a team through a two-day PI Planning event and executing as part of a team of agile teams. Prior to the introduction of this class, entering PI Planning was pretty scary for Scrum Masters. The ART expected a lot from them, but they had been given very little education to help them meet these expectations. We have certainly noticed the difference in PI Planning now that Scrum Masters have had role-based training prior to PI Planning.

At a minimum, the Scrum Masters and the RTE attend this class. If the train is particularly small you may not have enough people to fill a class of 12. In this case, I have seen organisations include aspiring Scrum Masters that will fill in for Scrum Masters when they take leave. Or on large SAFe sites advertise the class to others at the site that may not be on the train, as there seems to always be a need and can earn you good will with other initiatives.

---

[96] To learn more about the SAFe Scrum Master class check out: https://www.scaledagile.com/certification/courses/safe-scrum-master/ (Accessed 21 July 2019).

> **Tips for Globally Distributed ARTs**
> As always, we recommend co-locating for the SAFe Scrum Master class. This is an opportunity for the RTE and Scrum Master community to begin to bond as a team. If co-location is not possible, we recommend running the class in parallel and sending photos back and forth between the classes to try to make it feel like a shared experience.

Team Day

This is a repurposing of Day Five in the textbook Quick-Start, except for us it is the first day of the Quick-Start Week. The agenda for this day depends on some of the choices you have made about team formation and feature allocation.

> **Adrienne's Anecdote**
> Team day is also essential if you are rebooting an ART. If the ART is coming back to PI Planning but has had a really poor experience up to this point, we want this day to feel very different to the train. We ran this day for a client that called us in to reboot an ART they had launched on their own that had derailed. At the beginning of the day we could see the anxiety and stress in people as they were assembling into their teams, but by the end of the day people were smiling, excited, and told us they were surprised at how different this was.

Sample Team Day Agenda
- Speed-Meet with Personal Maps
- Self-Selection (optional)
- Train Theme and Name the Train
- Team Product Box (including Team Name)
- Feature Auction (optional)
- Agile Facilitation Skills Workshop (optional)
- Working Agreements (optional)

Speed-Meet with Personal Maps

It never fails to surprise me how a group of circa one hundred people who have been, in theory, working together for a number of years don't actually know each other. After tripping over this mistake numerous times, I have finally learnt to build this assumption into my ART launch approach. These days I kick off Team Day with a Speed-Meet inspired by a story from my friend Llewellyn Falco.[97] We kick off the morning by asking everyone to create a Personal Map.[98] We share Jurgen Appelo's template and tell people they can share as little or as much as they are comfortable with. We then use these Personal Maps for our Speed-Meet. The maps are then shared within the team, taking five minutes per pair until each person has met every other person on their team. The best part of this exercise is the amazing energy and buzz that is generated in the room!

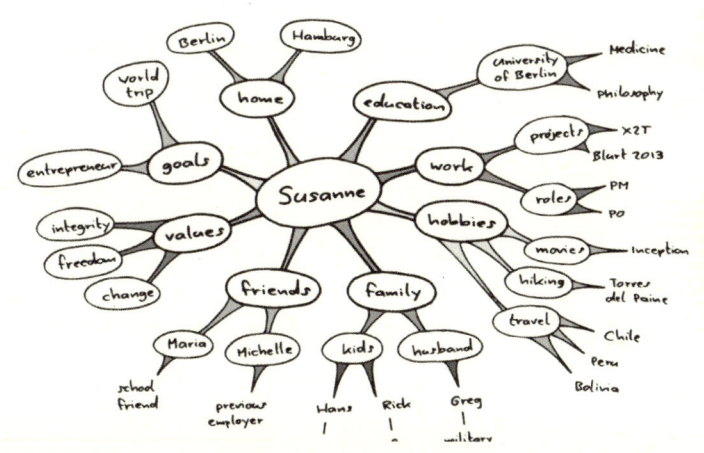

Figure 36 - Personal Maps[99]

---

[97] To learn more about Llewellyn's speed meet check out Llewellyn's blog: http://llewellynfalco.blogspot.com/2017/03/why-we-did-speed-meet-at-our-conference.html (Accessed 2 September 2019).

[98] To learn more about Jurgen Appelo's Personal Maps check out: https://management30.com/practice/personal-maps/ (Accessed 2 September 2019).

[99] Juregn Appelo, *#Workout, Games, Tools & Practices to Engage People, Improve Work, and Delight Clients*. (Rotterdam: Happy Melly, 2014). Kindle Edition. Location. 851.

Self-Selection

As I said in *Tribal Unity*, "... it is not mandatory to use self-selection, but if your goal is to improve the culture of your organisation and make it a truly great place to work, then I can't imagine a better place to start.[100] Following the case study in *Laying the Tracks*, there are a couple of additional tricks I would like to share.

First, due to time constraints we take a slightly different approach to the Speed-Meet with Personal Maps mentioned above. In the interests of time we ask people to bring pre-prepared personal maps with them to the event and then the Speed-Meet is across the whole train, similar to the 100+ person example in Llewellyn's blog post.

Second, use Scrum Master and Product Owner pairs as the starting point for each team. Hold a "speed-dating" session to allow the Scrum Masters and Product Owners to self-select into pairs.[101] Then have each Scrum Master and Product Owner pair pitched to the train, what life on their squad would be like at the commencement of the self-selection event. Matching features to teams is done after the teams have been formed.

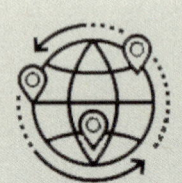

> **Tips for Globally Distributed ARTs**
> If you want to use Self-Selection as the approach to form teams for a distributed ART I would suggest being committed to co-located teams. You can then look to run events at each location. Time zone difference might make it more practical to have one site do their self-selection event the day before the other so that the time zone overlap time can be used for the team building components of team day.

---

[100] Em Campbell-Pretty, *Tribal Unity*, p. 12.
[101] See: http://blog.prettyagile.com.au/2017/08/re-squadification.html (Accessed 2 September 2019).

Train and Team Names

As I talk about in *Tribal Unity*, a shared identity is the first step in creating a one-team culture and it is my view that every train needs to see itself as a team. I like to start by giving the train a name and/or a theme. Teams then choose names based on the theme. Sometimes, the RTE chooses the theme, other times the teams nominate themes and vote for their preferred option. [102]

When asking teams to choose names, I usually post a sheet of flip chart paper at the front of the room and ask teams to add their team name as soon as it is decided. This prevents duplication and also provides an opportunity to vet the names for workplace suitability. I often find myself asking a team if they would be comfortable going home to their family and telling them that their new team name was [insert unsuitable team name here].

Team as a Product Box

The next activity, Team as a Product Box, is also straight out of *Tribal Unity*.[103]

> *This is an adaption of the product box exercise from Innovation Games*[104]. *In our variation, each team is asked to think of itself as a product and physically create the box that the team would be packaged in if it were to be sold on a supermarket shelf.*
>
> *The packaging should address the following questions:*
>
> - Who are your customers? (both internal and external)
> - What are the key services you offer those customers?
> - What are your customers saying about you?

---

[102] Em Campbell-Pretty, *Tribal Unity*, p. 28.
[103] Em Campbell-Pretty, *Tribal Unity*, p.30.
[104] Luke Hohmann, *Innovation Games: Creating Breakthrough Products Through Collaborative Play*, (Boston: Pearson, 2007), Kindle Edition, Location 1653

> - What are your "system" requirements? (i.e. what do you need to be able to deliver?)
> - What sets your team apart from your competitors? (both internally and externally)
>
> *All you need is the teams, some boxes, and some art-and-craft supplies. Give them the brief, set the time box, and you are good to go! When everyone is done and dusted it is time for the real fun, getting the teams to "showcase" their product box to the other teams in the tribe.*

Figure 37 - Team Product Boxes from an ART Team Day

Agile Facilitation Skills Workshop

The second half of the day starts with a crash course in facilitation, leveraging Jean Tabaka's material on Scaling Collaboration and Creating a Culture of Great Meetings. [105] This is a workshop about running great workshops. Very meta! We kick off the session with a quick lesson on Post-it etiquette from Michael Sahota.

---

[105] You can access the slides for the version of this workshop that Jean delivered at Agile Alliance 2015 here: https://www.slideshare.net/jeantabaka/the-secret-sauce-of-agile-a-culture-of-great-meetings-agile2015 (Accessed 2 September 2019).

All Aboard!

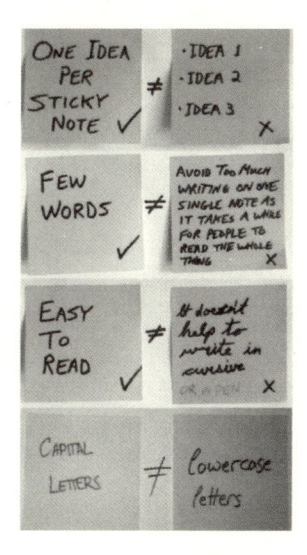

Figure 38 -Post-it Note Etiquette[106]

Then, we introduce some quick facilitation techniques like silent writing on Post-it Notes, dot voting, affinity mapping, and pass the pen. Given the teams are about to spend a lot of time in workshops with Post-it Notes this feels like a good investment. One recent client had such rich learnings about the communication challenges in his organisation that they immediately changed their video conferencing policy to enable smoother communication between their geographically distributed teams.

Working Agreements

For the final activity of the day we ask the teams to discuss and agree how they are going to work together and create a poster that captures what they agreed. We seed the discussion with the following questions:

- How will we communicate?
- How will we make decisions?
- How do each of us like to work?

---

[106] See: http://agilitrix.com/2013/10/how-to-go-fast-with-sticky-notes/ (Accessed 2 September 2019).

- How will we handle conflict?
- Think about things that <u>will</u> happen! e.g. illness, meetings, lateness, unexpected changes, problems, celebrations, etc.
- How will we hold each other to account on this?

Often teams choose to sign these agreements and post them in their team spaces when they return to the office.

Team Training

All In and All at Once

Our approach to *SAFe for Teams* training is to include everyone on the Agile Release Train.[107] This includes the Trifecta and Shared Services. Occasionally, we even get a senior leader or executive to join in, which the ART always interprets as a sign that the organisation is committed to SAFe. I once even had a CEO join the full suite of SAFe training (*Leading SAFe* (twice!), *Product Owner/Product Manager*, *SAFe Scrum Master*, and *SAFe for Teams*) as part of his organisation's first ART launch.

Often referred to as big room training, this approach to holding one large class for the entire train sounds crazy; however, it does have a number of advantages:

- The teams get to experience training as a team with their Scrum Master and Product Owner; the freshly trained Scrum Masters and Product Owners get the opportunity to reinforce their learning by supporting their teams' learning journey[108]
- Everyone hears the same message from the same trainer(s) at the same time

---

[107] To learn more about the *SAFe for Teams* class check out: https://www.scaledagile.com/certification/courses/safe-for-teams/ (Accessed 21 July 2019).

[108] I liken this to the Teach-Back techniques Sharon Bowman recommends in *Training from the BACK of the Room*. By teaching others what they have learned the Scrum Masters and Product Owners are deepening their understanding, increasing their long-term memory, clarifying their learning, increasing their confidence, and helping them

- When there is ambiguity about the go forward approach for the specific ART the leadership is there to answer questions and again everyone hears the same message at the same time
- The teams' participation in this training (and Team Day) is a shared experience and shared experiences over time helps teams build trust and trust is the foundation of teamwork.[109]

There is something about all the teams on a train, including the leadership team, learning together with their Scrum Masters and Product Owners that is just magical. Having spent many years convinced that training circa one hundred people at once was nuts, then going through the process a number of times, I have to say I was wrong. If Harvard Professor J. Richard Hackman is to be believed, 30% of a team's eventual performance is dependent on the initial launch of the team.[110] Personally, I cannot think of a better way to launch a team of teams than two days of learning together.

> **Protip**
> When training *SAFe for Teams* with the entire train you need to think about how many instructors you will need. A good rule of thumb is one instructor to every 25 – 30 people. You will need enough experienced SAFe folks in the room to coach the teams through the exercises.

This approach also has the advantage of being "just in time." Meaning that:

---

to master the new techniques. Source: Sharon Bowman, *Training from the BACK of the Room*, p. 177.
[109] Patrick. Lencioni, *The Five Dysfunctions of a Team : A Leadership Fable*, (New York: Wiley, 2002). Pages 194-7.
[110] J. Richard Hackman, Leading Teams: Setting the Stage for Great Performances, (Boston: Harvard University Press, 2002), Kindle Edition, Location 737.

- We know the potential Features for each team
- All of the features targeted for this PI should meet the definition of ready (as anyone working on getting the features to the definition of ready had to be finished before the class as they are expected to be in the class)
- We can use the team's real work (the features) for the training exercises giving the teams a head start on PI Planning
- There is an opportunity for gaps with feature readiness to be discovered and potentially addressed before PI Planning.

> **Tips for Globally Distributed ARTs**
> If you have been unable to co-locate your ART for the Quick-Start, you should still aim to deliver *SAFe for Teams* in parallel. We usually default to regular working hours so there is often a time lag between the classes. While there is no substitution for co-located big room training, we try and create as many connections as possible between the disparate locations by sharing data, photos, and videos from the various activities. These can include:

- Processing times from the penny game
- Estimates and actuals from the ball game
- Team presentations (video)
- Train role introductions (video).

The alternative is a number of smaller classes leading up to the PI Planning event. While we always ask for teams to attend as a team with their Scrum Master and Product Owner there is always some critical deliverable that stops this from occurring. The next problem is what does the team do after training and before PI Planning? Are they supposed to be SAFe now? Or should they continue working as they were before the training? Neither approach is going to feel great. Realistically, adult learners struggle enough retaining classroom training without adding these sorts of challenges.

> **Caution! Potential Train Wreck Ahead!**
> Organisations will resist training everyone. You will hear things like:
>> …but my teams are already agile …
>> … but I don't have the budget to train EVERYONE …
>> … you mean everyone except the vendor teams and contractors, right? …
>
> Do not compromise! Lack of training is the number one cause of train wrecks.
>
> While the organisation may think their teams are already agile, that is rarely true. They are more likely to be "Wagile" or "Fragile." Even if all the teams are truly agile, they are likely all doing their own version of agile and in SAFe we value alignment[111] therefore we want everyone to be doing the same version of agile. As for the budget argument, I doubt any organisation very much has the budget not to invest in training; train wrecks are expensive! As for vendors and contractors, of course, they need to be trained!

> **Protip**
> Don't ask your vendors to arrange their own training for their staff, include them in the training you offer your permanent staff. Many organisations will "buck" at the idea of paying for training for vendors. I know I was not at all convinced this was a good idea back when I was working in industry. It was my understanding that the reason we paid a premium for vendor staff was that they were highly skilled professionals, therefore I could not comprehend why we needed to provide training. Here's the rub: if the people are already inside your organisation,

---

[111] To learn more about SAFe Core Values check out: https://www.scaledagileframework.com/safe-core-values/ (Accessed 21 July 2019).

they likely have a good understanding of your systems. While you could replace these people with a team of folks that already have their SAFe certifications, the new people will not have any knowledge of your systems and that is going to be a much steeper learning curve!

My next instinct was to have the vendors arrange the training for their staff as I didn't think we should have to pay for it. This is great in theory, but in reality, it will likely create other problems. They will likely use a different training supplier and teams won't be trained as teams, resulting in alignment issues. In the end, the compromise I made with the vendors was that we would pay for the training, but they would not bill us for the time people spend in class. Remember, a common language and common understanding is critical to success.

Em's Anecdote

When I am invited into an organisation to review the health of an ART, I always ask to speak to the teams. In under half an hour it becomes clear to me that the teams have some significant gaps in their understanding of SAFe. So, I ask them if they had any training prior to the ART launch. The answer is almost always the same: "Some of the key leaders went on a training course." I probe, "Anyone else?" "No," they reply. At this point I am furious. In my view if you are going to tell your teams you want them to work differently, then you have a moral obligation to provide them with the education to be able to do so.

With this newfound insight I return to the folks who are sponsoring my engagement and ask some clarifying questions. "If I understand correctly, you decided to take circa one hundred people from across your organisation and asked them to work differently to how they have ever worked before?" "Yes," they

> reply. So, I'd ask "And you didn't give them any training in that new way of working? What did you think was going to happen?" Nothing good, is my guess!

Agreeing on the Definition of One

SAFe for Teams introduces the teams to SAFe's approach to Normalised Estimation:

1. ***Normalise story point estimation***: *Find a small story that would take about a half-day to develop and a half-day to test and validate and call it a "one." Estimate every other story relative to that "one."*
2. ***Establish velocity before historical data exists***: *For every full-time developer and tester on the team, give the team eight points (adjust for part-timers). Subtract one point for every team member vacation day and holiday in the iteration.*[112]

One of the challenges with this approach is that it anchors folks in the mindset of one point of effort equals one day to get a story to done. While I absolutely see the challenge of estimating capacity for five or six sprints without historical velocity data, I also see the challenge with time-based estimation:

- Humans are better at estimating relative size than absolute size.[113]
- Estimating in units of time can quickly become personal, as team members start to think in terms of how fast or slow they are compared to their teammates (and I don't think this creates a healthy team dynamic).

---

[112] To learn more about SAFe relative estimation model check out: https://www.scaledagileframework.com/iteration-planning/ (Accessed 21 July 2019).

[113] Mike Cohn, *Agile Estimating and Planning,* (New Jersey: Pearson Education, 2006), p. 55.

- Stakeholders are quick to judge estimates based on their view of what the estimate should be in days, which I also don't find to be a healthy dynamic.
- It is easier for management to slip into the anti-pattern of comparing teams.

After reviewing *Agile Software Requirements*,[114] I understand SAFe's estimation approach to be a hybrid of the two techniques outlined in Mike Cohn's *Agile Estimating and Planning*—relative estimation and estimating using ideal developer days.[115] I understand the intent to be using the concept of ideal developer days to estimate capacity while also wanting teams to use relative estimation and for this to work the 1-point story needs to be an ideal developer day.

Armed with this knowledge, we take a similar but slightly different approach when we get to this portion of *SAFe for Teams*. Instead of each team finding a story that takes one day to deliver and just running with it, we like to ask the teams to share their example 1-point stories. We will ask the teams to indicate which ones are equal and which ones are materially smaller or larger. We take the set that are seen to be equal and call them our "chickens" (a reference to the animal sizing game in *Leading SAFe*). The ART keeps the chickens as a shared definition of one to use going forward, adding more examples as they occur.

> **Tips for Globally Distributed ARTs**
> If you are not co-located for *SAFe for Teams* training, be sure to collect and share the chickens from each location so that you still end up with a calibrated "definition of one" for your ART.

---

[114] Dean Leffingwell, *Agile Software Requirements*, Location 2945.
[115] Mike Cohn, *Agile Estimating and Planning*, pages 35-46.

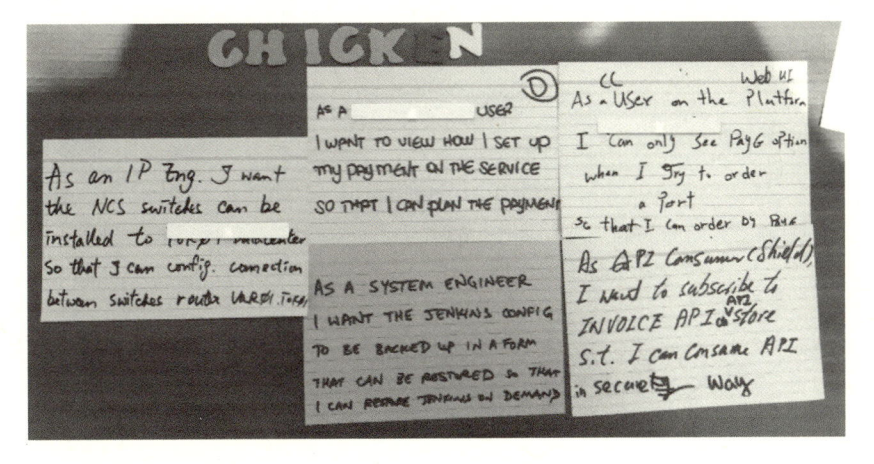

Figure 39 -Example of the "definition of one" stories (aka chickens) from one ART

Calculating Capacity (Velocity)

While we have everyone in the training room focused on the topic of capacity, we have them calculate their capacity for the full PI, so that we don't need to spend time on that during PI Planning. We often suggest that the ART should be encouraged to plan leave for the Program Increment prior to the Quick-Start so that we can factor leave into the planning.

We discussed earlier that humans are just terrible at estimation and newly formed teams will be even worse as they have no history of working together this way. Given we want the train to get a win out of the gate, we need to set these new teams up for success. We do this by asking the teams to reduce their capacity by 30% for every sprint in the PI.

For example, for an eight-person team with a full-time Product Owner and a full-time Scrum Master and no one taking any planned time off, the team's capacity would be 6 x 8pt = 48 pts. Thirty percent of 48 points is 14.4 points, which we would round up to 15. Forty-eight points minus 15 points is 33 points which is the maximum capacity we would ask the team to load their plan to.

The ART of Avoiding a Train Wreck

Program Increment (PI) Planning

Leading SAFe, Implementing SAFe, the Scaled Agile Framework website, and *SAFe Distilled* all provide very comprehensive coverage of SAFe's PI Planning event. Our intent is not to regurgitate that content here; instead, it is our hope to enhance your toolkit by sharing some additional tips and tricks we have learned over the years.

> **Protip**
> No one expects your first PI Planning event to be perfect. In fact, I'm not sure the "perfect" planning event is ever a realistic expectation. Every PI Planning event surfaces its own unique challenges that you will need to block and tackle.[116] The only constant in PI Planning is the mechanics. The first PI Planning event has a tendency to become the template for all future planning events. With this in mind, try not to skip any part of the agenda as the odds are you will continue to skip the same agenda items for every future PI Planning. Such is the imprint created on the ART by the first PI Planning event.

> **Caution! Potential Track Wreck Ahead!**
> Large scale training isn't the only thing that makes people nervous about launching a train. The PI Planning event can have a similar effect. Just the thought of 100+ people in a two-day workshop can be overwhelming. I have seen people use all sorts of funny shortcuts to help them deal with these nerves. The most common of these is one-day PI Planning. Personally, I find this to be a missed opportunity.

---

[116] A US expression often used in business, it is a reference to American football in which blockers and tacklers have the least glamorous positions but are critically important to the team as a whole.

One-day PI Planning doesn't provide the same opportunity for the teams to surface their challenges and have them addressed by management. I have also found that where there is one-day planning there is a huge amount of pre-work taking place to make it possible. Perhaps the biggest challenge with this (and other PI Planning shortcuts) is that a new train doesn't have the context with which to properly evaluate this choice.

Claire's Anecdote

A team on a train I worked with was so keen to make a good impression at PI Planning, they spent the week before PI Planning doing all of their planning. At the first break out on day one, they had nothing to do beyond Blu-Tacking up the pre-written stories. This was such a missed opportunity for them to work with their fellow train members to build a plan which could meet the ART's objectives. Also, I was shocked they had spent five days planning the PI, perhaps searching for the mythical perfect plan.

Aaron's Anecdote

Every client who has tried one-day PI Planning tells me, "Well, we're not doing that again!" For me, the goal of day one is to make adjustments in the management problem solving session, for the teams to sleep on their decisions, and digest the information. In one-day PI planning, this is completely lost! The last one-day PI Planning I was on resulted in the Business Owner giving a one in the confidence vote and an emergency re-planning at the office. That PI turned into the PI from hell with teams working weekends, business commitments missed, and unforeseen dependencies!

Case Study:
Good PI Planning is the Enemy of Great PI Planning

When I first met Dean Leffingwell, I had already launched the EDW Release Train without doing PI Planning. I was attending one of the early SPC classes in Boulder, Colarado. It was day three before I built up the courage to ask Dean the question that had been on my mind since I decided to attend the class: What should I do about the fact we weren't doing PI Planning?

My memory of Dean's response is that he was rather dismissive. With my 20/20 hindsight, I can see how I must have appeared to Dean. A youngish businessperson with no real experience leading large IT teams, suggesting that I knew better than a veteran of the technology industry, author of several books and creator of the Scaled Agile Framework. Looking at the situation through this lens, I find myself squirming with embarrassment at my own arrogance.

Fast forward to the present day, I am a SAFE Fellow and SPCT, making a living from helping enterprises implement SAFe. I encounter people every day who think they know better and I find myself bristling, perhaps in the same way that Dean bristled when I questioned the value of PI Planning.

While this could be the same arrogance I displayed back at that SPC class in Boulder, I hope the root cause is actually something different. I now believe. (Okay, I'm now channelling Agent Fox Mulder!) Seriously though, my experiences and those of others in the community who have chosen to share their experiences with me have convinced me that perhaps we should listen before passing judgement. I think Henrik Kniberg put it best in his talk about SAFe at Lego: "SAFe = Shu-level scaling."[117]

---

[117] See: https://youtu.be/TolNkqyvieE (Accessed 21 July 2019).

Figure 40 -Slide from "Is SAFe evil?" presented by Lars Roost and Henrik Kniberg at GOTO Conferences

Launching an Agile Release Train with that very first all-hands PI Planning event is a terrifying thought for many new to SAFe. Without an experienced SAFe practitioner on hand to lead the way through the courage of their convictions that it will work, new trains start to devise a plot for a "soft launch." Not unlike my first attempt at PI Planning with the EDW Release Train.[118] The end result often being equally as soft.

No matter how soft the launch, almost without fail, the team is inspired by big room planning. They decide to do it again in 12 weeks' time, or less, but this time better. But they are still not ready to go all in. They make some changes to make the next event a little more like textbook PI Planning. The second event is a raging success. Everyone is self-congratulatory. They have improved so much. They are making great progress. Clearly the more structured, full-scale PI Planning approach is for fools. In the end, it's all a matter of perspective. How can you be great if

---

[118] See: http://blog.prettyagile.com.au/2014/02/from-psi-planning-to-unity-day-and-back.html (Accessed 21 July 2019).

you don't know what great looks like? And there it is, just as Jim Collins observed—good is the enemy of great.[119]

The more underprepared PI Planning I see, the more I believe that the formula is almost fool proof. No matter how underprepared you are, or how many corners you cut, there is always a good outcome and a little taste of the magic. Perhaps it is just like sex and pizza: even when it is bad it is good. These days Dean likes to rib me about all the "workarounds" we did with EDW. It's all good-natured fun. We did what we did because we had no choice. Dean understands that, but he also knew something we didn't. If there is magic in SAFe, it is in PI Planning and you just have to experience it to believe it.[120]

Em's Anecdote

While I am convinced PI Planning is almost idiot proof, I think I may have also uncovered the exception to that rule. That is PI Planning without features. On one occasion I was helping out a colleague by being the SPC on the remote site for PI Planning. I was briefed that the features were not yet defined; however, there would be someone at my location with the information in their head and they would work with the team to flesh out the work that needed to be done.

When it came time for the team breakout sessions, I located the gentleman who had been nominated to define the feature and introduced him to the team. I kid you not, when we asked him to talk to the team about the work his open line was: "There is this guy named _____ and he knows all about this." Well, that

---

[119] Jim Collins, *Good to Great: Why Some Companies Make the Leap and Others Don't*. (London: Random House, 2001) p.1.
[120] Adapted from: http://blog.prettyagile.com.au/2015/12/good-pi-planning-is-enemy-of-great-pi.html (Accessed 23 September 2019)

> was no help to any of us. The person we needed to speak with was in another workshop at another location and could not be reached. So, we sent everyone home and there was no day two of PI Planning.

Preparing for PI Planning

If you are a certified SAFe Program Consultant or a certified SAFe Release Train Engineer the first thing you should do is go to the SAFe Community Portal and download the Program Increment Toolkit. It is free![121] It contains heaps of useful content that you can and should use. It amazes me how often we encounter SPCs and RTEs who have never downloaded the content, let alone used it! If you do not have the certification to access this content, don't panic! There is still a lot of completely free content available on the Scaled Agile Framework website including the ART Readiness Checklist.[122]

Here are some additional preparation items to consider:

- ❏ Get everyone's PowerPoint presentations in advance and load them to a single presenting laptop to reduce down time between presenters. Some folks even like to merge them into a single document.
- ❏ Remember to turn off all automatic updates on the presenting laptop. We had an iTunes update pop up once!
- ❏ Have the RTE call all of the presenters to the front of the room at the beginning of the event. Have the presenters stand in the order they will present so they all can see who will go before and after them. This way if you have to play pass the microphone, they can do that. This can be a huge time saver!

---

[121] As has been pointed out to me, it is not completely free, you did pay for the certification!
[122] To see the full SAFe ART Launch Readiness Checklist check out: https://www.scaledagileframework.com/prepare-for-art-launch/ (Accessed 21 July 2019).

- ❏ While the standard agenda suggests an 8:00 a.m. start, always consider the local context. For example, in Australia most PI Planning events start at 9:00 a.m. not 8:00 a.m.
- ❏ Consider how you want to capture the event. Photos? Video? Often organisations like to share the experience with those who could not attend as part of building some momentum for SAFe in the broader organisation.[123]
- ❏ Have a Time Timer[124] in the room and time box everything!
- ❏ Build a physical Kanban-style agenda in the room. This will allow the whole room to know at a glance how far through the event we are at and what is still to come.
- ❏ Put the dates of the sprints on the teams' sprint sheets and print the colour coding for the Post-its.

Darren's Anecdote

I always take lots of photos at PI Planning for my own reflection and learning. However, on one occasion I decided to put them into a video. Nothing fancy, an iMovie, with some sound or music and some text. Pleased with my effort I sent it to the client as a sort of "value add." They put it on their intranet, and it went viral. Before we knew it, we had more requests to attend the next PI than we could cater for. I always do a video now.

Adrienne's Anecdote

Sooner or later you'll have PI Planning around a fun holiday or event. So, why not have the train plan with a theme? Once, I was planning right before Halloween for that Solution Train I launched. The RTEs and I wore pink cowboy hats and masks.

---

[123] Here is an example of a PI Planning slide show created by one ART after their first PI Planning event: http://blog.prettyagile.com.au/2014/09/SAFe-ART-PSI-release-planning.html (Accessed 21 July 2019).

[124] See: https://www.timetimer.com/ (Accessed 21 July 2019).

One leader dressed up as a pill bottle where the prescription on the bottle was all about poking fun at the other senior members of the leadership team. As a side note, I still remember barely being able to read the "prescription" to the entire Solution Train because I was laughing so hard, and so were they! So, it's fun for sure so take advantage! But we also learned something unexpected. It was so hard for the RTEs and me to find each other in a sea of six hundred people until we had pink cowboy hats on! That became a pattern going forward to use colour to identify key people in the sea of people.

Tips for Globally Distributed ARTs

You will need suitably experienced facilitators at each location. The RTE will need people they can lean on to be they arms, legs, eyes, and ears in the remote locations. You will also need experienced SAFe coaches to support the teams in each location.

If there is a time zone difference between the locations try to shift the agenda so that the pain is shared equally by the locations. For example, when working across Australian Eastern Standard Time (AEST) and India Standard Time (IST) we might have Australia start at 11:00 a.m. which is 6:30 a.m. in India. This of course is only practical for the India site if everyone stays in the same hotel as the event or there is accommodation close by. We can't ask people to leave home at 4:00 a.m., travel for two hours and then do eight hours of PI Planning before another two-hour commute home. This does not demonstrate respect for people.

Map every agenda item across time zones to ensure there is adequate and appropriate breaks for snacks and meals at each location.

Determine the communication approach for every section of the agenda. How will dependencies be negotiated? How will you conduct a Scrum of Scrums with remote teams and Scrum Masters? How will plans be communicated and updated? How will the Business Owners rate the PI Objectives? Build your plan of attack in consultation with the train and once the approach has been agreed make sure it is communicated.

Have a contingency plan for when the technology fails you as it almost certainly will. Better still, plan in some redundancy if you can. Nothing is more embarrassing and infuriating than a technology failure with a 100+ people ready and expecting to collaborate.

Maarit's Anecdote

During training I usually get a lot of arguments about seriously suggesting a large globally distributed organisation should meet periodically. My usual response to that is that the decision of taking the cost of the global distribution is already taken. Our job is to make people who are already distributed to work together, and this we are going to do in the most efficient manner! Your choice is always to go back to co-located teams—or if that is not possible, at least consider how you could set up your ARTs in a bit more rational way.

Setting Up the Team Planning Space

Have the teams set up their planning space at the end of the second day of *SAFe for Teams*. If the venue won't let you stick flip chart paper to the walls, then you might like to purchase some corrugated plastic boards (also referred to as foam boards) for the teams to build plans on. This board is also great for building program boards and can generally be sourced from printers.

Teams should have printouts of the feature definition work, Solution on a Page, and Wireframes on hand. Often, I find teams like to stick these to the walls for easy visibility.

Some innovative team space ideas I have seen used by Scrum Masters I have worked with include:

- Creating swim lanes in their sprint planning sheets for features so the team can see which stories relate to each feature and which iteration of the feature is complete. This also helps with transferring features to the Program Board
- Having a sheet for questions so that they can be parked and then checked off as they are answered during the course of the planning session
- Draw a line through the middle of the risk sheet so that you have separate spaces for team and program level risks
- Have a facilitation plan with clear time boxes for the breakout sessions and make it visible to the team.

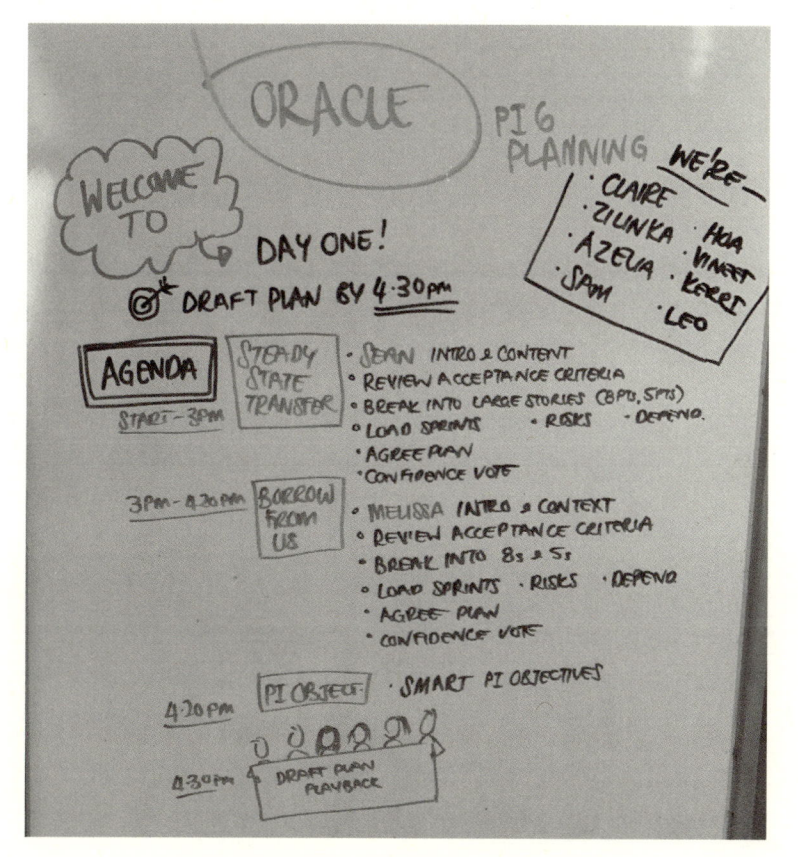

Figure 41- Example of Team Breakout Agenda

Business Context

For an ART's first PI Planning event, we recommend getting the most senior executive you can find that is willing to invest twenty to thirty minutes sharing with the ART the organisation's current business context and help the ART members understand how the work they do will contribute to the organisation. Often this briefing is provided by a VP or local equivalent but every so often a CEO steps up to the plate. Hands down the most impressive example we have experienced is the CEO that flew from Israel to Brisbane to deliver a forty-minute keynote at his organisation's first ART launch. Even if you do manage to get the CEO to present, still find time for both a senior business executive and senior technology executive to say a few words as well.

Product Management Briefing

In addition to the Product Vision, we like to see the Product Roadmap presented at PI Planning. We also have a preference to see all features in scope for the PI, even if that is more than ten. We coach Product Management to keep the feature briefings short. About three minutes per feature usually feels about right. We encourage them to have one slide for each feature that in a few words spells out the value of the feature. It can also be helpful to mention the team(s) likely to be working on the feature, the names of any SMEs that should be in the room that can be consulted and any known dependencies. Another model I have seen work well is Product Owners presenting the features. Sticking to the three-minute time box becomes both more challenging and more important with this pattern.

> **Protip**
> If your ART has a CX and/or UX Lead we like to see them included in the day one briefings to talk about things like the customer journey, the UX runway, and the UX standards for the ART. We have also seen the UX lead share videos of customers talking about or using the product, which is really powerful for the teams to hear.

Architecture Vision

In comparing notes from ART Launches over the years we have giggled how many times we both have witnessed a System Architect put up a slide and say, *"You can't read this but ... [insert important things teams need to know]."* The only logical conclusion is that there is an underground movement of SAFe System Architects conspiring to make Architectural Vision presentations impossible to read. ;-)

On a more serious note, keeping the architecture briefing at the right level is definitely a challenge. We suggest sharing the Solution on a Page for each feature in a way that illustrates where multiple features touch the same parts of the architecture. We also recommend the Architects use this briefing as an opportunity to remind the teams of any architectural guidelines that should be top of mind as they decompose the Features into stories.

> **Marc's Anecdote**
> The architecture briefing is a critical opportunity for Architects to "sell" the ART on their vision. Let's face it, in the Agile world, Architects can't simply decree that their vision be implemented, then govern teams' compliance. They need to get the teams on board or risk their best-laid plans falling on the floor. This is their opportunity to clearly articulate their vision, how it supports business objectives, and how they have set up the teams for implementation success. Of course, buy-in should be obtained at all levels prior to PI Planning so that the briefing is simply a formal announcement of the aligned architectural direction.

> **Em's Anecdote**
> In my experience, the Architects are often the folks most in need of strict time boxing. I once had an architect call in sick for an ART's first PI Planning event. The RTE decided to let him present remotely using Skype or Google Hangouts. The only problem was that it was impossible for him to read the room. After twenty minutes of people shifting restlessly in their seats, he asked if there were any questions and the room breathed a sigh of relief only to groan as he continued for another twenty minutes! I would definitely think twice before using that approach again!

Something else for the System Architects to consider is how accessible the architecture information is. Referring teams to a wiki or SharePoint won't be a good fit for PI Planning. If the teams will need to reference the information during planning, then it should be printed out and placed in their team space. Better yet, if they needed it for planning, they probably should have seen it before planning.

Development Practices

This briefing should include the ARTs Definition of Done (DoD). SAFe provides a good example[125] to get you started but you can't copy and paste this onto your slideware and call it done. In our view, the SAFe DoD is the bare minimum standard, which hopefully you can build upon. For example, the SAFe DoD states "no must fix defects" but we prefer "no new defects". Teams will push back and say that's not possible. This is often a sign of a cultural problem. It is also sometimes an indication that the current code base is extremely buggy and the idea of delivering "bugless" code is quite simply overwhelming, hence the choice to focus on no new bugs.

---

[125] To learn more about the SAFe Definition of Done check out: https://www.scaledagileframework.com/built-in-quality/ (Accessed 10 September 2019)

> **Adrienne's Anecdote**
>
> I used to build flight guidance systems, so bugs were a big deal. It's absolutely amazing to me how much an organisation can be haemorrhaging customers because of quality issues and still wants to debate this policy. What does a doctor do when a patient is bleeding out? Apply a tourniquet. What do you need to do if you have quality issues? Stop making it worse! It will be key in the organisation becoming predictable, reducing lead time and product support costs.

> **Adrienne's Anecdote**
>
> You may have your own rules for when to record a defect, but I only record bugs when they really are bugs. I have seen offshore testers write defects during the sprint to communicate issues back to the onshore developers. I've also seen testing organisations with a KPI to record as many bugs as they can! This doesn't help us understand if we are getting better at building quality in and it's not a very team centric behaviour. I prefer if a story doesn't meet the acceptance criteria and the team can't fix it before the end of the sprint then don't accept the story. Some will write a defect against the story and it's okay. If a story is accepted by the Product Owner and gets broken later that is a defect and should be logged.

The Development practices briefing should also address the expectations of the teams with respect to the built-in quality practices taught in *SAFe for Teams*. We need to see this clearly as the Definition of Done has an effect on how much effort it will be to realise a story. Will they be expected to pair? Or use Test Driven Development (TDD)? Is the organisation practising CI/CD? How will the DoD change over time to adopt XP practices and what does that mean to growing the capabilities of the train? No one is agile awesome day one but being able to articulate a roadmap here and the expectations PI over PI will be key.

Planning Context

The SAFe Program Increment Toolkit will provide you with the basic textbook briefing. There are some slides that will need your input so don't leave looking at this until the last minute. Here are some additional practices that we recommend to our clients and include in our briefings.

Managing Noise

One of the challenges with 100+ people PI Planning in a single room is a lot of noise. It can be very hard for the team to hear each other. Therefore, we recommend reminding the room of this and asking that any conversations not being held with a team are held away from the teams. I always tell the Scrum Masters that they are empowered to tell anyone (including me!) who is having a conversation in or near their team space to "sod off"[126]! I also like to ask SMEs and observers to wait for the teams to come and get them, rather than hovering around the team spaces waiting to be engaged.

Categorising the Work, Capacity Allocation, and Colour Coding

SAFe guidance categorises the work of the teams into the following buckets:[127]

- User Stories (Green)[128]
- Maintenance (Purple)
- Exploration Enabler aka Spikes (Yellow)
- Infrastructure Enablers (Orange)
- Risks and Dependencies (Red)

---

[126] "Sod Off" is a British saying for go away.
[127] Richard Knaster, *SAFe Distilled* p. 101.
[128] Sometimes we have changed this to be yellow as you can buy a lot of canary-yellow Post-its!

Maybe all of these make sense to you, maybe they don't. Take a moment to consider what makes the most sense in your context.[129]

> **Protip**
> Index cards are generally a much better option than Post-it Notes if you want user stories written in User Voice.
>
> In addition to the categories and colour suggested in SAFe, there are some additional categories we use including:
> - "Bring out your dead"[130]
> - Discovery
> - Innovation
> - Upskilling
> - Bug Fix/Maintenance.

"Bring out your dead"

While in theory everyone on the ART is 100% on the ART and focused on the ART backlog, this is rarely 100% true for every team member. At the beginning of the first PI Planning event we ask each team member to create cards for any work they are bringing with them and size it in points. The goal is to visualise all the work the team is doing, even if it is not specifically related to the train's backlog. This helps the team (and the train) see it's true capacity and creates the option to deprioritise (or prioritise) this work in the context of the train's backlog for the PI.

For example, on one train there was a guy who spent every Wednesday morning manually generating a report for a senior executive. Making this visible allowed the team to adjust their capacity to reflect reality

---

[129] Also, double check you can source Post-it Notes in the right colours! In Australia a five-pack of Post-its comes in green, blue, yellow, orange and pink or red, orange, yellow, blue and purple!

[130] If you are not familiar with this saying you should check out the film *Monty Python and the Holy Grail* (1975).

and it enabled the RTE to investigate if the report was still needed and if so, could it be automated.

Discovery

As you know we prefer teams to have seen the features prior to PI Planning. Ideally, we want them to participate in feature definition and provide a job size in story points for inclusion in the feature prioritisation. We also don't want this to be a crazy rush at the end of the PI. Our rule is that planning for next PI begins day one of Sprint 1 of this PI. For the teams to play a part in this they will need to hold some capacity. Most ARTs hold 10% or 15% of the team's capacity each sprint to "discover" features for next PI.

> **Protip**
> The refinement of the program backlog for next PI needs to begin immediately following PI Planning for this PI. Product Managers that are really on top of their game bring their top priority features for discovery in Sprint 1 to PI Planning and ask the teams to pull the Features they find most interesting into their plan.

> **Caution! Potential Train Wreck Ahead!**
> If Product doesn't have Features Ready for teams to discover then teams tend to use this time for delivery work. This is a slippery slope, as once that time is gone you can't get it back. The end result being a huge bow wave of discovery needing to be completed just before the next PI Planning and/or teams not getting the opportunity to participate in feature definition and sizing. Also, no one on the ART has the authority to use discovery time for anything other than discovery (including the Product Owners).

Innovation Time

In *Tribal Unity* I recommend allowing teams to allocate 10% of their capacity every sprint to innovation.[131] My motivation is twofold: tapping into people's intrinsic motivation thereby creating a working environment that people want to be a part of and secondly seeding a culture of learning.

There are only three rules for Innovation Time:

1. The team can use the time any way they want as long as they are making an investment in the team and/or train getting better.
2. The team must be transparent about how they plan to use the time by including stories in their sprint plan and sprint review.
3. No one can "steal" your Innovation Time, including your team!

For some ARTs innovation time is also bug fix time. Teams with no new bugs get all their innovation time. Teams that deploy code with bugs get the bugs returned to them for fixing during their innovation time. The premise being "you broke it, you fix it."

> **Protip**
> You will get push back on this one. The idea of giving up 10% of the ART's delivery capacity will be terrifying in some organisational contexts. In my experience the payback is always significant. As an example, I once had a team automate a task that would take a week once every couple of months, reducing it to half a day. If you are looking for something more concrete my friend Llewellyn Falco uses a similar approach called Learning Hour which he talked about at the Agile 2017 conference. Using the concept of compound interest, he projects that an hour a day invested in learning that delivers a 1% increase in output will pay for itself in 28 days.[132]

---

[131] Em Campbell-Pretty, *Tribal Unity*, p. 67.
[132] See: https://www.slideshare.net/llewellynfalco/roi-on-learning-hour (Accessed 7 August 2019).

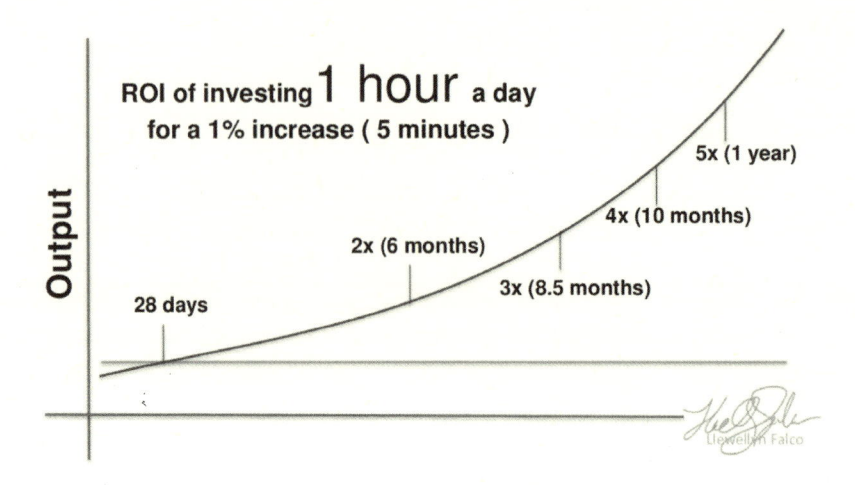

ROI of investing 1 hour a day for a 1% increase (5 minutes)

- 28 days
- 2x (6 months)
- 3x (8.5 months)
- 4x (10 months)
- 5x (1 year)

Figure 42 - Return on Investment for team learning 1 hour-a-day

Upskilling Time

Often cross-skilling is a significant challenge for a new ART that has traditionally worked in functional teams or component teams. One way to start to address this is by allocating capacity to this activity. This sends a clear message to the ART that you value cross-skilling and that you are prepared to invest in making it happen. As with innovation time, I ask teams to tell us how they are using their upskilling capacity each sprint. I have also seen this approach used to support teams in learning and adopting new practices such as TDD.

Bug Fix/Support

In environments where there has not historically been a culture of "built-in quality" the teams may already be spending a significant proportion of their time "fixing bugs." As undesirable as this may be, it is always best to "confront the most brutal facts of your current reality."[133] So, work out how much time is being spent, or how much time you want to allocate and have the teams hold this capacity. This

---

[133] See: https://www.jimcollins.com/concepts/confront-the-brutal-facts.html (Accessed 10 April 2019).

goes hand in hand with the "zero new bug policy" we suggested you include in your DoD.

> **Caution! Potential Train Wreck Ahead!**
> If you have been working in a world where 80% of your development organisation's capacity is currently being used to address customer support tickets, you need to take this into account when setting the capacity allocation for working on support tickets. Twenty percent is probably unrealistic and leaving it at 80% doesn't help you claw back capacity for development. Try for something more middle of the road, maybe 40% or 50% of capacity. If you under bake this your PI plan will be completely blown before the end of the first sprint.

> **Protip**
> One way to start to address known problems is have your Architects and Technical Leads review the feature roadmap and identify opportunities to address known bugs while working on the business's priority features. It is an excellent XP practice to refactor the code base to keep it healthy as you build the new features. This is a win-win as we incrementally refactor and improve the code as we deliver features! As for the known bugs that don't align with the feature roadmap, Product Management and the System Architect will need to collaborate on prioritising and burning down this list. Unlike our "you broke it, you fix it" approach to new bugs this work should be evenly distributed across teams on the train.

Don't forget to include a slide in your Planning Context Briefing that shows the teams the categories, the allocations, and the colours. The first activity we ask the teams to do once the Team Breakout session starts is to create placeholder cards (or Post-it Notes) using the correct colour, with the category's name written on it and how many points it is. We do this for every sprint, except for the IP Sprint.

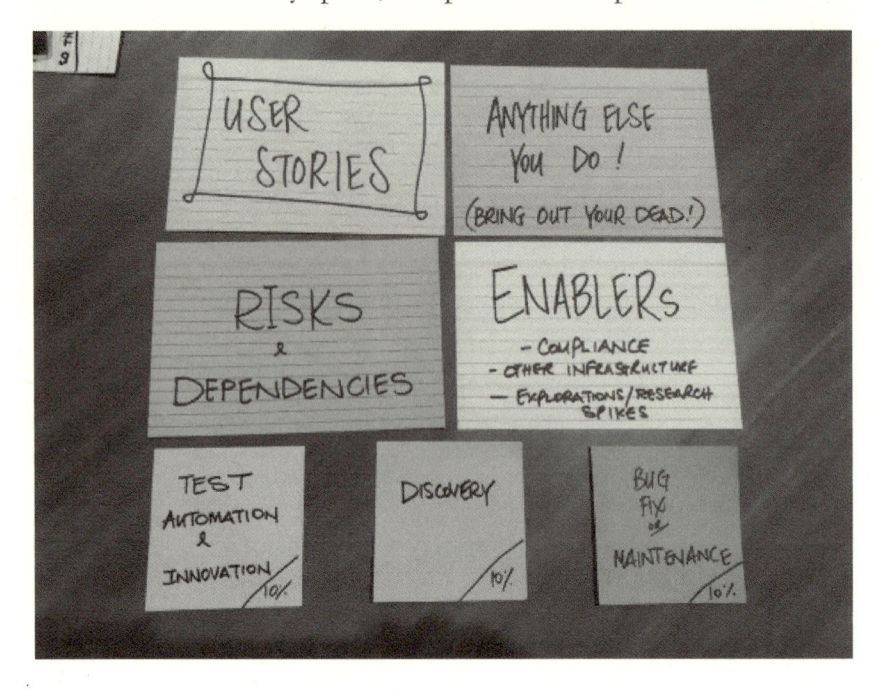

Figure 43 -Colour coding of index cards and post-it notes

Feature Kanban Board

Physical Kanban Boards are awesome information radiators. At the beginning of PI Planning you will have ten to twenty features that need to be planned and five to twelve teams making this happen. We find it useful to have a simple Kanban to help us manage this. It has four states: Backlog, In Planning, Draft Plan, and Final Plan. We write up three cards (one white, one yellow, and one blue) for each feature as per the example below. The cards are Blu-Tacked[134] or clipped together and placed in priority order from 1 to "n" in the Backlog column.

---

[134] For those not living in Australia or the UK: https://en.wikipedia.org/wiki/Blu_Tack (Accessed 10 April 2019).

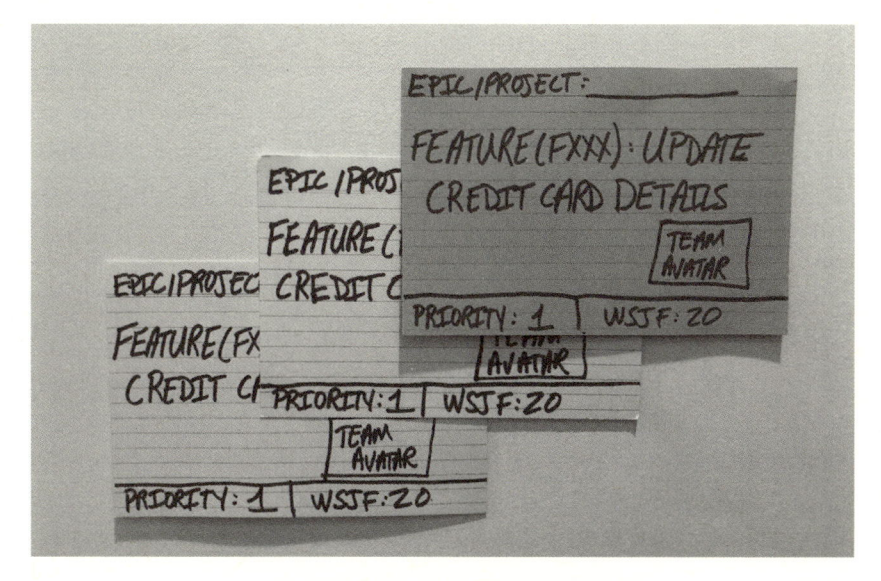

Figure 44 – Features cards for planning

Teams are encouraged to have a WIP limit[135] of one feature "in planning." When teams are ready to start work on a feature, they come to the Feature Kanban and select their highest priority feature as per the feature prioritisation. The white card is taken by the team and the yellow and blue cards are placed in the "in planning" column. Often teams use the white card to label a swim lane for that feature on the team plan.

Protip:
Ask the teams to "bring out the dead" and add the capacity placeholders for discovery, innovation, etc. <u>before</u> pulling their first feature into planning so that they understand their true capacity for feature work before loading the sprints.

---

[135] To learn more about WIP limits check out SAFe Principle #6: https://www.scaledagileframework.com/visualize-and-limit-wip-reduce-batch-sizes-and-manage-queue-lengths/ (Accessed 10 April 2019).

Once the team has finished planning a feature, they return to the Feature Kanban. The yellow card is moved to "draft plan" and the blue card is placed on the Program Board in the sprint in which the feature will achieve the Definition of Done. Our goal is to have all features in "draft plan" by Draft Plan Review at the end of day one. However, it is not uncommon for some features still to be in the "backlog" or "in planning." As part of wrapping up day one, it is good to understand why these features did not make it to "draft plan." Did the team run out of capacity or did they run out of time? On day two, the teams should progress their features from "draft plan" to "final plan" and make adjustments to the program board as necessary.

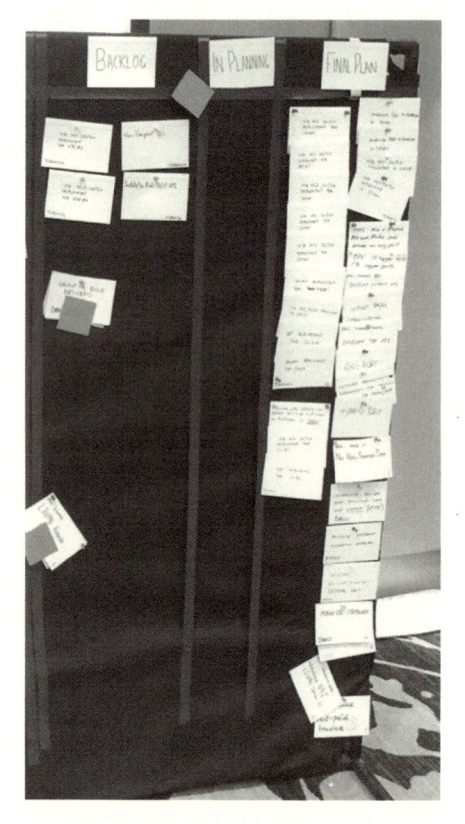

Figure 45 - Program Kanban for Features; Blue, White and Yellow cards at the end of day two

> **Protip**
> The ART needs to have a clear and consistent definition of what it means for a feature to be plotted as completed on the Program Board. For some ARTs this means released to production (our preferred definition), for other ARTs it means deployed to production (our next preference), and for some it means ready to deploy. Whatever you decide, remember to brief the ART as to your expectations.

Plotting Dependencies on the Program Board

As you know, the whole point of the Program Board is to visualise dependencies. Every feature should be owned by one team, even if multiple teams will be contributing to delivering it. Normally, this is the team that has the bulk of the work. This team is responsible for putting the feature on the Program Board and getting the dependencies agreed and added to the board. As simple as this sounds, it is not unusual for teams, eager to get their features on the board, to plot dependencies that have yet to be agreed. This challenge coupled with a desire to make the program board more usable post PI Planning resulted in one client designing a dependency card.

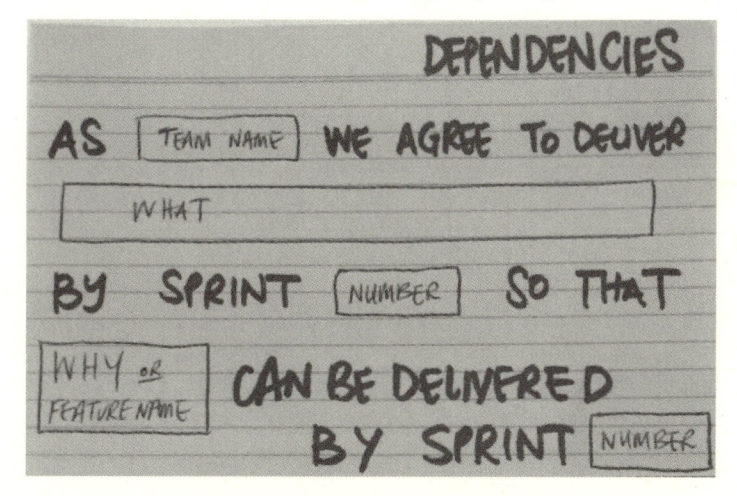

Figure 46 - Example dependency card

The ART of Avoiding a Train Wreck

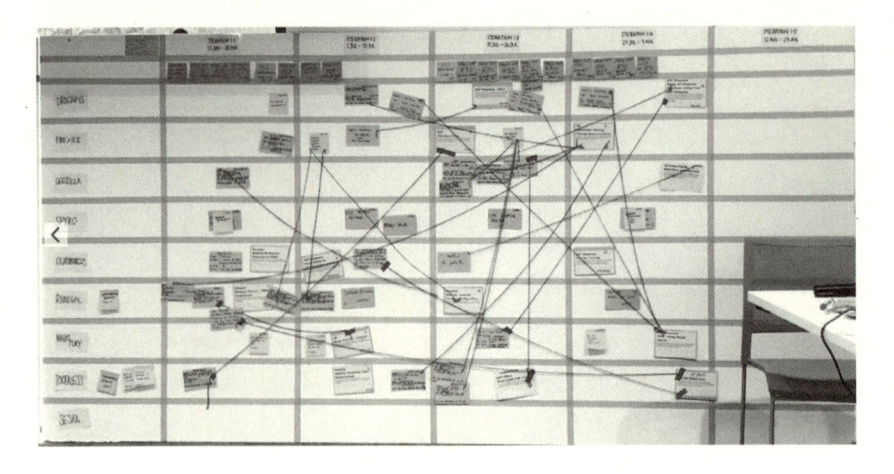

Figure 47 - PI Planning Program Board

For a card to be completed, the team needing the dependency needs to go and visit the team that would deliver the dependency, agree on the timing, and collect a team avatar to put on the card. When a completed dependency card contains both team avatars, connected by red yarn to a feature, or to another dependency, that signalled to the RTE that the dependency had been agreed by both parties.

> **Caution! Potential Train Wreck Ahead!**
> Be on the lookout for backward dependencies, where the blue feature card is plotted in an earlier sprint than the pink dependency card. Also watch out for same sprint dependencies as these rarely work out well for Scrum teams.[136]

---

[136] In Scrum teams commit to delivering by the end of the sprint. While we encourage teams to progressively deliver completed stories during the sprint, this practice often comes with experience. New, more inexperienced Scrum teams are likely to suffer from "student syndrome" and complete delivery of their stories on the last day of the sprint. This means any team with a mid-sprint dependency on a new Scrum team is likely to end up disappointed.

Live Risk ROAMing

The standard PI Planning agenda has the Program Risks session (also known as ROAMing the risks) on the afternoon of day two. By the time we get to these risks there is often a very long list. While the transparency created by sharing the full list of Program Risks with the room is awesome, the process of trying to read people's handwriting, understand the nature of the risk, and find a path forward is slow and painful. It occurred to me that what we were doing was creating a big batch.[137]

This inspired us to try a more flow-based approach. We build a ROAM board with the column heading Backlog, **R**esolved, **O**wned, **A**ccepted, and **M**itigated. We ask the Scrum Masters to bring their Program Risks to the Scrum of Scrums and we discuss them at the meet after and work to get them closed out. Often a risk will start with someone owning it and over the course of the two days the risk gets moved to resolved. In top heavy organisations this also gives the managers something valuable to do to support the teams during PI Planning.

To help with the clarity of communication we use a standard form for the risk cards that includes feature name, team name, description of risk, impact, ROAM outcome, and the name of the person who owns the ROAM action.

---

[137] To learn more about why big batches are bad check out SAFe Principle #6: https://www.scaledagileframework.com/visualize-and-limit-wip-reduce-batch-sizes-and-manage-queue-lengths/ (Accessed 23rd September 2019)

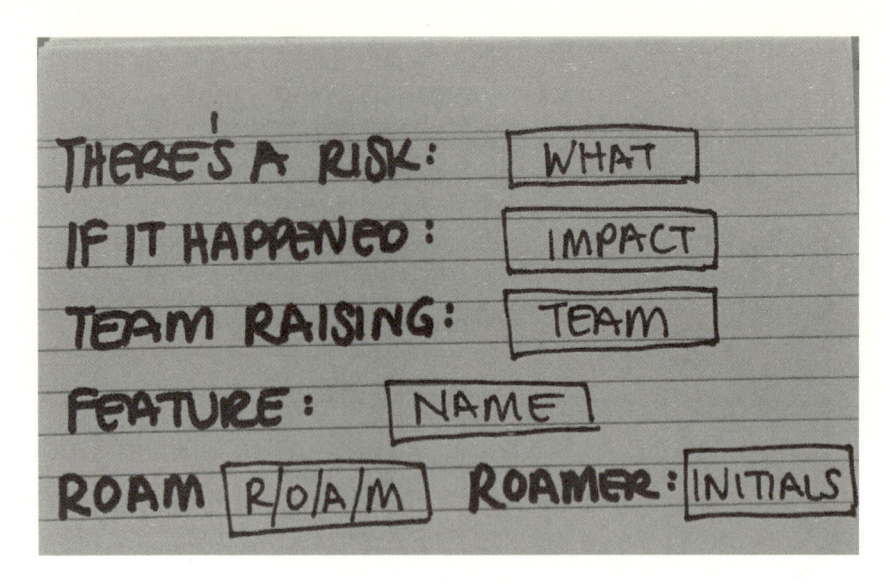

Figure 48 - PI Planning Risk Template

Scrum of Scrums (SoS)

The SAFe Program Increment Toolkit includes a Scrum of Scrums PI Planning Radiator, with a comprehensive set of questions to ask at each SoS. We recommend taking a less-is-more approach. Every question on the list adds more time to the amount of time the Scrum Masters are away from their teams.

We like to run the SoS from a whiteboard, which gives us maximum flexibility when deciding what questions to ask at each SoS. For example, a question that was answered in one SoS with a mixture of yeses and nos you might like to leave on the board and only ask the Scrum Masters that said no last time for an update.

We like to make the "Definition of Done" for each day visible on the board so everyone knows what the goal is. We also start each SoS with a reminder of the amount of time remaining in the time box. As we get closer to the end of day one, we ask the Scrum Masters to give us a "fist of five"[138] for their level of confidence that they will have a draft plan by the end of team breakout #1. We repeat this pattern as we get closer to final plan review on day two.

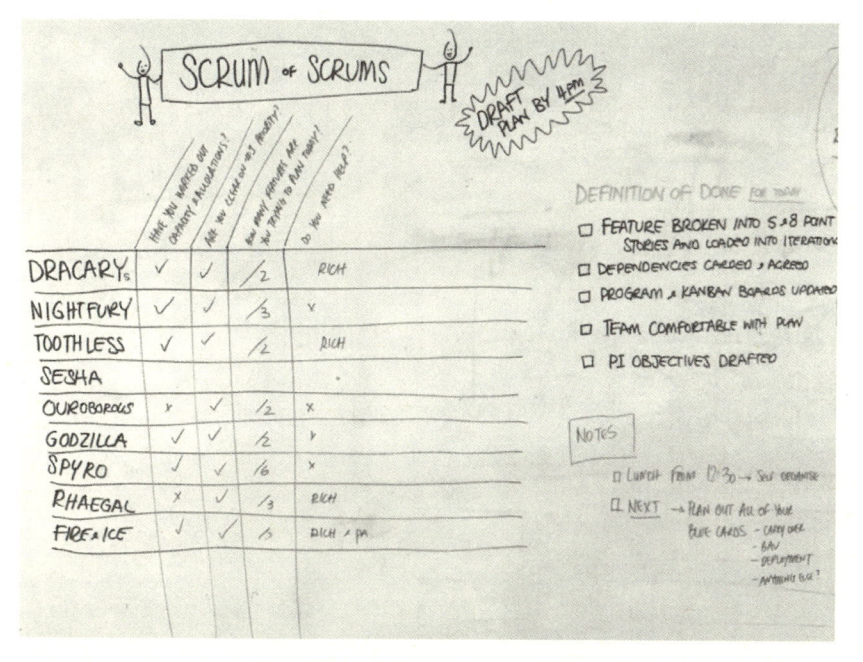

Figure 49 - Scrum of Scrums Template

> **Em's Anecdote**
> Before my first PI Planning, another coach told me not to bother with the Scrum of Scrums as it was a waste of time, so I didn't. That is an experiment I never ran again. There was no way to gauge what was going on in the room and which teams were struggling. It was simply horrible.

---

[138] The "Fist of Five," is a quick and simple technique to gauge confidence. The way is works is each participant holds up his or her hand and votes using their fingers where five fingers means a high level of confidence and one means "we are doomed."

> A few years later I was working with a client that was running their 14th PI Planning event! They had decided that the SoS was too disruptive to the planning process, so they decided to post the SoS questions on a sheet of flip chart paper and asked the Scrum Masters to keep it updated as they progressed. It was a nice idea, but it didn't get updated! My feedback to them was to reinstate the SoS.

> **Tips for Globally Distributed ARTs**
> You will need video conference facilities and a quiet space at each location to make this work. Take a photo of the Scrum of Scrum board at the main location and replicate it at the other location(s) so that the Scrum Masters can read the questions. In cultures where English is not everyone's native tongue some folks find it easier to read in English than to listen. Often the proxy RTE at the remote location asks the questions locally to improve the fidelity of the conversation. However, all teams still need to attend one session not two separate sessions (unless the time zones make this truly impossible).

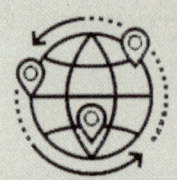

Team Breakouts

For some teams the Team Breakouts on the first day of their first PI Planning event may well be the first time ever, or perhaps in a very long time, that they have been asked to do their own detailed design, estimation, and planning. If your teams are used to having detailed designs handed to them, they may be of the view that the feature definition work done prior to PI Planning does not contain enough detail for them to plan. In the first PI Planning this is often true as the features have a tendency to be under prepared but even in future PIs the features won't arrive with the same level of detail as they may have come to expect from their previous, less agile world.

You will need to support the teams with this change in approach. In worlds where teams are used to being "beaten-up" for non-delivery you may also have a culture of fear, leading to teams being uncomfortable to commit to a plan. Leaders that have been guilty of this behaviour in the past will need to address this. It will take time to generate trust and, let's face it, all leaders will at one point or another revert to their old ways because they aren't perfect. Don't give up on them! If you see them slip just take a moment to have a kind conversation with them and help them see what they are doing.

> **Caution! Potential Train Wreck Ahead!**
> In the retrospective for the first and, maybe even the second PI Planning, the teams will probably tell you that there were not enough details in the features for them to be able to plan. They will suggest that for the next PI they should write all of the stories and complete detail design before PI Planning. Please don't go down this road.
>
> Instead, make sure you are protecting the discovery capacity allocation as the most common cause of "not enough detail" is actually a lack of familiarity with the feature. You should also look at the level of detail the teams are getting into during PI Planning. Eight to twelve weeks of 1- or 2-point stories is way too detailed! We like to see teams plan 5- and 8-point stories.[139] We want the teams to create a plan with an acceptable level of risk and surface dependencies to be able to deliver PI Objectives, not deliver individual stories. Remember PI Planning is about working out what business outcomes fit in the PI and flushing out the risks and dependencies. By draft plan review on day one, we want to know what fits, what does not, and who has spare capacity.

---

[139] Teams should use Backlog Refinement and Sprint Planning meetings to get to 1-, 2-, and 3-point stories post PI Planning.

> **Protip**
> Sometimes teams start spinning in place during PI Planning. There is a lot of debate, but nothing is getting written down. I will often try and break the deadlock by handing a whiteboard marker to whoever is currently on the soapbox and tell them to stop talking and start drawing! If they tell me they can't draw, I tell them just to try. The whiteboarding tends to bring focus and alignment, breaking the deadlock.

Writing Team PI Objectives

In the last fifteen minutes of the day one Team Breakouts, the teams will usually turn their attention to writing their draft PI Objectives. Teams often get tied up in knots over PI Objectives. According to scaledagileframework.com *"Team PI objectives are a summary of a team's plan for the PI."*[140] Hence, it makes sense to write them at the end of the day based on the plan that has emerged. PI Objectives are a communication tool that amongst other benefits help the Business Owners understand the plan. Consider being a Business Owner for an ART of five teams, where each team has planned circa forty stories for delivery over the PI. This is just too much detail for the Business Owners to be able to consume, and frankly far more detail than they need.

Writing good PI Objectives is something a lot of teams struggle with. I have seen everything from "The team will deliver feature 123" to "The team will deliver an intuitive, easy-to-use interface", with neither extreme being particularly SMART.[141] We like to coach teams to think about what they intend to demonstrate and when,

---

[140] To learn more about PI Objectives check out: https://www.scaledagileframework.com/pi-objectives/ (Accessed 8 August 2019).
[141] SMART stands for: Specific, Measurable, Achievable, Realistic and Time-bound. See: https://www.scaledagileframework.com/pi-objectives/ (Accessed 8 August 2019).

then simply describe it without any fluffy marketing language. For example, we had a client that wanted to enable customers to view invoices via their mobile app, so that PI Objective was something like "Customers can view last month's invoice via our Mobile App." We usually recommend team write between three and five objectives for a PI. Be conscious that every PI Objective will need to be demonstrated in the PI System demo at the end of the PI and if there are too many objectives it is going to be a VERY long and boring meeting.

Every PI Objective also needs to be demonstrable. Even enablers where you might be learning what to do next. You will need to coach the teams to think about this when writing PI Objectives. We like to ask team "How do you plan to demo that?" For example, if there was an objective relating to a security audit, we would expect the findings and the resolution of any identified issues to be demonstrated.

Another trap trains fall into is writing PI Objectives that the team can't possibly influence, such as a software team writing objectives about delivering an increase share price or an improvement in customer satisfaction. While these may well be the outcomes that Product Management and the Business Owners hope to achieve from the Features they have prioritised, I'm not sure these are outcomes that a software team can commit to. As a side note, Business Owners should be accountable for the features they prioritise delivering on the benefits they promised.

> **Protip**
> One approach we have used to help teams write S.M.A.R.T. PI Objectives and deliver incrementally is ask them what they plan to demo at the end of each sprint. Once they can see the holistic outcomes from each sprint then they can write a holistic PI Objective. While this objective might deliver in Sprint 3 (timely) it doesn't mean teams should write objectives for each sprint.

Uncommitted PI Objectives

Uncommitted objectives (previously known as stretch objectives) seem to cause no end of confusion. Probably because we are all conditioned to think of everything in a plan being committed. In SAFe uncommitted are part of the summary of the team's plan but the team won't be committing to these. Uncommitted objectives relate to work that the team has the capacity to deliver and intends to deliver; however, there is a level of uncertainty where the team is unable to commit to delivering. Often this is the feature that descends on a team out of nowhere, with no context and no warning on day one, or even worse, on day two of PI Planning.

> **Protip**
>
> We coach teams to have at least one uncommitted objective as any team that commits to delivering a 100% of their plan and delivers on it every time isn't stretching themselves. We want the teams to stretch and grow, in the same way your personal trainer encourages you to do just one more sit-up than you think you can. By calling this stretch an uncommitted objective we are able to manage the expectations of the ART's Business Owners. We want the teams to make commitments that they can keep. When the team delivers on their commitments it builds confidence in the train and the process.

Draft Plan Review

One of the debates Adrienne and I have often had is who should do the read-out. The two most common patterns seem to be that it is either the Scrum Master or the Product Owner. We settled on them to do it together or even better have the whole team present; after all, it is the team's plan.

Often team members comment that this portion of the day is boring. My suggestion is to encourage teams to work as a team to frame their read-out in terms of what they think folks on other teams need to know or would like to know about their plan. It is particularly valuable to have team members think about their peers with the same skill sets in other teams and what information will be valuable to them.

We always project the draft (and final) plan review questions in the room so each speaker has a clear guide to follow. In addition to the standard draft review agenda, we like teams to anchor their read-out by sharing the names of the features they have been working on. We also like to see teams talk to who they are dependent on and ask the dependent team to acknowledge they have the dependency in their plan. It's very cool to see teams supporting each other in draft plan review when the dependent team is nodding their heads to a dependency that is in their plan. It can also be somewhat amusing and enlightening when the nodding doesn't occur!

> **Protip**
> Before the draft plan review remind the Business Owners that they should be listening intently, asking questions and taking notes in preparation for the Management Review and Problem-Solving session. One organisation we know of has developed a one-page document for the Business Owners so that they know, step by step, what is expected of them in PI planning.[142]

---

[142] Thanks to Cécile Auret for the one-page document tip.

> **Darren's Anecdote**
> I started a new ART with feature teams which included front-end developers and back-end developers (both Java). However, the back-end developers were considered a more senior role. When it came to the work for the first PI for one particular team, the work was primarily front end. During the Draft Plan Review I noticed that the capacity had suddenly reduced for the PI and Load was far in excess. I asked, "What has happened here?" The answer was the work is all front end and we only do back-end work!! I reminded them of the concept of team work that we talked about in SAFe for Teams and also maybe in the next PI they may have more back-end work that they can cope with and would like the support from the front-end guys.

Post the Draft Plan Review we ask each team to take a sheet of flip chart paper and write a letter to the Management Team listing the items they need addressed in the Management Review and Problem-Solving Session. We find this brings focus to the discussion and ensures all of the team's key issues are addressed.

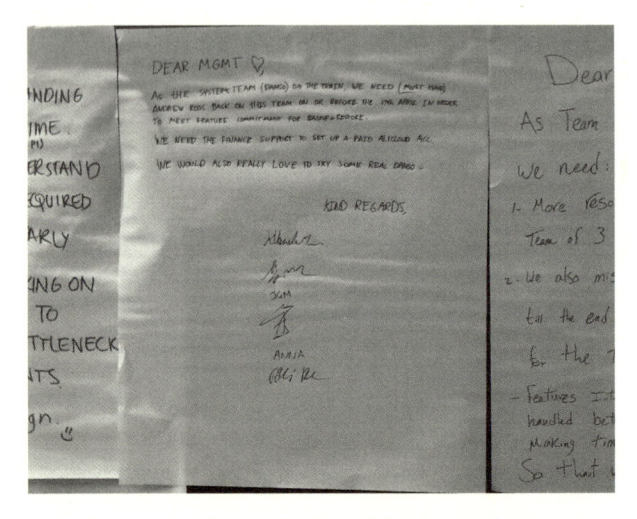

Figure 50 - Dear Management Letters

Management Review and Problem Solving

First a word of warning: while the SAFe guidance suggests this session will only be an hour, this has never been my experience, especially early in the life of a new ART. The most common pattern we see is a two- to three-hour session. So, make sure the Trifecta and the Business Owners plan to be with you until around 9:00 p.m. (for a co-located or single time zone ART). This also means you need to provide food, as a roomful of "hangry" managers rarely makes for a productive meeting!

> **Em's Anecdote**
> A Business Owner on an ART I launched insisted that they were awesome decision makers and they did not need to order dinner as they would be done by 6:30 p.m. I suggested to them that in my experience there is no way they will be done that quickly; of course they knew better! At 8:30 p.m. the session was still going, and no one had eaten. They didn't make that mistake **again**.

> **Caution! Potential Train Wreck Ahead**
> When it comes to providing meals for the Management Review and Problem-Solving Session there are two traps to be aware of. The first is alcohol. Many ART leaders feel like they have "earnt a drink" at the end of day one of PI Planning. While this may be true, as someone who has facilitated dozens of these events, let me tell you, alcohol does not improve the speed or quality of decision making at these events! The second trap is letting the venue provide you a formal sit-down three-course dinner. This will also do nothing to improve the speed or quality of decision making!

SAFe guidance suggests the RTE facilitates this session. While we can see the logic in this, as the RTE is the facilitator of the train ceremonies, we also think it is impossible to be a good impartial facilitator and a participant at the same time. In our view a good RTE is going to want to advocate for their teams in this session. This can be a good place to use an external facilitator or to "borrow" an RTE or SPC from another train. We like the facilitator of this session to be someone who is comfortable challenging executives and sometimes an internal staff member will struggle with this.

> **Protip**
> While some ARTs like to ask Scrum Masters and Product Owners to stay back for the Management Review and Problem-Solving session, we prefer to let them go home and get some rest. They have probably been on their feet all day and they will need to do it all over again tomorrow. We recommend that the RTE and Product Managers have a way to contact the Scrum Masters and Product Owners, if necessary. Often this is via a group chat on a messaging app.

> **Em's Anecdote**
> One RTE I worked with decided he could handle the Management Review and Problem-Solving session without support from the Business Owners. One of our big learnings during day one of planning was that approximately half the people on the ART were still working on an in-flight initiative. The ART needed a priority call made. Should they keep working on the in-flight initiative or should they pivot and focus on the Program Backlog for the ART?
>
> As there were no senior leaders present at the event, I asked the RTE if he could call someone to get a decision. He assured me that this was not necessary as he knew that the priority was the ART's Program Backlog; however, he would have this decision ratified at the steering committee next week. By this point my

> blood was boiling, as a decision at the Steering Committee next week was not going to help the teams complete their plans tomorrow. I asked again if there was someone he could call but he was adamant he was making the right decision and there was nothing to be concerned about.
>
> On day two the train continued to plan in line with the RTE's guide that the ART's backlog should take priority over the in-flight program of work and committed to PI Objectives that correlated to this directive. The Steering Committee meeting the following week was cancelled, which meant that the prioritisation decision was not tabled for another two weeks. Unfortunately, when it did get tabled the RTE had made the wrong call. It was the in-flight program of work that was the priority, resulting in the PI Plan being abandoned and a sprint of lost work. The moral of the story—if the key decision makers can't attend the Management Review and Problem-Solving meeting, they at least need to be available to take a call!

We always start the session by creating four flip charts with the following headings:

- Things I observed today that made me proud of the ART
- Things I am concerned about and we MUST discuss this evening
- Things I am concerned about and we SHOULD discuss this evening
- Things I am concerned about and we COULD discuss this evening

We then give each participant a Sharpie and a pad of Post-it Notes and ask them to review their notes, read the management letters, study the team boards, the Program Board, the Feature Kanban, and the Risk Board, and create a Post-it for each item they want to discuss. We usually allow a ten-to-fifteen-minute time box for this activity.

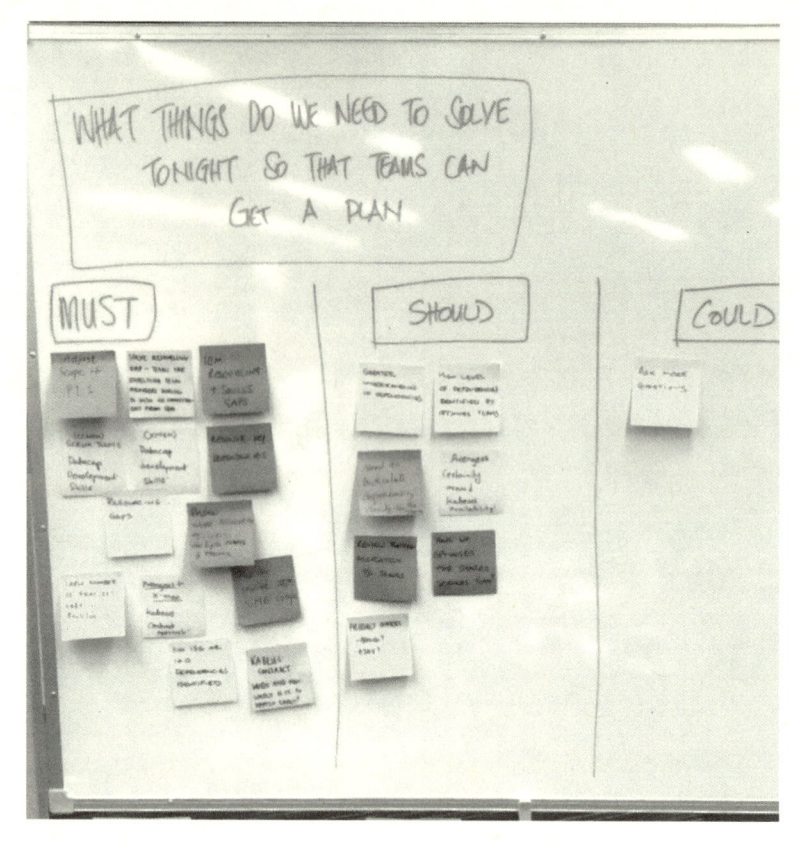

Figure 51 - Management Problem Solving - What must, should and could be discussed

The rest of the session is a facilitated review of the flip charts starting with "what made me proud" then moving on to the MUST items. As a rule, the items on the MUST list have to be discussed before we leave for the night. After covering the MUST discuss items we move our attention to the Feature Kanban, the risk board, and the management letters, as these must all be addressed before we can leave. The SHOULD and COULD items tend to only get covered if we have time before 9:00 p.m. We find by 9:00 p.m. everyone is pretty much brain dead and it is time to call it a night.

The most common discussion topic for any new train is what to do about the imbalance between demand and supply as there is always too much demand and not enough supply. When the Business

Owners see the reality of what is and is not likely to be included in the PI, there is often some last-minute horse trading. This can sometimes result in a feature that a team spend all day planning being deprioritised for something that no one has started to plan but needs to be delivered. It is my belief that you can only blow up a team's day one plan so many times before they lose confidence in the system.

Sadly, these situations are often avoidable. I am always completely baffled when a Business Owner chooses the Management Review and Problem-Solving meeting to share that they think priority 27 is more important than priority 6. (Yes, this really did happen to me!) While occasionally something we learn in PI Planning changes the priorities, most of the time these situations are foreseeable.

> **Protip**
> Review the items on the Feature Kanban that are in the "backlog" and "in planning." Can or should any of these Features be parked for this PI? Sometimes Product Management and Business Owners can be reluctant to remove anything from the backlog, even if it is clear as day it is never going to get done. "I would prefer to leave it there just in case the teams find some capacity," they say while we stare at the overflowing team plans.
>
> This is the perfect coaching moment: try to help the Business Owners see that the teams, being eager to please, have already taken on too much. The right leadership action at this point is to save the teams from themselves and relieve the delivery pressure by descoping the Features that we already know won't fit.

Make sure a clear action or decision is captured for each item and you know who is going to share the outcome in the Planning Adjustments session on day two. We like to capture the actions and decisions on flip charts so that the discussion is transparent to the teams. Don't forget to nominate someone to share the "what made me proud" Post-its as well!

The ART of Avoiding a Train Wreck

Figure 52 - What the Leaders witnessed that made them "proud of the train"

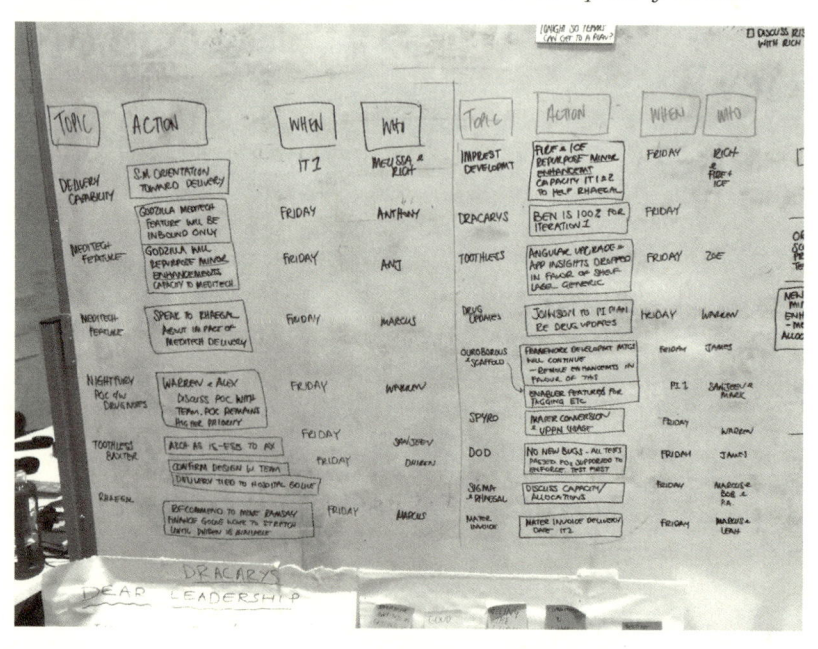

Figure 53 - Planning adjustments decision board

> **Caution! Potential Train Wreck Ahead**
> One more word of warning. While SAFe suggests moving of people is a potential outcome of this session, we recommend avoiding this if at all possible. There has been a rare occasion on which there was a clear error in the team or team formation that would necessitate this. However, the suggestion to move people between teams often seems to come up as a classic way to solve this problem. In which case I remind the group that in lean we move the work to the people not the people to the work.

> **Tips for Globally Distributed ARTs**
> You will need the RTE proxy at each location to attend this session to represent the teams at that location. The proxies will need to be diligent in making sure the information being radiated at their location is fed into the conversation. Often, we ask the remote locations to send us their "Post-it Note" observations via a messaging app so we can replicate them and create a single backlog for discussion. The facilitator will need to be very deliberate in their facilitation approach so that voices from all locations are heard. The proxy RTE(s) will need to make sure they are clear about the planning adjustments required so that they can support their local teams on day two. You will of course need video conferencing in place for this session too.

Planning Adjustments

It is advisable for the folks who attended the Management Review and Problem-Solving Session to arrive at least half an hour before the kick-off of day two. They can use this time to remind themselves of the discussions, decisions, and actions taken the night before and prepare to share with the ART. Product Owners and Scrum Masters often choose to come in early too, to get an early insight as to the changes that could impact their team.

It is important that the Business Owners take responsibility for the decisions made during the Management Review and Problem-Solving Session and don't just leave the RTE to deliver the news. For instance, if the Business Owners made a mistake with prioritisation, which means a team will need to throw away a plan or significantly rework it, the right leadership behaviour is for the Business Owners to admit their mistake. Remember one of SAFe's core values is transparency[143] and transparency is how we build trust. If we want our teams to be transparent with us about their challenges and mistakes, we need to lead by example.

Once the actions and decisions have been shared, have them displayed near the Scrum of Scrums board so that progress can be updated at the Scrum of Scrums over the course of the day.

Team Breakout #2

Once we start Breakout #2 the train is on a countdown to the confidence vote. The SoS are key to helping bring focus and ensuring the teams will be ready for Final Plan review. This isn't the time for the Business Owners or the Trifecta to decide to take other meetings. A singular focus to get the best possible outcomes from the event is all that matters now.

Something to watch for is teams overloading their plans. I often find teams that are overly confident and eager to please will go "just one or two points over" each sprint in order to squeeze in some deliverable business desperately wants. While this is extremely admirable, we prefer to set teams up for success and insist they work with their Product Owners to pull some scope out of the plan.

Another thing teams will do in a well-intended effort to deliver more is override the capacity allocations. Stealing time from discovery, maintenance, or innovation to work on business features. This

---

[143] To learn more about SAFe's Core Values check out: https://www.scaledagileframework.com/safe-core-values/ (Accessed 10 September 2019)

is not a team level decision and generally we advise the Business Owners against making this compromise as there will be flow-on consequences to future PIs.

> **Protip**
> Sometimes the best thing a team can do is to help another team finish something rather than start something new. This is something to watch for during the Scrum of Scrums. As teams complete planning, some might have capacity to pull in another features. Before they do that, encourage them to offer to support the other teams on the train.

Assigning Business Value to PI Objectives

Assigning Business Value to PI Objectives[144] may well be the most often skipped component of PI Planning. I know I didn't do it for the longest time as I just could not get my head around the point of the whole exercise. I think at least in part, I found it hard to see how this was different to the Business Value conversation that is part of WSJF prioritisation. If the number of times we get asked about the point of this is any indication, we are thinking that a lot of folks struggle with this, so let's take a moment to explore this topic through the lens of the questions that we are most frequently asked.

What is the point of Assigning Business Value to PI Objectives?

For us, the value of this activity is the alignment conversation. What could be better than the people who do the work talking to the people that are sponsoring the work about the work? In our experience, both groups gain insights and clarity from this interaction. The other

---

[144] To learn more about Assigning Business Value to PI Objectives check out: https://www.scaledagileframework.com/pi-objectives/ (Accessed 10 September 2019)

reason to take the time to assign business value at PI Planning is that it provides a useful mechanism to understand how well expectations were met at the end of the PI. However, the process of assigning business value is not without its challenges.

Isn't this Business Value thing rather subjective?

While this may well be true, I'm not sure how much it matters if the approach is consistent and the same group of people assign all the values. Perhaps Jennifer Fawcett and Drew Jemillo put it best in their presentation at the SAFE Summit in 2018: *"Ultimately, it turns out that business value is just that; it is what the business values RIGHT NOW."*[145]

Didn't we already do this as part of WSJF?

Well, you did, and you didn't. WSJF tells us what Features we should bring into PI Planning. PI Objectives come from the teams and represent a summary of the Team's PI Plan. While some PI Objectives align to Features, many do not, so we are unlikely to have a 1:1 mapping here. For example:

- Features may be split across teams
- Objectives might relate to independent stories (not originating from Features)
- The nature of the feature may evolve during PI Planning[146]

Isn't the morning of day two a little late in the piece to be having an alignment conversation?

Perhaps, but having the conversation before the team has a plan to summarise seems premature too. At least by doing this on the morning of day two, we can uncover any misalignment while there is still time to adjust the plan.

---

[145] See: https://2018.safesummit.com/?ddownload=6348 (Accessed 20 August 2019).
[146] Adapted from "Measuring Business Value" by Jennifer Fawcett and Drew Jemillo https://2018.safesummit.com/?ddownload=6348 (Accessed 20 August 2019).

How do I know what is the most valuable objective, if I haven't read all the objectives?

You don't! So, if practical, we ask the Business Owners to visit all of the teams and read their objectives before they assign any values. This gives them a chance to align on where they see the 10s in the room.

Do I give a 10 to every team?

Well, you can if you like and that is a pattern that some folks choose as they don't like any team to think that their contribution isn't valuable. We prefer only giving 10s for the most valuable things on the ART, so that if/when there is a delivery challenge with a high ranked objective the entire train knows where it needs to focus its efforts if we are to ensure the best business outcome.

> **Em's Anecdote**
> At one ART's first PI Planning event we had the head of the department assigning business value. There were four aspects to his approach I really liked. First, when he visited the teams, he took the time to have a discussion and help the teams see the business value of what they planned. Secondly, he provided guidance on how they could make the objective more valuable. Thirdly, each time a team had an objective about team building he rated it a 10. Lastly, for the teams that did not have a team building objective he asked them to write one!

Final Plan Review

The SAFe playbook for PI Planning says:

> *"During this session, all teams present their plans to the group. At the end of each team's time slot, the team states their risks and impediments, but there is no attempt to resolve them in this short time box. If the plan is acceptable to the customers, the team brings their program PI objective sheet*

> *and program risk sheet to the front of the room so that all can see the aggregate objectives unfold in real time."*[147]

I have always struggled with the concept of the business "accepting the plan" prior to the risks being addressed, the team having an opportunity to express their confidence in the plan and accepting the plan in a piecemeal way. It always felt backwards to me. At a tactical level empowered Product Owners were part of building the plan and the Business Owners have already agreed to the objectives, so the question seems redundant at this point.

We prefer to wait until after the Program Risks have been ROAMed and after all the teams and the train have completed the confidence votes, then ask the Business Owners if they accept the plan. If they say yes, I will ask them to shake hands, and provide a thumbs up or a fist of five in front of the Program Board while we take a photo. ARTs love this sign of commitment and support from their leaders. Many ARTs I work with proceed to print the photo on an A3 sheet of paper and hang it above their Program Kanban as a reminder that everyone is in this PI together.

Figure 54 - Business Owners accepting the plan

---

[147] See: https://www.scaledagileframework.com/pi-planning/ (Accessed 11 April 2019).

Program Risks

If you followed our advice and constantly addressed risks as they have been raised over the past two days this should be relatively painless. If any additional risks emerged as part of the final plan review, you should ROAM them now. I then have the RTE do a lightning-fast walk through of all the Risks raised and the ROAM outcome, for the purposes of transparency and alignment. Once the full list has been shared, I ask everyone with their name on a Risk that is being Owned or Accepted to come to the front of the room and stand with the Risk Board while we take a photo of them owning and accepting the risks for the ART.

Figure 55 - Risk Kanban board for ROAM

> **Protip**
> Don't let teams raise risks about the ability of other teams on the ART to deliver on their commitments. This is not how you build a one-team culture. The inter-team dependencies should be clearly displayed on the Program Board and talked about in the Team PI Objectives which should be sufficient.

Confidence Vote

With any luck this goes well. Often Scrum Masters will intermittently gauge their team's temperature multiple times throughout the two days, just to get an idea of where we are before the big vote. You are asking the teams their level of confidence in delivering on the PI Objectives they wrote to summarise the plans they created; objectives that the team does not have confidence in should be uncommitted and the leadership have owned or accepted the open risks. Even though the official SAFe guidance states that "if the average is three fingers or above, then management should accept the commitment,"[148] we prefer to see the entire train voting are three or above.

If anyone votes a one or a two, we pause and ask that person to share their concerns. These can range from someone just wanting to be heard and acknowledged, to serious misses that require the train to put another thirty minutes on the clock to do some re-planning. Sometimes the person (or team) voting a one or two struggles to articulate what is bothering them. Try asking them what you can do to improve their confidence, creating a bias to action. If they are still lost for words, that is okay too. Just make sure you look out for that team as you go into PI Execution. In my experience their gut instinct is probably right even if they can't articulate the problem.

> **Protip**
> Try positioning a vote of three as "I can live with it <u>and</u> support it." We often describe this as committing not to "bitch and moan" about the plan for the entire PI.

---

[148] See: https://www.scaledagileframework.com/pi-planning/ (Accessed 11th April 2019).

Adrienne's Anecdote

The other facilitation technique I use is to share with the train before the vote that voting a one or two is entirely okay. No one is going to beat them up. If anyone does vote this way, we are going to stop and address the issue before the train gets to move to the event retrospective. Which means we are going to ask that person to be able to share what the issue is that they see.

When someone does vote a one or two, the first thing I do is thank them for being brave enough to do that in front of their peers and maybe some high-powered executives. I'll even have the train give them a round of applause! Then I'll ask them to share what's on their mind with the rest of the train. I have had an entire team vote a two once. It's important to solve the issue now. The train is in its best position to solve a problem now as the context of the plan is fresh in everyone's mind and we are still at full strength.

Em's Anecdote

I remember working with an RTE at a particularly rough PI Planning where one of her teams was really struggling and there was a difference of opinion between the RTE and the team on the way forward. When it came time for the confidence vote the team voted a two. The RTE brushed over it and did not give the team an opportunity to explain their vote. After the confidence vote they approached the RTE to express their disappointment that she had not followed the process and given them a chance to comment. This was not only damaging to the team morale, but it put a dampener on the day for the entire train.

Carl's Anecdote

During a confidence vote at the end of a first PI Planning for a new ART everyone was still a bit careful/shy and voted three or higher. However, in the back of the room the most recent addition to the ART, a junior tester, was voting a one despite everyone else's high confidence. When asking him about it he explained to everyone that it was clear to him that the existing plan did not have enough room to handle potential performance problems that most likely would be caused by a large inflow of new users to one of the core applications that the ART was developing mid-PI unless the plan was adjusted. After some quick adjustments were made, planned work was removed to create buffers for managing the potential problems. Everyone re-voted and now, he gave us the "go" with a higher vote.

During the execution of the PI it was evident that his input was critical and saved the PI/ART ... and in the next PI Planning confidence vote everyone was much more brave/honest and voted both one and two to share concerns and solve problems together.

Protip

Beyond asking everyone who votes one or two why and addressing/solving these concerns, be sure to ask the people who voted four and five why they have such high confidence in the joint plan for the PI. These positive voices can be very helpful for the ART culture as they show that we can be confident and sometimes even proud in our joint work as a team of teams.[149]

---

[149] Thanks to Carl Starendal for this Protip.

Retrospective

I like to use the end of PI Planning retrospective as an opportunity to seed new retrospective data gathering techniques in the train. There is nothing more boring than asking every two weeks "What went well?", "What didn't go well?" and "What should we improve?"

My favourite technique that I will almost always use for a first PI Planning is called the 4Ls.

Have each team take a big easel-size Post-it Note and divide it into four quadrants. Then write the following headings in each quadrant: Liked, Learnt, Lacked, Longed For. Have everyone on a team use a Sharpie and some Post-its, one suggestion per Post-it. The RTE can then facilitate a two-minute time box per quadrant for people to populate the quadrants with "What they liked, what they learnt, what was lacking, and what they longed for" over the two days of PI Planning. Once all of the feedback is captured, you can have all teams bring their sheets to the front of the room and the RTE can invite people to wander through to have a look at the feedback.

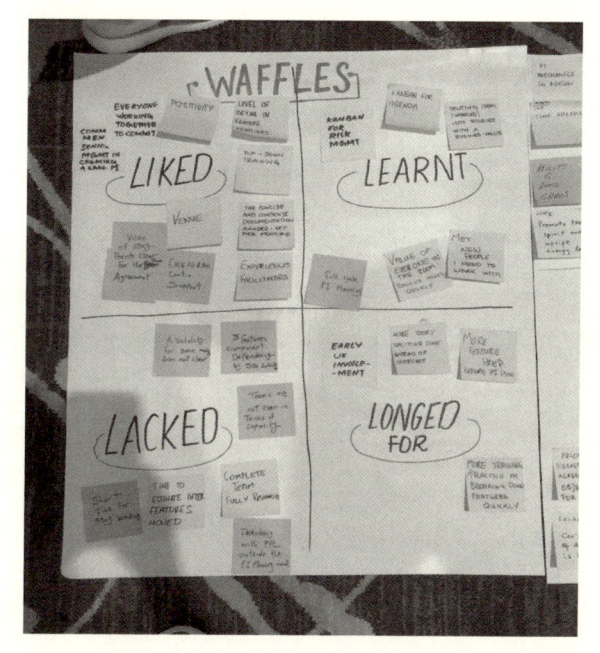

Figure 56 - PI Planning Retrospective Feedback

Post the PI Planning event the Trifecta and the Scrum Masters should review the feedback and determine what they plan to do differently next PI Planning. The RTE can then update the train with these commitments at Unity Hour.

Closing PI Planning

Everyone is completely exhausted by this point. Have the most senior person, or persons, in the room thank the train for their hard work and transparency. This won't be hard. ARTs do an amazing job of pulling together to get to a great outcome.

Now might be a great time to have a celebration as a team of teams. Just let people know beforehand so that arrangements can be made for pets, kids, partners, etc.

What Happens After PI Planning?

With two days of intense planning behind you, it is now time for the ART to deliver on its commitments!

> **Protip**
> One client we worked with (Adrienne's first Australian Train!) had a great communications person. The RTE was really on top of keeping the train connected through a newsletter. This particular train was in Australia and India. After each PI Planning, the new committed PI Objectives were shared along with some photos from the event. There was also a newsletter after each System Demo summarising what had been happening across the train.

All Aboard!

> **Sprint 1 Newsletter**
>
> *Welcome to the first edition of the* **<Train Name> Sprint Newsletter.** *This newsletter will be released at the end of each sprint to share important updates, highlight key deliverables, and acknowledge achievements within the Train. We hope you enjoy the first edition—so sit back, relax, and if you have anything you would like to add to future Newsletters, please contact <RTE Name>.*

If you are using the IP Sprint patterns we discussed earlier, you will be able to leverage the last Monday and Tuesday of the IP Sprint to do some backlog refinement for Sprint 1 of the PI. When we come out of PI Planning, we have some quite chunky stories in our plan. They are probably more 5- and 8-point stories, with the occasional 1-, 2-, or 3-point story. They won't have acceptance criteria and probably aren't written in the usual "as a ___, I want ___, so that___" language. These chunkier stories are fine for PI Planning because we are driving out risk and dependencies to get to a list of committed PI Objectives. But teams can't execute a sprint with these. They don't meet the definition of ready, so some refinement is required.

Chapter Summary

Launching an Agile Release Train is a big endeavour for an organisation. In this chapter we discussed:

- Using our Quick-Start method to generate a focused launch including the logistics to make the event go well
- Conducting role-based training for the Scrum Masters and the broader Agile Release Train.
- Starting to build a team and train culture through the Team Day pattern including
  - Creating and sharing Personal Maps
  - Naming the Train and creating a train theme
  - Building Team Product Boxes
- The detailed success patterns we use for every part of the Program Increment Planning two-day event
- Creating communication patterns for sharing information about PI Planning, ART execution, lesson learned, etc.

PART 6
STAYING ON THE TRACKS

Staying on the tracks (also known as PI Execution) is the Continuous Delivery Pipeline in action. The ART should be both preparing for its next PI Planning and executing on the commitments it made in the last PI Planning. This means operationalising the timetable you set prior to PI Planning.

The Program Kanban

When it comes to keeping your ART on the tracks, an effective Program Kanban System that enables demand management using visualisation and flow is the key. Your ART's Kanban will also support your organisation in operationalising the process of "preparing the cargo."

Normally when designing a Kanban it is best to "start where you are." For many organisations, just the act of visualising demand is a huge step forward. Writing the name of each idea/initiative/epic/feature on an index card and getting it up on a wall is a good first step and can be done at any time. Then once you have your first cut of your Kanban process you can place these cards on the Kanban board and use this activity to test the process.

Designing an effective Kanban System for your ART requires both knowledge of SAFe and an understanding of the way your world works today. When you launched your first ART you changed the way some of your world works but my guess is you have created an agile bubble, and the rest of the organisation is continuing just the way it always has. This means designing the Program Kanban for your ART will require you to walk a fine line between reflecting the way your world works today and the new way of working that you have introduced.

The Scaled Agile Framework provides "A typical program Kanban" as an exemplar to help get you started.[1] It has eight states: (1) Funnel, (2)

---

[1] To learn more about the SAFe Program Kanban check out: https://www.scaledagileframework.com/program-and-solution-kanbans/ (Accessed 2 September 2019).

Staying on the Tracks

Analysing, (3) Backlog and (4) Implementing, (5) Validate on Staging, (6) Deploying to Production, (7) Releasing and (8) Done. It also provides some guidance on what activities are likely to occur in each state. There is also an example of "A typical Program Epic Kanban" with three states: (1) Funnel (2) Reviewing (3) Analysing.

> **Protip**
> Before we dive into the details a quick word of advice on the use of the term Analysing. In our experience, many folks associate analysing with the need to produce large and detailed documents. Of course, this is not our intent. However, no matter how much you coach this point the use of the term analysing always seems to end up driving document-writing behaviour. We prefer to use the term Discovery instead as the intent of the activity is to learn enough information to decide if and how to proceed. On this basis, for the purpose of this book we will use the term Discovery instead of Analysing in our discussion of the Program Kanbans.

Funnel	Reviewing	Discovery	Backlog	Implementing	Done

Figure 57 - An Exemplar Program Epic Kanban. When the features have been identified for the epic they get added to the Program Feature Kanban below

Funnel	Analysing	Backlog	Implementing	Validate on Staging	Deploying to Production	Releasing	Done

Figure 58 - An Exemplar Feature Program Kanban

Before you run off and implement your new Kanbans "out of the box," can I suggest you pause and consider how it applies in your context. If you just blindly create a beautiful wall, exactly as depicted in SAFe, it is likely you will find it very difficult to move anything

The ART of Avoiding a Train Wreck

through the system as it does not reflect the way your organisation works. Hence my earlier advice to "start where you are."

When designing your Program Kanban the trick is to take the typical Program Kanban from SAFe and overlay your own context. For example, how does an idea get from "concept to cash" in your organisation? Often no one person in the organisation can answer this question so a small workshop is often the best approach to nutting this out. Personally, I like to take a pile of index cards, a Sharpie, and some Blu-Tack and build the flow on the wall as the group debates the process. This exercise will highlight the areas in which your process needs to change to implement SAFe as well as identifying where you might need to adapt SAFe to your context. We take a pragmatic approach in applying Lean here. It's best to start with where you are, not where you wish to be.

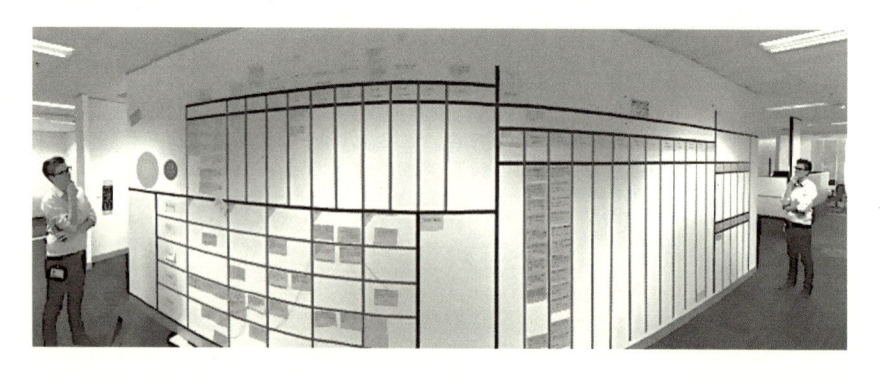

Figure 59 - A Program Epic Kanban (top left) flowing into a feature Kanban (middle right). The Feature Kanban has both feature cards (blue) and dependency cards (pink). This wall also houses the Program Board from PI Planning (bottom left, with string), bug fixes (far right middle), and the open ROAM cards from PI Planning (far bottom right)

When defining Program Kanbans, it is important to clearly define where the process starts and ends. While it can be tempting to boil the ocean, what we really need initially is to understand where the ART begins and ends. As the ART's processes improve you may choose to begin to tackle the processes upstream or downstream of the ART.

Staying on the Tracks

So, how does this work in practice? Let's look at how you might tackle this by stepping through the states of the exemplar Kanbans and considering how we might need to refine or adjust to better fit your organisational context. Specifically, you need to consider if there are additional states needed, what WIP limits make sense, and what the exit criteria is for each state.

> **Protip**
> Always use physical Kanbans. A good physical Kanban will generate conversation. People will gravitate to it when they are discussing the work. It radiates information all the time unlike electronic tools (also known as information refrigerators) and it is fun! It enables a completely different conversation and you observe things on a physical wall that you don't just in an electronic tool. It's really obvious you have a WIP problem or a flow problem on a physical wall. In a tool you scroll to see more. But that is a typical user behaviour that doesn't generate alarm bells as it probably should in a flow-based system.

Figure 60 - Visualising excessive WIP using a physical wall

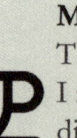

Maarit's Anecdote
The physical Kanban wall creates collaboration! I recently worked with a Product Manager who did not want to use a physical wall. His meetings were boring ones! We scrolled through the features backlog in a tool. At the end of the meeting he was complaining about the lack of participation from the Product Owners. I could see he was dedicated and wanted to work in an agile manner, but he just could not see how his belief that "sticky notes on the wall are not professional way to work" hindered the Product Team working as a team and being fully engaged. If you want people to engage, you need a physical wall and some facilitation skills. If you are like this Product Manager, go and ask RTE or some of your SPCs to help you with the facilitation!

Tips for Distributed ARTs
In most cases the physical program Kanban is at the same site as the RTE and I have rarely seen it replicated at other sites. Some organisations choose to replicate the Kanban in their electronic tool; however, they still hold their ART Sync in front of the physical wall.

Defining the States of the Program Epic Kanban

We will start with the epic program Kanban as most ARTs start in a world with a backlog of projects, initiatives, or ideas that are going to take longer than a PI to implement and are therefore classed as epics. If this is not your world then you can skip ahead to the Program Feature Kanban.

For the states of the Program Epic Kanban we start with Funnel, Review, and Discovery as the overarching states an epic will pass through before it reaches the Backlog state where it will wait for the ART to pull it in.

Epic Funnel

While SAFe advocates that all ideas are welcome, this may or may not hold true in the context of your organisation, particularly if this is your first instance of SAFe. Often an organisation's first ART is a "carved out" piece of the organisation and therefore there may well be existing protocols regarding what ideas are welcome and who is empowered to raise these ideas. This might not be ideal, but it may well be reality. So, for now I would just roll with it.

A common pattern we have found useful for the funnel is to split it into three states:

- Inbox: Where new ideas or requests enter the system

- Validate Entry: Where the Epic Owner determines if the idea or request meets the "definition of ready" for the ART Trifecta to review it

- Ready for Review: Where the epic waits for there to be capacity in the Review state.

The "definition of ready" for review could be something as simple as a phrase on an index card and the name of the person who came up with the idea. Some ARTs like to receive ideas in the form of a draft Epic Hypothesis Statement. I like this as it makes the requestor think a little bit about the outcome of the epic. If your ART doesn't have its own funding source, you might want to know if the epic is funded. Alignment to strategic themes[2] is one exit criteria I think belongs in every funnel and if the answer to this is no then the trash bin might be the best place for this idea.

---

[2] To learn more about Strategic Themes in SAFe check out: https://www.scaledagileframework.com/strategic-themes/ (Accessed 24 August 2019).

> **Caution! Potential Train Wreck Ahead!**
> An ART adrift in a world where there are no strategic themes is likely to grind to a halt under the weight of the organisation's expectations. One train I worked with moved business units in its first year but could not get any clarity on how this impacted the strategy they were enabling. This created a situation whereby they were receiving demand from both the old and new business unit and had no way to filter the demand against the Strategic Themes, resulting in the ART being six times oversubscribed. This meant if they did not accept a single new request it would take them eighteen months to clear the existing backlog.

Exemplar Epic Funnel		
Inbox	**Validate Entry**	**Ready for Review**
Suggested WIP limit = none	Suggested WIP limit = 1 per Epic Owner	Suggested WIP limit = none
Potential Exit Criteria: • Date of entry is recorded • Epic Owner assigned • The Epic Owner has capacity to validate the entry	Potential Exit Criteria: • Epic meets the definition of ready for Review • Product Management is willing to invest in an Epic Writing Workshop and solutioning for this idea	Potential Exit Criteria: • There is capacity in review • If there are multiple items queued here the Business Owners and/or Product Managers should prioritise

Figure 61 - Example of the Epic Funnel with suggested WIP limits and potential exit criteria.

Epic Review

The goal of the review state is to get clarity on the epic hypothesis, have a first pass at Weighted Shortest Job First (WSJF), and determine if you want to invest in discovering this epic. We prioritise the demand using WSJF in the same way we did when we were preparing to launch the ART. However, this time we don't want a big batch. Try to ascertain how often new projects, initiatives, or big ideas descend on your train and put in place a cadence-based session with the Business Owners that enables a flow-based approach to prioritisation.

With the above context in mind some of the states we might use as part of the review state include:

- Prepare for Epic Writing Workshop: Where Epic Owners coordinate the Business Owners, Product Management, and System Architect to attend a two- to four-hour Epic Writing Workshop. If your ART receives a high volume of epics, say one a week or one a fortnight,[3] then you may find it easier to have a predefined cadence for these workshops.

- Epic Writing Workshop: Where the Epic Hypothesis Statement is created and agreed. Many epics might come out of this. Some might need to go back to funnel and some will move to epic solutioning.

- Epic Solutioning: Where the Solution on a Page is created. We really like to get the first pass of this as a part of the Epic Writing Workshop but there is always some follow-up work that needs to take plan to get the Solution on a Page to done.[4]

- Ready for WSJF: A wait state to hold epics between cadence-based WSJF sessions.[5]

- Waiting for funding approval: In some organisations the decision to move an epic into discovery is also a decision to release some seed funding. Even if this is not the case in your organisation it can be helpful to pause and consider if you want to invest in discovering, as regardless of how your ART

---

[3] For US readers a fortnight is a period of two weeks.

[4] When it comes to the initial estimate or sizing, it is important you don't invest too much time here. Perhaps you already have people in your organisation whose role it is to provide a "wag" (wild arse guess), a VVROOM (Very Very Rough Order of Magnitude), or even an Order of Magnitude Guess (OMG). If so there is no reason to stop using this process unless it is slow or requires extensive effort. If you don't have an existing mechanism for this try using some version of the Fibonacci sequence such as 100, 200, 300, 500, 800, 1,300 points.

[5] This serves as a "time box" for the ART's effort in analysing/discovering the epic.

and epics are funded there is always a cost, even if that is just consuming labour involved in analysing an epic. This is likely a wait state to hold epics waiting on approval.

- Ready for Discovery: A wait state in which approved epics wait for the ART to have capacity to start discovering them.

Exemplar Epic Review State						
Prepare for Epic Writing Workshop	Epic Writing Workshop		Epic Solutioning:	Ready for WSJF	Waiting for funding approval	Ready for Discovery
Suggested WIP limit = 1 per Epic Owner	Suggested WIP limit = 1 per Epic Owner		Suggested WIP limit = 1	Suggested WIP limit = none (wait state)	Suggested WIP limit = none (wait state)	Suggested WIP limit = none (wait state)
Potential Exit Criteria: • Workshop schedule • Room booked • Invitees have confirmed their attendance	Potential Exit Criteria: • Epic Hypothesis Statement complete including a S.M.A.R.T. Business Outcome Hypothesis and Leading Indicators • Description of possible cost of delay considerations is captured		Potential Exit Criteria: • Solution on a Page complete, including an understanding of the alignment between the epic scope and the ARTs skill sets • Ballpark-size guestimate provided in points • Peer review complete	Potential Exit Criteria: • WSJF complete	Potential Exit Criteria: • Epic approved to proceed to Discovery • Funding provided/released • A story point "budget" allocated for Discovery	Potential Exit Criteria: • A team on the ART has the capacity to start discovery

Figure 62- Example of the Epic Review State with suggested WIP limits and potential exit criteria.

Discovery

This is where the rubber starts to hit the road. Moving from Review to Discovery is a decision to make a small investment in progressing the epic. The definition of small tends to vary by organisation. In many cases the size of this investment is determined by accounting rules and the balance the organisation wants to achieve between capex and opex expenditure! I have seen this investment be anything from 5 – 20% of the "guestimated" size of the epic. In the absence of any finance guidelines 10% of the "guestimated" size of the epic in the review stage should suffice.

The goal of this state is to discover just enough information to enable the Business Owners to decide if they should invest in building the MVP for this epic. As we did when we launched the ART, we use Impact Mapping to break down the Epic into Features.

Some potential Kanban states for Epic Discovery might be:

- Prepare for Impact Mapping A wait state in which approved epics wait for the Epic Owner to schedule the session
- Impact Mapping Workshop In this state the epics are split into features and potentially new epics are created
- UX Design/Wireframes is a state we use when UX is not in the teams. If they are in the teams then developing wireframes will be part of the team's discovery effort
- With Team(s) for Feature Definition This is where the epics sit while the teams are working through discovering the epics. Here we see features appear on the Program Kanban for the first time. The detail of how this works is in the Program Kanban discovery state. The epic stays on the Epic Kanban
- Lean Business Case The Epic Owner should have been iteratively collecting the data for this since the epic entered the review state. This state is for the final wrap-up and review of the Lean Business Case

- Waiting for Go/No-Go Decision This is a waiting state for the next cadence-based meeting with the Business Owners.[6]
- Ready for WSJF A wait state to hold epics between cadence-based WSJF sessions.

Prepare for Impact Mapping	Impact Mapping Workshop	UX Design/Wireframes	With Team(s) for Feature Definition	Lean Business Case	Waiting for Go/No-Go Decision	Ready for WSJF
Suggested WIP limit = none (wait state)	Suggested WIP limit = 1	Suggested WIP limit = 1 per UX person or UX Team	Suggested WIP limit = 1 per team on the train	Suggested WIP limit = 1 per Epic Owner	Suggested WIP limit = none (wait state)	Suggested WIP limit = none (wait state)
Potential Exit Criteria: • A 2-4 hr meeting and room has been scheduled and the Business Owners, Trifecta, Product Owners, UX and technical leads, and interested parties have all accepted the meeting • All attendees have been trained on what impact mapping is	Potential Exit Criteria: • A completed impact map where the features that are related to the ART are drafted • A candidate MVP is identified, and the feature/enabler(s) associated with it are drafted and agreed • The Solution on a Page and/or the epic hypothesis are reviewed and revised • If necessary new epics are created and added to the backlog	Potential Exit Criteria: • There are wireframes for the features included in this epic	Potential Exit Criteria: • The train has completed discovery for all of the features from impact mapping in the epic • The discovery outcomes have been accepted by the ART	Potential Exit Criteria: • The Lean Business Case is complete, reviewed, and accepted by the Trifecta as ready to present to the Business Owners	Potential Exit Criteria: • Cadence-based meeting with the Business Owners to approve the epic(s) • Capacity on the release train to move to the Program Backlog	Potential Exit Criteria: • WSJF complete

Figure 63 - Example of the Epic Discovery State with suggested WIP limits and potential exit criteria.

---

[6] Epics that are below the LPM threshold can skip this state. To learn more about LPM epic approval thresholds check out: https://www.scaledagileframework.com/guardrails/ (Accessed 3 September 2019).

Defining the States of the Program Feature Kanban

Funnel

The SAFe guidance suggests that the Program Kanban has a funnel where all new features are welcome.[7] As with the Program Epic Kanban we would usually split this into an Inbox and a Verify Entry state.

- Inbox: Where new features enter the system either from the Program Epic Kanban or directly.
- Validate Entry: Where the Trifecta determines if the idea or request meets the "definition of ready" for the teams to commence discovery.

Discovery

This is a lightweight time box activity. The goal is to understand enough about the feature to provide a reasonable estimate of the effort to feed into WSJF session and if applicable the Lean Business Case. At the end of the time box the team needs to provide evidence of discovery to the ART for feedback and acceptance.

Some potential Kanban states for Feature Discovery might be:

- Ready for Discovery: Wait state for features to be further elaborated by a team.
- Feature Definition: In this state the teams complete the feature definition and solution work we described above. Discovery must be documented, demonstrated, and accepted by the teams on the train as the team that discovers the feature is not always the one that ends up delivering it.
- Discovery Review: The team demos their feature discovery outcomes to the rest of the train in a cadence-based session. Representation from each team attend this session to provide feedback and acceptance. This is an alignment session.

---

[7] See: https://www.scaledagileframework.com/program-and-solution-kanbans/ (Accessed 24 September 2019)

- Discovery Complete: As the features for an epic will be discovered progressively the completed features will wait here.

Backlog

Here features that are part of epics wait for the epic to be approved. Features are prioritised and the features with the highest WSJF score are queued for PI Planning.

Some potential Kanban states Backlog might be:

- Waiting for Epic Go/No-Go—This is the easy one. We are just waiting for the epic to be approved.[8]
- Ready for Feature WSJF—The Product Manager has a regular cadence meeting to WSJF with the Business Owners, the other members of the Trifecta, POs, and tech leads.
- Ready for PI Planning—As PI planning approaches the teams need to know which features they are actually taking into the event. This is described in Preparing for PI Planning.[9]

SAFe in a Project Driven World

When working with projects, the feature sizes from Discovery are often used as the "budget" for the feature. If the feature is found to be larger during PI Planning the Product Owner would seek guidance from Project Management and/or the epic sponsor as to whether to proceed or if the feature should be scoped back. Under no circumstances should the teams ever be asked to re-estimate the work to make it "fit." This will not change the size of the actual work to be done and results in teams over commitment and either having to work overtime to meet their commitments or failing to meet their commitments.

---

[8] Features not related to an epic skip this state.
[9] If the person who wants a feature can't come to PI Planning, they don't want their feature badly enough!

	Exemplar Feature Funnel			Exemplar Feature Discovery State		
Inbox	Validate Entry	Ready for Discovery	Feature Definition	Discovery Review	Discovery Complete
Suggested WIP limit = none (wait state)	Suggested WIP limit = all features from a single epic or 1 stand-alone feature.	Suggested WIP limit = none (wait state)	Suggested WIP limit = 1 per team on the train	Suggested WIP limit = 1 per team	Suggested WIP limit = none (wait state)
Potential Exit Criteria: • Date of entry is recorded • The Trifecta has the capacity to validate the entry	Potential Exit Criteria: • Features meets the definition of ready for discovery • Product Management is willing to invest in Feature Definition and solutioning for this idea	Potential Exit Criteria: • Capacity in a team and the highest WSJF	Potential Exit Criteria: • The entire team has participated in refining the feature and sizing in points to meet the Definition of Ready for the feature • Their findings have been documented in a lightweight template	Potential Exit Criteria: • The train accepts the discovery with confidence vote of three or above	Potential Exit Criteria: • All features in the epic have completed discovery review • Business outcomes have been clearly articulated and validated • The feature set has been reviewed as a whole to ensure completeness

Figure 64 - Example of the Feature Funnel and Discovery States with suggested WIP limits and potential exit criteria.

Exemplar Feature Backlog State			
Waiting for Epic Go/No-Go	Ready for Feature WSJF	WSJF'd Backlog	Ready for PI Planning
Suggested WIP limit = none (wait state)	Suggested WIP limit = none (wait state)	Suggested WIP limit = none (wait state)	Suggested WIP limit = 2 features per team
Potential Exit Criteria: • Epic "go" decision	Potential Exit Criteria: • WSJF complete	Potential Exit Criteria: • Highest WSJF • There is capacity in the PI Planning Backlog	Potential Exit Criteria: • The external dependent parties for the feature are confirmed they are coming to PI Planning

Figure 65 - Example of the Feature Backlog State with suggested WIP limits and potential exit criteria.

Implementing

Features move into the Implementing state post PI Planning. It is possible that some of the Features changed shape as a result of PI Planning. If so, write new cards and put them on the board. Features that were descoped, or split should also be written on cards and put into the backlog for refinement. We also like to write cards for the dependencies that were visualised on the Program Board. As the cards move across the board you will be able to see the plan coming together on the wall without all the string. Features related to uncommitted objectives should be on the wall, too.

The states in the Implementing section of the Kanban will depend heavily on the context of the train, the technology stack, and the maturity of the DevOps practice. Our advice is to remember to build the board based on what you can do now. With time, and the delivery of enablers, you'll build more DevOps capability. Which will mean you will be able to go faster, and your states will change accordingly. It is always fun to look back on your first Kanban after a year of SAFe and marvel at how different it is and how far you have come.

You will need to tailor steps to what you can actually do. Here are just some possibilities to get you started:

- Development and Test: For cards that the team has started to work on. We suggested a WIP limit of two cards per team (feature or dependence cards). Some potential exit criteria could include:
    ◦ All user stories are accepted.
    ◦ The feature meets the current Definition of Done.
    ◦ Dependencies have been accepted by the dependent team.

> **Protip**
> While most teams will plan to deliver more than one feature in the Program Increment, we prefer to WIP limit teams to two features in flight at a time to encourage cross-skilling and enable better flow. This can be particularity challenging for new feature teams so if you are pushed to widen to increase the WIP limits be very careful you don't end up making a decision that keeps everyone busy but results in lower throughput. That's making a resource efficiency decision when there is a better flow efficiency decision to be made.

- Integration Testing: If you need a dedicated integration step maybe because you are working in a hardware context or you are just starting to build out your DevOps capability.

- NFR validation testing: This is usually intensive testing and done later after the functionality is working.

- Deploy to Production: Exit criteria might be all the tests pass including NFR tests, customer service is trained, compliance packages are complete and accepted by all of the certifying authorities.

- Release: This might have many states. Is it a dark or canary release? Or a full customer base release?

Additional States

Some ARTs choose to add states between Implementing and Done. What makes sense for you will be highly dependent on your train context. Some examples for you to consider are listed below:

Operating/Warranty
What happens after you release to the world? Some trains we have worked with have a warranty and/or stabilisation period before the code is transitioned to an external support team.

Bug Fix
If defects are found in production, and you apply the "you broke it, you fix it" paradigm,[10] as we do, you will want to be able to see this failure demand.[11]

Stakeholder NPS
About six to eight weeks after a feature has been released, I like to collect an NPS score from the person who requested the feature. This can be accomplished via a phone call, email, or survey. There are only two questions:

1. On a scale of 0 to 10, where 0 is not at all likely, and 10 is extremely likely, how likely would you be to recommend the delivery services of the Agile Release Train?
2. What is the main reason you gave that score?

Benefit Realisation
A state for monitoring the leading indicators you might have written as a part of the feature benefit hypotheses or the epic business outcome hypothesis.

Done
Doesn't every Kanban need a done state? All kidding aside, it's a nice bow on a journey that hopefully is getting faster and more predictable. Also, a great time for a celebration when an epic or feature is done!

---

[10] "You broke it, you fix it" means the team that created the bug gets to fix it.
[11] "Failure demand is demand caused by a failure to do something or do something right for the customer." Source: John Seddon, *Freedom from Command and Control: Rethinking Management for Lean Service*, (New York: CRC Press, 2005), Kindle Edition, Location 367.

> **Protip**
> A consistent approach to the use of size, colour, index cards, and Post-its will help make your walls easier to consume. A good Kanban is self-explanatory. There is an example of this in the section on Kinder Surprises below.

Dealing with (Kinder) Surprises

While we would hope that Features added post PI Planning are more an exception than a rule, for some trains it is very common. There will always be a need to respond to the market, but most of the time most features can be identified well ahead of PI Planning.

> **Em's Anecdote**
> We had an ART that had so many "surprise" features in their first PI that they decided to call them "Kinder Surprises."[12] This particular train was part of a consumer retail brand. They launched at the end of October without any Christmas-related features in their backlog for PI1. When the product folks realised Christmas was coming (!) it rained "Kinder Surprises." To help illustrate the impact of the never-ending stream of "Kinder Surprises" to the ART's Business Owners, the Trifecta gave them their own category of card on the Program Feature Kanban.

---

[12] For US audiences a Kinder Surprise is a chocolate egg that contains a small "surprise" toy that often needs to be assembled https://en.m.wikipedia.org/wiki/Kinder_Surprise (Accessed 25th August 2019).

Staying on the Tracks

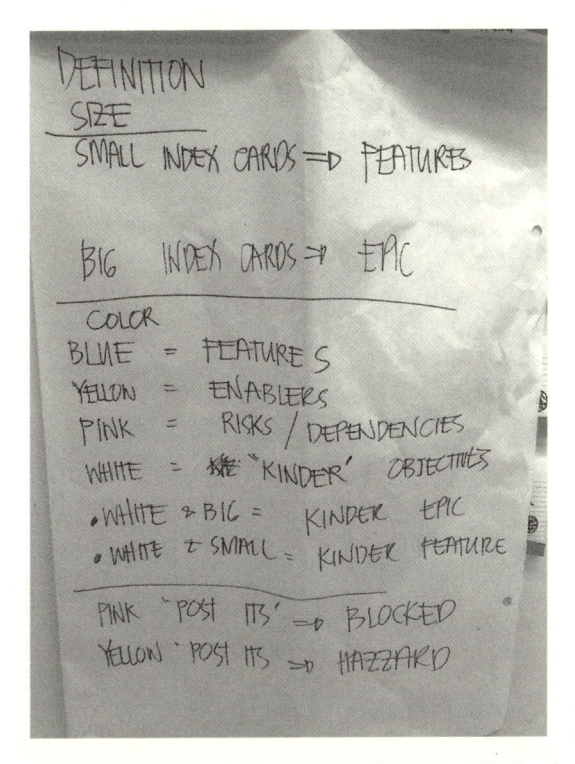

Figure 66 - Kinder surprise colour coding for the program Kanban board

A question we get asked in almost every class is, *"What do we do if a new, urgent feature arrives after PI Planning?"* It's a good question and something that many organisations don't handle very well. We coach the ART to respond by first asking, *"Can it wait until next PI?"* While often the answer is no, there is no harm in asking. Think of it like a sprint in Scrum. At the end of sprint planning the team commits to deliver and the Product Owner commits not to change their mind for an entire sprint.

In textbook Scrum, if the Product Owner wants to introduce a new story into a committed sprint backlog then the sprint plan is null and void and the team re-plans. A Program Increment is in essence an uber-sprint, so the same logic applies. Of course, in the same way teams rarely re-plan sprints for new stories, ARTs rarely re-plan PIs for new features. But if the change is significant this might sometimes be necessary. In which case you will want to validate with the ART's Business Owners that commercially it makes sense for the ART to down tools to re-plan to include this new feature or features.

The more common pattern for a Scrum team whose Product Owner requests a new story post sprint planning is that the team takes on the story in exchange for the Product Owner removing a larger, not yet started story from the backlog for that Sprint. If necessary, we can apply that same pattern to "Kinder Surprises." However, this is not an invitation to skip discovery.

Consider the amount of refinement that goes into getting a feature to "ready" for PI planning. "Kinder Surprises" generally don't have any of that. This is a recipe for disaster; teams struggle to deliver features that don't meet the definition of ready. In a flow-based system this will stand out like a sore thumb, as it should! Our advice is if a Kinder Surprise is coming at the train, the Trifecta needs to intercept the request, pressure test the time criticality of it with the Business Owners need, and then if truly urgent, ask a team to start discovery next sprint.

If political pressure or some other factor prevents you giving the teams some time to discover the feature then we suggest you allow the team to size the feature, double their estimate, and pull out of their PI plan enough features and stories to free up that amount of capacity. Now you're wondering why double it? Because the work is under baked, the estimates will be very rough, and scope will be fuzzy around the edges. This needs to be agreed before anyone actually starts working on the Kinder Surprise.

Of course, if there is too much volatility in your system then shorten the batch size. If you are having a lot of Kinder Surprises with a 12-week cadence, try reducing it to ten- or eight-week. Yes, there will an increase in transaction cost—but you are already paying that via the Kinder Surprises!

Operationalising the Program Kanban with Cocktail Hour and ART Sync

As we mentioned in *Setting the Timetable* we like to see a Cocktail Hour with an ART Sync happen every day.[13] For me a daily ART Sync is the heartbeat of the Agile Release Train. Every morning the who's who of the train share their progress and challenges with their peers. Visitors are always quick to comment on both how transparent everyone is and the energy of the train. This stand-up is always peppered with lots of good-humoured jibes and comedic antics designed to start the day with a laugh. Of course, the real magic is the speed of the information flow. Within the first hour of the day, all the blockers across all the teams have been surfaced and the remedial actions have commenced.

You might think we are crazy but the difference in latency and action orientation when compared to a weekly ART Sync or Scrum of Scrums is significant. For those wondering how moving from a weekly ART Sync to a Daily ART Sync is in alignment with SAFe, all you have to do is think about the principles. A daily ART Sync is a weekly ART Sync on steroids. Faster feedback (Principle 4)[14] and smaller batches of information (Principle 6)[15] combined with cadence and synchronisation (Principle 7).[16]

The key to making a daily ART Sync work is to keep it under fifteen minutes. You do not want a blow-by-blow update on the last 24

---

[13] ARTs that have Unity Hour on day one of the sprint tend to skip Cocktail Hour on day one of the sprint.

[14] To learn more about SAFe Principle #4 check out https://www.scaledagileframework.com/build-incrementally-with-fast-integrated-learning-cycles/ (Accessed 21 July 2019).

[15] To learn more about SAFe Principle #6 check out https://www.scaledagileframework.com/visualize-and-limit-wip-reduce-batch-sizes-and-manage-queue-lengths/ (Accessed 21 July 2019).

[16] To learn more about SAFe Principle #7 check out https://www.scaledagileframework.com/apply-cadence-synchronize-with-cross-domain-planning/ (Accessed 21 July 2019).

hours from each team. This session should always be held in front of the Program Feature Kanban, which I strongly recommend being a physical wall. Start at the end of the right-hand side which is the closer to delivery of value and walk the wall to the left. Not every card needs to be talked about every day. Instead, as you walk the states of the Kanban from right to left team representatives should call out blockers, issues, risks, and requests for help. I like to have the person speaking walk to the wall and touch the card they are talking to in order to bring focus to it. This approach moves the conversation away from status updates, instead bringing focus to how we create flow.

Some RTEs like to have a whiteboard on hand so that they can note the follow-up actions. This can be a useful visual reminder that ART Sync is a stand-up not a problem-solving session. Once the wall walk is complete you can ask if anyone has anything else to add. This is a good time to move to the meet after pattern described in SAFe, too.[17]

Most ARTs will probably need to grow into this and realistically there won't be much to talk about in the early sprints of the first PI so another pattern that is useful for new ARTs is to focus on sharing learnings.

---

[17] Adapted from: http://blog.prettyagile.com.au/2015/03/leaning-into-safe-with-feature-flow.html (Accessed 21 July 2019).

Scrum of Scrums Questions

- What information from your world do you think the other teams need to know?
- What hurt your team the most yesterday?
- What are you most worried about for your team today?
- BONUS QUESTION: What was the most valuable thing your team learnt yesterday?

@PrettyAgile

Figure 67 - Example ART Sync Questions for your first PI with a focus on learning

Tips for Globally Distributed ARTs

For distributed ARTs you may need to adjust the timing so that all locations can attend post their team stand-up. You will also need a video conferencing solution to support communication between sites. Portable video conferencing units are awesome for this. Another option I have seen work well is a portable program Kanban board that can be wheeled into a room with video conferencing facilities. One thing you'll want to avoid is having multiple stand-ups in a day to accommodate all of the locations. We want alignment and having many stand-ups for different subsets of the train isn't as helpful.

Sprinting

While sprinting in SAFe is much the same as sprinting in Scrum, we want to briefly draw your attention to some of the nuances we consider important.

Sprint Planning

While the Scrum Guide[18] suggests sprint planning may take up to four hours, in our experience, teams that have been through PI Planning and are doing regular backlog refinement won't need four hours every sprint. The exception is when teams are using tasks, which is a common pattern that new teams use when getting to know one another and how they each contribute to getting stories to done.[19] Tasking can also be useful if you have a significant percentage of staff that are more expereinced than the rest of the team. New folks coming in learn the domain significantly quicker when they experience the decomposition of a problem with senior people repeatedly.

The Scrum Master should bring into sprint planning the team's capacity based on their historical weighted velocity adjusted for planned leave. For the first PI we don't bother too much with this and just use the discounted normalised capacity from PI Planning for the whole PI.

Calculating Weighted Velocity

When planning agile teams generally use "yesterday's weather"[20] to predict their velocity/capacity for the next sprint (or sprints in the case of PI Planning). The idea is that: yesterday's weather is the best predictor of today's weather. When applied to agile this is taken to mean last

---

[18] Insert footnote: See: https://scrumguides.org/scrum-guide.html#events-planning (Accessed 24 September 2019)

[19] To learn more about sprint planning in SAFe check out: https://www.scaledagileframework.com/iteration-planning/ (Accessed 9 August 2019).

[20] See: http://www.scruminc.com/yesterdays-weather/ (10 August 2019).

sprint's velocity is the best predictor of the next sprint's velocity. Where team velocity is the total story points delivered by a team (planned and unplanned work). Of course, this approach does not take into account that a team's capacity is not equal from sprint to sprint, as it is affected by both planned and unplanned leave. I have observed that ARTs tend to solve for this by re-setting their capacity every sprint using SAFe's normalised estimation approach[21]—which drives me batty!

Frustrated by the misuse of SAFe's normalised estimation approach, I started to play with the concept of weighting velocity to improve the accuracy (not precision) of team and train planning and forecasting. I have come to call my approach weighted velocity. It is a way of adjusting velocity information so that it more accurately reflects capacity. This entails collecting the attendance data for a team or ART and expressing it as a percentage of the team's normal capacity.

For example, if a team usually has eight full-time team members and one was on leave for five days of the ten-day sprint then the team percentage attendance would be 93.75%, e.g. 75 days/80 days = 93.75%. I then take the velocity for the same team (or ART) for the same period and divide it by the % attendance. For example, if the velocity for the given sprint was 45 points and the percentage attendance was 93.75% then the weighted velocity would be 48.

This approach can also be used to address the impact of working overtime on velocity, too. (Before all you Agilists out there go on the attack, we all know there should not be overtime on an agile team!! And I tell my clients this all the time but sometimes these things still happen …) For example, the team has eight full-time team members and they all came in for a half day on a Saturday. The team would have attended 84 of 80 days making their % attendance 105%. If the velocity for this sprint was 50 points, the weighted velocity would be 48 (i.e. 50/105%).

---

[21] To learn more about normalised estimation in SAFe check out: https://www.scaledagileframework.com/iteration-planning/ (10 August 2019).

By always weighting the team or (ART's) velocity we remove the variation caused by planned and unplanned leave, providing a more realistic view of yesterday's weather for planning and forecasting. Perhaps more simply, we are reverse engineering what the velocity would have been if the team had been at full capacity (100%) for the sprint. Of course, when using weighted velocity as yesterday's weather for planning purposes, I suggested taking an average over four or five sprints, then adjusting the number down for any planned leave using the same percentage of attendance approach used above.[22]

During sprint planning we expect the teams to replace the placeholder cards from PI Planning with specific stories for innovation and discovery. We would also expect the innovation and discovery outcomes to appear in the team's sprint goals. The discovery effort for a team usually takes the form of some workshops with product management, subject matter experts, and users. The goal of these workshops is to get the features to meet the definition of ready for prioritisation for PI Planning.

> **Protip**
> It is important that the entire team attends these workshops so there is shared understanding of the ask and the solution. Even though the outcome will likely be documented in some way, as Jeff Patton says, good documents are like vacation photos: if you were there when the photo was taken you can fill in the missing detail.[23]

---

[22] Adapted from http://blog.prettyagile.com.au/2019/01/weighted-velocity-approach-to.html (Accessed 10 August 2019).

[23] See: https://www.jpattonassociates.com/read-this-first/ (Accessed 11 August 2019).

Caution! Potential Train Wreck Ahead!

Some trains struggle to have enough work ready for discovery each sprint. So, we just give the team a vacation, right? We tell the Product Manager they need to start the cadence of refining the backlog of the train day one of Sprint 1. This is the "continuous" part of continuous elaboration of the continuous delivery pipeline. Did we mention continuous?

Falling behind on discovery is a sure-fire way to put your train into the ditch. Or derail it, or pick your metaphor. So, if the teams don't have a feature to discover this should be brought up at the ART Sync, over, and over again, until a feature shows up. But it will only take a few days of the affected teams mentioning to the Product Manager that they don't have features that it will create enough noise that the Product Manager will get the point. The RTE should probably have a quiet conversation with the Product Manager to find out what needs to be done to move this along. The RTE doesn't want the train going into the ditch in the first sprint, either.

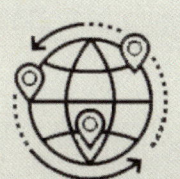

Tips for Globally Distributed ARTs

Let's be really clear where a single team is split across two locations, or more, that is the slowest configuration there is. In this arrangement there is a hidden tax the organisation is paying on throughput and culture. Now that the public service announcement is over, let's move on to helping these people become a team!

There are some key elements to care for. First, there are no second-class citizens on a team or train. The timing of team events needs to balance the pain between the sites. It makes no sense to have anyone up in the middle of the night trying to be a part of team! The team might have to rotate that pain depending how many time zones are separating them.

Using video conferencing is best to help these people see each other and form a team. Next best is voice calls and last is chat apps. If there is need to prioritise access to video conferencing, we recommend putting these teams first.

Creating working agreements that acknowledge the time zone challenges is key. Working agreements that bias the team to use to face-to-face conversation are going to be best. The smaller the "overlap" of working hours in the day (US and India, for example) the more deliberate and focused these teams will need to be. These hours should be looked upon as sacred team time.

We still use physical Kanban boards for teams in this configuration. The team co-located with the board sends photos to the remote team members when the board is updated. So, everyone can still see all of the plans no matter what team you are on or what location you are in. The remote team members have buddies that are co-located with the physical board who can update the board for them when required. This might also be a good working agreement.

Melissa's Anecdote

A large government agency had a distributed train across five Australian states with most teams having a member in each state. The whole day was spent on wireless headsets. Individuals quickly worked out it was easier to sit at your desk than physically join stand-up with one or two people with the remainder on the phone. The quality of the communication and pace of delivery slowed to a grinding halt whilst everyone dialled in constantly tripping over each other and getting mixed messages. Eventually, we got a hold of telepresence rooms and booked all our team rituals. People couldn't believe how much more work we got done when we could actually communicate!

Reunification

At the end of sprint planning day, we hold Reunification. The Scrum Masters, Product Owners, Chapter Leads, and Technical Leads will gather at the Program Kanban with the Trifecta to share their sprint goals. Sometimes the entire train will join in. Just like in PI Planning we are using a mass peer review to make sure the team dependencies are cared for and everyone is in alignment.

Daily Stand-Up

Each team should have a fifteen-minute daily stand-up where they align on their priorities for the day ahead and surface any blockers that will prevent them from reaching their sprint goals. Some ARTs like to synchronise the team stand-ups so that they occur immediately before the daily ART Sync. Others like to cascade the stand-ups so that interdependent teams can visit each other.

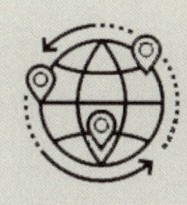

> **Tips for Globally Distributed ARTs**
> When the train is spread across multiple time zones, stand-ups tend to be at the start of the day local time. When a team is split across multiple locations the team may choose to sync more than once a day.

Backlog Refinement

The teams should schedule backlog refinement on an agreed cadence. A common pattern is to use the same time block on day six of the sprint that the team uses on day one for sprint planning. Another pattern is to spend an hour on this on days three, five and seven each sprint. Some trains like to synchronise this so that dependencies between the teams can be agreed.

> **Em's Anecdote**
>
> A team on a train I was coaching invited me to sit in on their retrospective one day. They told me that the same problem was coming up every retrospective. The problem was that sprint planning was taking three days—every sprint! Clearly surprised, I asked them why and they explained that there were always questions that could not be answered during sprint planning and these questions would take a couple of days to close out. My next question was "Do you do backlog refinement?" The blank stares answered that one for me. So, I explained that they should try holding backlog refinement meetings a few days before sprint planning!

Discovering the Cargo for Next PI

Each sprint the teams should be working on refining and sizing features for the next PI; this is the Discovery work we reserved capacity for during PI Planning. This effort is time boxed in story points.

When a feature comes to the team for some sizing feedback it can be very tempting for the team to spend their discovery time box writing a mass of detailed stories that meet the definition of ready for a sprint. This is too much detail even for PI Planning. The outcome we want from the teams is a really high-level estimate, alignment on the outcome for the feature, and to iterate on the architectural approach.

There are lots of ways to do this. One way is to spend an hour working up a story map with the people who know about the feature as described in Jeff Patton's book *User Story Mapping*.[24] These are really, really rough stories. No user actor voice, no acceptance criteria.

---

[24] Jeff Patton, *User Story Mapping,* Pages 67 -77.

Just a single sentence or a few word description to describe what the story is. From there the team can use the white elephant method of sizing.[25] Once that is done you add up the story points, jot down questions, feedback, and risks for the Trifecta and get ready for the discovery playback.

Sprint Review

Your teams must demo at the end of each sprint. Perhaps you use the ART Show model we talked about earlier or maybe you use the more traditional Sprint Review either way the team needs to demonstrate what they have delivered so that they can get feedback.

> **Em's Anecdote**
> Back when I worked in industry, my team would occasionally approach me to ask if they "had to" demo this sprint as they had nothing to show! I would always respond by suggesting that they must have been doing something for the last two weeks and they should share what they had been working on. For me this is a matter of transparency and building trust between the team and their stakeholders.

A question we always ask our clients, is how safe is it to be transparent in your organisation? For example, if one of the teams on your ART had accidently deleted what they had been working on and did not have a backup, would they turn up at the Sprint Review with PowerPoint (smoke and mirrors) or would they be transparent about the mistake that have been made? If your answer is PowerPoint, have a think about why that might be. How do leader's respond to mistakes in your organisation? Do they respond with retribution, or genuine concern? I like to think leaders will respond

---

[25] To learn about the White Elephant Sizing planning game, check out: https://www.tastycupcakes.org/2009/09/sizing-game/ (Accessed 24 August 2019).

to these times of accidents with a learning mindset. Perhaps asking, "What did the team learn and how will they work differently in the future?"

> **Protip**
> The best way for a team to be sure to have something to demo is for the team to decide in Sprint Planning what they will demo at the end of the Sprint. Ideally, the Product Owner should be the voice of the demo, providing context to stakeholders about the new functionality delivered by the team. We also like the whole team to be present, to help drive the demo, answer questions and hear the feedback. After all, agile is a team sport!

Sprint Retrospective

There is a lot of guidance and plenty of books on the subject of agile retrospectives. In addition to the traditional reflection on what happened during the sprint and the opportunities to improve next sprint, consider what data the team should be reviewing and what data the team needs to provide to the RTE.

The end of sprint retrospective is also an opportunity for the team to reflect on their estimations from sprint planning. I ask teams to look for where they feel there was significant variance between the initial estimate and the actual effort involved in completing the story. Where these variances occur, I suggest the team has a discussion about why they think the estimation varied (i.e. what did they learn through the delivery of the story) and how they may be able to use this learning in future planning sessions. If you are using cost per story point[26] you will also want the Scrum Master to record these variances as an input.

---

[26] To learn about how we calculate Cost per Story Point check out the White Paper: http://bit.ly/CostPerPointWP (Accessed 10 August 2019).

Bubble-Up

We ask the teams we work with to capture issues raised in their retrospectives that are outside of their control outside of their control to bring them to Bubble-Up. Some teams like using the Circles and Soup retrospective format.[27]

Operationalising the Chapters

Now that the teams have started sprinting, it is time to get the Chapters operational. The Chapters should meet at least twice a sprint, although twice a week is my preference. There are two discussions I like to see Chapters having on a regular basis. The first is peer review. Chapter members share what they are working on and the approach they are taking and seek feedback from the Chapter. The second is a more organic knowledge exchange using the Lean Coffee[28] technique to build the agenda. These can be two separate meetings or both discussions can be held in each meeting.

If the Chapter Leads are also the line managers of the chapter members, they will also want to establish regular 1:1 coaching and mentoring sessions with each chapter member.

Executing the Innovation and Planning (IP) Sprint

So, we know there are two events that will happen every single IP Sprint: Inspect and Adapt (I&A) and PI Planning—what we do with the rest of the time is generally a matter of context. Most trains in their first PIs will be using at least some of this time for contingency, to help them deliver on their committed PI Objectives.

---

[27] See: https://www.innovationgames.com/circles-and-soup/ (Accessed 3 September 2019).

[28] To learn about how to facilitate a Lean Coffee check out: http://agilecoffee.com/leancoffee/ (Accessed 11 August 2019).

As you might have gathered I am a huge advocate of using some of this time for additional training. When we launch a train using the Quick-Start approach, we throw a lot of information at the train in a very short period of time and of course not all of it sticks. In terms of bedding in the learning from *SAFe for Teams*, I have found the SAFe Team Self-Assessments to be a useful tool as illustrated in the case study below.

> ### Case Study: Facilitating SAFe® Team Self-Assessments
>
> As part of an Agile Release Train's commitment to relentless improvement it is necessary for all the teams on the train to reflect and assess the effectiveness of their Agile practices on a regular cadence. For most once a PI seems to be a logical frequency. The Scaled Agile Framework provides a self-assessment tool to support this process and makes it freely available for download at: https://www.scaledagileframework.com/metrics/
>
> I have found clients often want to do self-assessments by sending them out as an online survey for team members to complete individually. Personally, I am not keen on this approach for a number of reasons. Firstly, most new agile teams don't have a clear and consistent understanding of what good looks like, therefore, they tend to overstate their level of maturity. (The first time I did this on an Agile Release Train, the most mature team gave themselves the lowest score and the least mature teams gave themselves the highest score!)
>
> Secondly, by completing online surveys the team doesn't have an opportunity to discuss their different perspectives and reach a shared understanding. In my experience self-assessments provide an excellent coaching opportunity, especially if you are the only SPC supporting an ART and doing so part time. Often this can be as simple as reminding them of what a five looks like and resetting their anchors. Even though an RTE can take a

DIY approach to this, an external facilitator can be very valuable and as an SPC this is your opportunity to ensure the assessment is only used for good and not evil.

A few years ago, I was getting ready to facilitate the first round of self-assessments for a new train and I got thinking about my approach to facilitating these sessions. My priority was to ensure that every team member got an opportunity to express their individual point of view. Which led to me contemplating how Planning Poker uses the simultaneous reveal to prevent anchoring. One idea I had was to create cards numbered with the 0 to 5 rating scale, but that felt a little boring. Then it came to me—the perfect combination of silent writing on Post-it Notes and a big visible information radiator …

During my lunch break I raced out to Officeworks and purchased a box of Sharpies, an eight-pack of super sticky Post-its, and a pad of flip chart paper. I made it back to the office and found the meeting room with moments to spare. I quickly drew a large star, like the axes of a radar chart, on five sheets of butcher's paper. I gave each poster a heading as per the areas in the SAFe Self-Assessment: Product Ownership Health, PI/Release Health, Sprint Health, Team Health, and Technical Health. I then labelled each axis A through E and marked the numbers 1 through 5 along each axis. I then took a sixth piece of poster paper and wrote up the rating scale. I attached the posters to the wall, put a Post-it pad and Sharpie out for each team member and waited for the team to arrive.

Once the team had settled in, I provided a brief introduction, reminding everyone that the purpose of self-assessment is to reflect on where the team is at and identify opportunities for improvement. The self-assessments would not be used to compare teams, nor would they be used by management to "beat up" the teams. Then came the instructions:

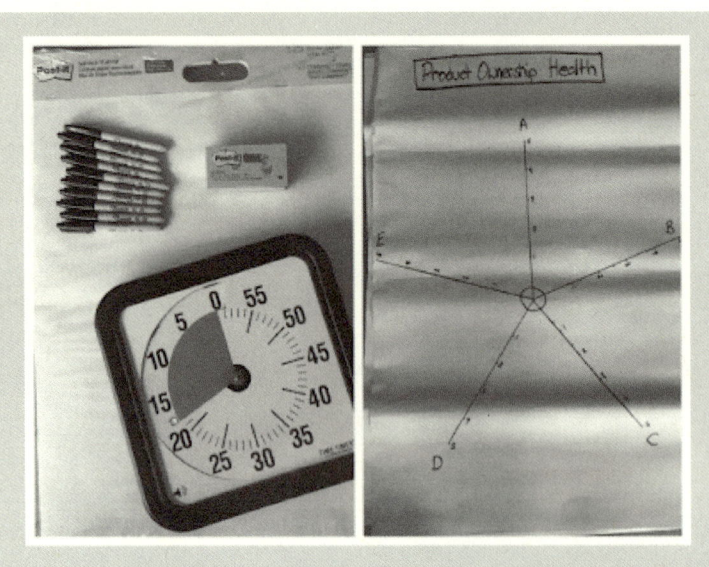

Figure 68 - Supplies for the Team Self-Assessment

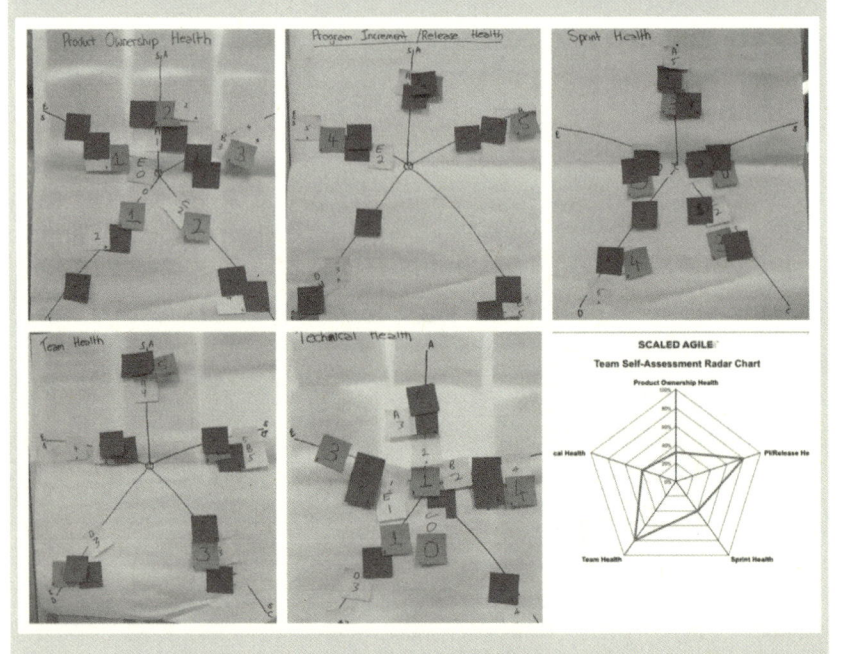

Figure 69 - Results of the Team Self-Assessment

"We are going to work through each of the five sections using the following approach. Each section has five statements, which I have labelled A through E. As I read out each statement you will need to write the letter corresponding to the statement and your score using the rating scale provided. This will be a silent writing exercise. Once everyone has provided an assessment for all five statements for a given area, you will each place your responses on the chart. Then we will go through and discuss the responses and reach a consensus on the overall score for the team."

Section by section the teams created visualisations reflecting their assessment of the current state. In some areas the team was close to 100% aligned and on others their opinions could not have been more varied. As each section was completed, I facilitated a discussion with the group about the results. Where there were clear outliers, I would start by asking for someone to comment on them. For the most part, the discussions tended to result in convergence on a shared assessment that I could record in the template. When the team struggled to reach consensus, I ask them to "re-vote" by holding up the number of fingers that reflect their current view and I recorded the mode. Once I had completed all five assessment rounds, I also had the data to complete the summary radar chart.

The first few times I used this approach I struggled with the time box and did not leave enough time for the most important step: identifying the actions the team would take to improve. These days I use a two-hour time box and always make sure the team leaves the session having committed to actioning their key learnings. I like to try and get one improvement focus or action from each of the five areas.

I think one of the strengths of this approach is its alignment to the brain science about how adults learn. In her book *Using*

Brain Science to Make Training Stick,[29] Sharon Bowman, creator of "Training from the Back of the Room," talks about six learning principles that trump traditional teaching:

- Movement trumps Sitting: In order to learn the brain needs oxygen. The best way to get oxygen to the brain is to move
- Talking trumps Listening: The person doing the most talking is doing the most learning
- Images trump Words: The more visual the input is the more likely it is to be remembered
- Writing trumps Reading: The team will remember anything they write longer than anything you write
- Shorter trumps Longer: People will generally check out within twenty minutes
- Different trumps Same: The brain quickly ignores anything that is repetitive, routine or boring.

This approach to facilitating self-assessments includes: Movement in the form of standing up and placing answers on the chart; Talking in the form of the discussion that the team have amongst themselves on the results; Images in the form of the posters; Writing in the form of the written response; Shorter in the form of the twenty-minute time box for each area; and Different to filling out an online survey!

As the SAFe Self-Assessment is very practice centric, teams will probably outgrow it as they move through Shu-Ha-Ri. You will probably also find that after the first assessment, results will often go down rather than up as teams begin to understand what good looks like and they hold themselves to a higher standard. As a rule, I am not a fan of "agile maturity" surveys, as they have a tendency to end up on performance dashboards and scorecards re-

---

[29] Sharon Bowman, *Using Brain Science to Make Training Stick: Six Leaning Principles That Trump Traditional Teaching*, (Glenbrook: BowPerson Publishing, 2011).

sulting in teams being pressured to improve their scores and the system most likely being gamed. The real value is in the conversations. Reaching a shared understanding of each team member's experience and consensus on the next actions the team should take as part of their commitment to relentless improvement.[30]

If you would like to try this approach yourself, you can download a facilitation guide from: http://bit.ly/SelfAssessmentWP

Tips for Globally Distributed ARTs

This facilitation approach is a little trickier for a team that is distributed across two sites. In this scenario I have used Survey Monkey to gather the inputs and created the visualisation before the session. The discussion of the differences and aligning on a value and actions is the same but takes place using video conferencing facilities.

Post ART Launch Training

The SAFe classes we encourage trains to invest in after their first couple of PIs include the *SAFe DevOps* class[31] and the *SAFe Agile Software Engineer* class.[32] We also like to see the *SAFe Advanced Scrum* Master class[33] delivered about a year after the ART launch. We have found this class

---

[30] Adapted from: http://blog.prettyagile.com.au/2015/08/facilitating-scaled-agile-framework-safe-team-self-assessments.html (Accessed 24 September 2019)

[31] To learn more about the *SAFe DevOps* class check out: https://www.scaledagile.com/certification/courses/safe-devops/ (Accessed 8th August 2019).

[32] To learn more about the SAFe Agile Software Engineering class check out: https://www.scaledagile.com/certification/courses/safe-agile-software-engineering/ (Accessed 8 August 2019).

[33] To learn more about the SAFe Advanced Scrum Master class check out: https://www.scaledagile.com/certification/courses/safe-advanced-scrum-master/ (Accessed 8 August 2019).

re-energises the Scrum Masters and that energy subsequently affects the entire train. Another learning activity we used is *getKanban* board game.[34] Some ARTs like to bring teams into software dojos to top them up and refocus where they may have gotten into some bad habits.

In the case of new team members, often we choose to onboard them during the IP Sprint and run them through *SAFe for Teams* before their first PI Planning.

> **Adrienne's Anecdote**
> One train we were working with was coming up to their first I&A when the Scrum Master approached us about taking her team back through *SAFe for Teams*. She had a few new people on her team including a new Product Owner. The team was struggling to gel and the relationship with the new Product Owner was strained. There was a definite divide on the team. While sending the new folks on training was a no brainer, I thought the idea of bringing the whole team back to the training room was a great play by this Scrum Master.

Innovation

In addition to the Innovation Time capacity allocation we also like to see some of the IP Sprint used for innovation; after all, it is called the innovation and planning sprint! This will often be in the form of a Hackathon[35] or Ship It Day.[36] Although in our context there are not 24-hour events with no sleep, as that doesn't gel with our Lean-Agile values such as sustainable pace and Respect for People. We like to see teams being given 24 hours over three days. The subject of the

---

[34] See: https://getkanban.com/ (Accessed 8 August 2019).
[35] See: https://en.wikipedia.org/wiki/Hackathon (Accessed 8 August 2019).
[36] See: https://www.atlassian.com/company/shipit (Accessed 3 September 2019).

hackathons vary greatly from technical debt remediation to solving customer facing problems.

A great way to inspire innovation is gemba time. Teams taking a day to do ride-alongs with the people who use the products and services they deliver. This is always insightful.

If you really want to ramp up your investment in culture, you could always try a "breakaway day."[37] In *Tribal Unity*, I talk about this being an end-of-year, fully paid, day out of the office (for both contractors and permanent staff) to play games and share a meal in a local public garden, but there is no reason you can't take a day out to have fun at any time of year!

> **Claire's Anecdote**
> One large Australian enterprise I worked with enthusiastically embraced the idea of an Innovation Day as part of the IP Sprint. After much discussion and planning amongst Chapter Leads, the date was set, and teams were invited to "Go Innovate"! The "deer in the headlights" look on the face of team members said it all. The next IP Sprint, business leaders introduced a set of Customer Problems to solve. This was a much more inspiring and successful approach.

Inspect and Adapt

SAFe guidance suggests this is a half day every IP Sprint; however, I have found that allowing the better part of a day is better investment.

The PI System Demo

We are often asked how this demo differs from the sprint-based System Demo. Rather than reinvent the wheel we thought we might try and level set everyone with some words from the SAFe website:

---

[37] Em Campbell-Pretty, *Tribal Unity*, p. 42.

The PI System Demo is the first part of the I&A, and it's a little different from the bi-weekly ones that precede it, in that it is intended to show all the Features that the ART has developed over the course of the PI. Typically, the audience is broader, for example, additional Customer representatives or Portfolio representatives may choose to attend this demo. Therefore, the PI system demo tends to be a little more formal, and some extra preparation and staging are usually required. But like any other system demo, it should be time boxed to an hour or less, with the level of abstraction high enough to keep stakeholders actively engaged and providing feedback. During the PI system demo, Business Owners, customers, and other vital stakeholders collaborate with each Agile team to rate their actual business value achieved.[38]

We like to think of this event as a celebration of all that was achieved during the PI. If PI Planning was one book end of the PI, this is the other. While SAFe suggests a 45-60-minute time box for this, depending on the size of the train we will sometimes choose to have a 90 minute- or two-hour time box.

In PI Planning the teams committed to deliver on a set of PI objectives. These objectives were also given business value ratings by the Business Owners. The PI System Demo is the opportunity for the teams to demonstrate how they delivered on those objectives to the train's Business Owners. Depending on the size of your organisation and the seniority of the Business Owners, they may or may not have attended the System Demos during the PI. Either way now is the time for the Business Owners to tell the teams if the value they promised has been delivered.

---

[38] See: https://www.scaledagileframework.com/inspect-and-adapt (Accessed 19 June 2019).

> **Protip**
> Ask the teams to self-assess the actual value before asking the Business Owners for their view. Teams are often harsher on themselves than their Business Owners. This tends to ground the teams in reality before they demo and can sometimes result in the teams being pleasantly surprised by a higher value from the Business Owners.

The PI System Demo is an opportunity to "showcase" your ART. This is particularly important if the ART is one of the first in your organisation, as part of your role is to inspire the organisation and build momentum for the SAFe transformation.

At a minimum we would have expected everyone who was at PI Planning to be at the I&A, especially the Business Owners. Assuming some of the features delivered will be used by internal stakeholders or sold to external customers it would be typical to have people representing these groups attend the demo including folks from Sales and Marketing. If you include people in this demo that have not been part of the PI Planning process you will need to brief them on the event so that they understand the context.

Demonstrating Objectives

This is where having a huge number of PI Objectives for the ART is going to prove challenging as you will struggle to get through the content in an hour. Focusing on completed objectives will help with this. In terms of the narrative, we have often seen these demos set in the context of the epic to which they belong, with the product team demonstrating the customer experience. Context is king—especially with a non-technical audience.

Business Value Rating

The same people who assigned the Business Value provide the teams with feedback on the Actual Value during I&A. When assigning actual business value, we would expect that if a team has delivered on their commitment then the full business value is assigned, even if the Business Owners have deprioritised the feature. For an incomplete objective where the part of the objective that is complete is potentially shippable and meets the DoD, we would expect partial credit to be given. However, if only "design" has been completed or "it hasn't been tested" then zero value would be applicable.

One temptation is for teams to want to negotiate for a higher actual value on their PI Objectives. They might say something like, *"We really knocked it out of the park. Can't we get eight points instead of seven?"* There are a lot of reasons this might happen but pragmatically speaking, whatever the Business Value that was assigned at PI Planning is what was assigned.

> **Caution! Potential Train Wreck Ahead**
> If the features have changed over the course of the PI—perhaps some got removed and others got added—do not change the PI Objectives! We use these and the associated value delivered to measure predictability. If the features change and objectives get missed, the system is unpredictable, and this should be reflected in the PI Predictability Measure. Remember PI predictability is not a reflection on the teams but on the system!

Quantitative Measurement

The SAFe Program Increment Toolkit that certified SPCs and RTEs (in good standing) have access to has a recommended set of metrics to include in this section. We won't revisit the entire list here; rather, we will explore the metrics we modify, add, and exclude from the Quantitative Measurement portion of the Inspect and Adapt.

Modifications to Quantitative Measurement

Rather than Features Planned and Features Accepted we prefer:

- #Features committed at PI Planning

- #Features uncommitted at PI Planning
- % Features Delivered
- # Features added post PI Planning (e.g. #Kinder Surprises)

Program Velocity

When showing velocity numbers for the ART we prefer to use **Weighted Program Velocity**.[39] This is a way to adjust the train's velocity for holidays and unplanned leave. This helps us understand the rate the train can burn down a backlog allowing us to match capacity and demand.

Additional Metrics

Feature Cumulative Flow Diagram (CFD)[40]

Given this is a flow-based system measuring this over time is a good choice. Especially if you want to think about how you achieve a faster, predictable flow.

Employee NPS (eNPS)

If you have not already done so you should start measuring eNPS. Even if your first PIs have been bumpy it will be good to understand the trajectory you are on.

Software Quality Metrics

You should also see an improvement in your code quality metrics as your XP practice gets stronger. We would recommend starting to measure:

- Code churn
- Code coverage
- Test by type coverage
- Cyclomatic complexity
- # of automated and manual tests by type

Metric Exclusions

---

[39] To learn how we calculate Weighted Velocity check out: http://bit.ly/WeightedVelocity (Accessed 8 August 2019).
[40] See: https://www.scaledagileframework.com/metrics/ (Accessed 9 August 2019).

User Stories or enabler stories planned and accepted.
This metric appears counter cultural to us. We expect trains to deliver on PI objectives not individual stories, so counting the total number of stories planned and accepted at the end of the PI makes no sense. Including this measure in the Inspect and Adapt can result in the teams on the train seeing it as a measure of performance, resulting in them getting into too much detail during PI Planning and being afraid to add stories during the PI. Also, given we fully expect teams to add stories during the PI as they learn more and break down the chunkier stories, this metric does not seem useful.[41]

> **Adrienne's Anecdote**
> In one organisation I was surprised the day that the technology leader stood up at the second Solution Train PI Planning and told the development teams that their performance goal for the year ahead was to deliver on their sprint commitments 24 out of 26 sprints. That meant that they could only miss their sprint commitment twice in an entire year. I was floored. This organisation did have delivery problems, but it wasn't because these folks were bad developers.
>
> The business was supporting ten versions of the product, the architecture was hacked to do this, and the technology leaders didn't invest in DevOps training to allow the teams to create any automated testing. The code was a mess! The morale of the story here is be careful what you measure. What's the way to go faster and get predictable? Apply a tourniquet to the practices that create technical debt. What would I do in this case? Performance goals around learning XP practices and a train goal to reduce the lead time to deliver.

---

[41] Teams should keep track of this at a sprint level to help them understand how well they are able to plan and deliver.

⚠ **Caution! Potential Train Wreck Ahead!**
Whatever metrics you choose to share, never share team level metrics in this forum. No matter how much you coach leaders not to compare teams, the temptation will be impossible to resist when team-by-team data is presented. Remember: *"Metrics are very sharp tools. They are great at helping us focus, but they can hurt us badly if we focus on the wrong things."*[42]

Problem-Solving Workshop

The key to a successful Problem-Solving Workshop is clearly articulated real world problems and good facilitation. Neither thing is particularly easy to achieve.

When it comes to identifying the problems to solve, we have a few different approaches we like to use depending on the circumstances. The first and perhaps most straightforward is to use the backlog from "Bubble-Up." This approach is particularly useful if you have a distributed ART. A second lightweight approach we use is the SAFe's recommended problem statement format and a facilitation approach called thirty-five.[43]

---

[42] Adzic, Gojko, Impact Mapping, Location 352.
[43] Image source: https://thiagi.net/archive/www/pfp/IE4H/march2008.html# Framegame (Accessed 8 August 2019).

What

When

We discovered three significant design problems in the October deployment of the new EMV vehicles at the Thrills Amusement Park.

Impact

Where

The design flaws caused us to recall the vehicles and invest three months in materials, redesign, and testing. We delivered late, paid substantial penalties, and lost credibility with the customer.

Concept contributed by Beth Miller

© Scaled Agile, Inc.

Figure 70 – The anatomy of a well-phrased problem[44]

We ask each individual to write the problem statement, using SAFe's format, for the thing they believe most impeded delivery during the PI. We do this post the demo as we believe the demo and metrics segments help folks see the challenges more clearly. While the format is hardly mission critical, it does focus the problem solving on a specific event which is useful when using fishbone diagrams and the five whys as a problem-solving technique. We then use thirty-five as a way to identify the ideas that people are most passionate about. When I have the time, I will facilitate a "Timeline"[45] retrospective to get people thinking before playing "Thirty-Five."

Thirty-Five Facilitation Guide[46]

1. **Ask the question.** For example: *"What was the most significant impediment to the ART delivering on its commitments this PI?"* or *"What is the most important problem we need to solve if we want to improve flow?"*

---

[44] See: https://www.scaledagileframework.com/inspect-and-adapt (Accessed 8 August 2019).
[45] Esther Derby and Diana Larson, *Agile Retrospectives: Making Good Teams Great*. (Pragmatic Bookshelf, 2005). Kindle Edition Location 871.
[46] Adapted from: https://thiagi.net/archive/www/pfp/IE4H/march2008.html#Framegame (Accessed 9 August 2019).

2. **Invite written responses.** Distribute an index card and a Sharpie to each participant. Ask the participants to record their answer using the recommended SAFe format, legibly on one side of the index card.
3. **Walk around.** Ask participants to hold their cards with the written side down. Tell them to walk around and exchange cards with one another. Ask them not to read the responses on the cards at this time. Play some fun music for 30 to 60 seconds.
4. **Find a partner.** Stop the music. Ask participants to pair up with someone nearby. (Note you will need an even number of participants for this to work.)
5. **Score the responses.** Ask each pair of participants to review the responses on the two cards they have. Instruct them to distribute seven points between these two responses where seven is the most significant issue and 0 is the least significant, e.g. 4 and 3, 5 and 2, 6 and 1, or 7 and 0. Tell participants to avoid using fractions or negative numbers. Have the participants write the scores on the back of each card.
6. **Repeat steps 3 through 5 four more times.** Ask the participants to record their scores for each round on the back of the card below the previous number.
7. **Conclude the evaluation process.** At the end of the fifth round, ask participants to return to their seats with the card they currently have. Ask them to add the points from the five rounds and write the total.
8. **Conduct a countdown.** After pausing for the totals to be computed, explain that you are going to count down from 35. Begin counting down to identify the card with the highest score. When a participant hears the matching total on the card, they should stand up and read the response from the card. After the participant reads the response from the card, lead a round of applause. Repeat the countdown process until you have identified the top five to ten responses. Make sure to pause on potentially duplicated cards and ask the group if they should be merged and counted as one. (To work out how many responses

I need for the Problem-Solving Workshop I divide the number of people at the workshop by seven and round down.)
9. **Conclude the session.** Thank participants for generating and evaluating useful responses.

Now we have our top five to ten issues to problem solve. Prior to the I&A workshop we normally run a preparation workshop with the ARTs extended leadership team (the Trifecta, Product Owners, and Scrum Masters). One of the activities in this preparation workshop is to identify a handful of facilitators for the Problem-Solving Workshop. We will often default to using the Scrum Masters for they are probably the folks with the strongest facilitation skills. We have also found UX people and Six Sigma practitioners to be good at this. We have these facilitators practise facilitating the "five whys" root cause analysis method.

When it comes to forming the problem-solving teams, we ask each facilitator to take a problem statement and then we ask the room to move to the problem that they are most interested in or can best contribute to solving. We tell them that the groups cannot be any larger than eight people. If some problems end up with no people, we take that as a sign that the problem is not as significant as the others and don't continue working on it.

> **Caution! Potential Train Wreck Ahead!**
> Facilitating populating the fishbone diagram and root cause analysis using the five whys is just plain hard. People seem to get themselves "wrapped around the axle" at almost every step of the process! First, it is the labels on the bones on the fish. I like to coach people that the labels are prompts to help you think about possible causes of the problem.

> The second challenge is people critiquing each other's responses. Basically, someone in the group suggests a cause and someone else says "no, that's not it" and then things start to spiral out of control while the accuracy of the suggestions is debated. I try to encourage teams to withhold judgement and start by getting all the possible causes on the diagram. The third challenge is staying out of the doom loop and avoiding circular references during the five whys. I think the trick here is to always remember to frame the why in the context of the previous why. It can also be prudent to remind people that this is not the "five whos".

> **Protip**
> One way to stop everyone from debating the validity of a cause is for everyone to have a pad of Post-its and a Sharpie. Each person writes down what they think their why is. This will save the facilitator from running out of the room and gets people to think about their why before they get caught up in trying to get their point heard. Now the facilitator can invite people to put their whys on the board, affinity group where you can, and proceed.

At the end of the Problem-Solving Workshop, make sure the suggested solution(s) have owners and, where required, the right messages. The RTE needs to make sure the backlog items make it into PI Planning the next day. As my friend Inbar Oren would say, "Don't Inspect and Forget."

Em's Anecdote

Back when I was a GM working in the business and feeding the technology money fire, when there were issues with delivery the technology team was quick to point the finger at me. They said that it was "a lack of business engagement" that was at the heart of our delivery issues. Eventually, this excuse got old and I decided to take a leaf out of Lyssa Adkins' book and "take it to the team.[47]"

We ran a program-wide retrospective, using the Timeline approach from Esther Derby and Dianna Larson's *Agile Retrospective*[48] books. We asked the teams to reflect over the last couple of months leading up to their last release what had gone wrong, what had gone right, and what were the things that the program needed to help them solve if they were going to be successful. Then we asked, *"If we wanted to increase throughput, if we wanted to double our throughput, what would we need to do?"* No idea was too bad or too big or too scary. Anything was up for grabs.

When we aggregated the results, strangely enough, business engagement didn't make it to the top five. Instead it was a raft of technical issues, with the most challenging being environment stand-up and test data provisioning. It was taking six to eight weeks to stand up an environment for a development team. Essentially, the agile teams were treading water for weeks, waiting for these environments to be stood up. It is this finding that was the catalyst to create a new team which, in due course, would become our first System Team.

---

[47] Lyssa Adkins, *Coaching Agile Teams: A Companion for ScrumMasters, Agile Coaches, and Project Managers in Transition,* (Boston: Addison-Wesley, 2010) Kindle Edition. Location 1052.

[48] Esther Derby, *Agile Retrospectives,* Location 871.

Adding Teams to the Train

While not an overly common pattern, from time to time, some ARTs need to add new teams. Ideally new people and teams are onboarded during the IP Sprint so as not to disrupt the teams while they are in the middle of delivering on the PI commitments.

There tends to be two main reasons trains need to grow. Either (a) some teams that belong on the ART were not included in the initial ART launch for some reason, or (b) your ART needs to grow to better balance supply and demand. If it is scenario (a) then we recommend you Quick-Start them on to your Agile Release Train, i.e. have a team formation day, followed by *SAFe for Teams* and PI Planning with the rest of the train.

In the second scenario we generally do not advise adding new people to the train as teams; rather, we recommend you sprinkle the new folks across the teams to enable them to learn the environment. Of course, you will also want to provide *SAFe for Teams* training for the new folks.

> **Caution! Potential Train Wreck Ahead!**
> One RTE we worked with had heard us loud and clear when we said the teams on the train should be stable. When he needed to add three new teams, he literally added three whole new teams to the ART. The people on these teams had no context about the company, the product, or the architecture of the systems they were going to work on. It was evident from the moment we started to decompose features during *SAFe for Teams* training that this would not be a good approach. How can you size work when you have no context? Quite simply you can't, and this became clear as these teams found it impossible to create meaningful PI Plans that they were comfortable committing to.

Case Study:
How to Grow an Agile Release Train

Most Agile Release Trains are established as a fixed capacity model. This means if demand is outstripping supply you have a few options: do nothing, add other team(s), or add people to the existing teams. One train I was working with that had five permanent feature teams decided it would experiment with adding people to the existing teams.

The teams on this train were all eight-person feature teams consisting of one Scrum Master, one Technical Lead, one Quality Lead and five Developers. Given the optimal size of an Agile team is considered to be 7 ± 2, we theorised we could add another developer to each team and increase throughput. The idea was appealing, it seemed logical. Worst case should our experiment fail we could always go back to teams of eight by launching a sixth team.

The RTE discussed the concept with the Scrum Masters and everyone agreed it seemed like a great idea. So, we went about recruiting five new developers. After a few iterations all the teams had an additional developer and we watched and waited to see what would happen.

Four iterations (eight weeks) went by and we were surprised to find that nothing happened! Throughput did not increase, nor did it decline, it essentially remained constant. It appears Brook's was right: nine women can't make a baby in one month! Having long been an advocate of Brook's law,[49] it was fascinating to see it materialise in front of me.

The RTE took the data to the Scrum Masters and asked them what they had observed since the addition of an extra developer

---

[49] See: https://en.wikipedia.org/wiki/Brooks%27s_law (Accessed 10 August 2019).

to their teams. Their observations were consistent: team members had become more focused on their areas of specialisation and the team had started to lose the cross-skilling that had been central to our early agile success. The consensus was that we should return to eight-person teams and consider experimenting with even smaller teams in the future!

It was time to execute "Plan B" and move from five teams of nine to six teams of eight. Again, we watched with interest to see what happened and this time the throughput of the Release Train went up!

While we did not get the result we hoped for, our experiment did provide a solid approach for growing an Agile Release Train. By adding an extra person to each team in the first instance, new developers were immediately immersed in our culture and ways of working, quickly acclimatising. When we finally made the call to create an additional team, we weren't adding a new team from scratch, avoiding much of the teething pain that a brand-new team of brand-new developers was anticipated to cause us.[50]

Speeding up the Train with DevOps

Recently I was asked if I have ever tried running a SAFe transformation and a DevOps transformation in parallel. Puzzled by the question, I responded – yes, all the time. Since my very first Agile Release Train, I have found DevOps to be one of the key enablers to success with SAFe. In fact, I am forever telling people that the only way to achieve the amazing productivity results claimed in the SAFe case studies,[51] is to practice XP and DevOps.

---

[50] Adapted from: http://blog.prettyagile.com.au/2013/09/how-to-grow-agile-release-train.html (Accessed 10 August 2019).

[51] See: https://www.scaledagileframework.com/case-studies/ (10 September 2019)

If you have not done so already, the first thing you will want to do is value stream map your development process.[52] Once you can see the process, identify the biggest bottleneck and start the process of improving it. Remember the words of Eli Glodratt: *"an hour saved at a non-bottleneck is worthless."*[53] If you aren't sure how to address a bottleneck, run an Impact Mapping session with train. After all, the people who do the work know the most about it!

> **Protip**
> Improving the frequency of release (or deployment) is one of the outcomes most organisations expect from their DevOps transformation. One way to start to improve this is by leveraging the existing "hot-fix" windows. Almost every application can deploy, and release, changes once or twice a week. If you keep your changes small, you should be able to release more frequently by leveraging this.

With your Program Increments now operationalised, and your closed feedback loop systems working, you should be well placed to keep your ART on the tracks. You'll also have some tools in your toolbox to reset any accidental derailing.

---

[52] There is an example of this in the section on the System Team.
[53] Eliyahu M. Goldratt, *The Goal: A Process of Ongoing Improvement.* (Great Barrington: North River Press, 1984). Kindle Edition. p.259.

Chapter Summary

Keeping an Agile Release Train on the tracks, healthy and thriving, is a very big job! In this chapter we talked about activities, tools, and ceremonies that will help you steer the train. We explored:

- Using Program Epic Kanban to manage the flow of epics onto the ART through to being done
- Using the Program Feature Kanban to manage features onto the ART
- Start Sprinting off on the right foot including specific operational ceremonies we use to keep the train on the tracks
- Getting Chapter meetings operationalised
- Guidance on successful patterns to use in the Innovation and Planning sprint to help the ART get better together
- A reminder that DevOps is the key to unlocking speed.

SAFe Travels

Everyone underestimates the time commitment required to successfully launch an Agile Release Train. We have the same conversation with every new client. "Be prepared to clear the decks," we say. But this message is rarely heeded. Almost every time after we get through the launch the client says to us, "Oh, you really did mean clear the decks …"

Clients are often looking for someone to do the work for them. In our view this does not lead to sustainable outcomes. If the organisation truly wants to change and adopt a new way of working, then it is the organisation that needs to make the change.

We think that the journey is pretty straightforward. We see it as following the proven recipe:

- PI Planning
- PI Execution
- Inspect and Adapt

What is often lacking is the discipline to stick to the recipe, even when times are tough. Adrienne and I had the good fortune to visit Japan last year on a Lean Study Tour with Katie Anderson and Isao Yoshino. One of the significant discussions during the tour was what makes Toyota exceptional. While Toyota are of course the creators of Lean (or as they call it the Toyota Production System (TPS)), Lean is widely practised, especially in Japanese manufacturing. Even so, Toyota still stands out from the crowd. At the end of the week Mr. Yoshino, 40-year Toyota veteran (and John Shook's first manager at Toyota) let us in on the secret—Discipline.

When thinking about SAFe and its foundations in Lean and Agile it is important to remember the people on the journey. As Dean says: *"People do all the work,"* Great cultures lead to places that people like to work. Who doesn't want to work somewhere fun, where they are respected for their skills and contributions? For the more economically minded, there is also a huge economic upside to having a great culture.

With that lens we leave you with our final thought: *If you have the discipline to make decisions with respect for people as front of mind you can't go wrong.*

Figure 71 – One ARTs internal case study

SAFe travels friends! It's all about the people!

Appendix

PI Planning Stationery

Per Table
1 x box of 500 coloured ruled index cards 152 x 102mm
2 x packet of super sticky Post-its
1 x roll of blue painters tape
1 x Post-it flip chart paper
1 x box of black Sharpies
1 x packet Blu-Tack[54]
1 x packet coloured whiteboard markers
1 x packet of coloured flip chart markers
Planning Poker Cards
1 x Stationery Container that can hold all of the above items
1 x Time Timer[55]
Big visible sign on each team table with team name
Printouts of feature definition work, Solution on a Page and Wireframes
Lots of bottled water or reusable water bottles (keeping track of who is using which glass is impossible)
A storage box per team to pack up everything into
A folio or poster container for team plans

Per Agile Release Train
Lots of team avatars for putting on feature cards
3 prepopulated index cards for each feature (one blue, one white, one yellow)
- Index card should have on it:
    - Feature number
    - Feature Name

---

[54] https://en.wikipedia.org/wiki/Blu_Tack (Accessed 21 July 2019).
[55] https://www.timetimer.com/ (Accessed 21 July 2019).

- Project/epic name
- Unique Priority Ranking
- Room for a team avatar (or avatars in the case of an ART of component teams)

2 x rolls of blue painters tape

Large foam boards for the program board, planning Kanban and risk board (so you can easily take them back to the office)

Spare stationery

Name stickers for all attendees

Red Wool

Scissors

Prepopulated floor plan

Time Timer

Push Pins (if pinning to a board)

Appendix

Checklist for Avoiding a Train Wreck

Ticket to Ride

- ❏ Determine which implementation path makes sense for your organisation
- ❏ If "Going All In" run a *Leading SAFe* with the executive team and facilitate a *Value Stream and ART Identification Workshop*
- ❏ Choose the first ART to launch
- ❏ Conduct empathy interviews with key stakeholders
- ❏ Choose the metrics you want to track and baseline them

Laying the Tracks

- ❏ Run a *Leading SAFe* class for the ART's extended leadership
    - ❏ Select an instructor and book a venue
    - ❏ Decide the participants, send a calendar invitation and the pre-reading
    - ❏ Line up someone to introduce the session
    - ❏ Remind students to take the exam

- ❏ Design the Agile Release Train:
    - ❏ Identify the Business Owners, Release Train Engineer, Product Manager(s) and the System Architect(s)
    - ❏ Decide the shape, size and locations for the Agile Teams
    - ❏ (If applicable) Decide what vendor model applies and brief your vendors
    - ❏ Identify a Scrum Master and a Product Owner for each Team
    - ❏ Determine if the Features Owner or Chapter model adds value in your context
    - ❏ Build the System Team
    - ❏ Identify who needs to be in the Shared Services team on the ART
    - ❏ (If applicable) Decide the approach for the UX team and Business Change Management

- ❏ Confirm all Line Manager, Project Managers, and business analysts have been cared for
- ❏ Evaluate the option of holding a self-selection event
- ❏ Set a date to launch the train
    - ❏ Build the plan to get to launch
    - ❏ Establish the operating rhythm for the launch team
- ❏ Deliver *SAFe Product Manager/Product Owner (POPM)* training

Preparing the Cargo

- ❏ Identify possible Program Epics
- ❏ Define a handful of Program Epics using the Epic Hypothesis Statement
    - ❏ Have a single clear Business Outcome Hypothesis for each epic
    - ❏ Identify the MVP and Leading indicators
    - ❏ Align enabler epics to the business roadmap
- ❏ Create an Architecture on a Page for the ART and a Solution on a Page for each epic
- ❏ Have the Business Owners prioritise the epics using estimating poker and WSJF
    - ❏ Agree the cadence for this session during PI Execution
- ❏ Validate the ART has the skill sets to deliver the priority epics
- ❏ Decompose the priority epics into features using Impact Mapping
    - ❏ Split out the MVP feature set into a separate epic
- ❏ Create the ART's Definition of Ready for Features
- ❏ Create the ART's Definition of Done (DoD) for stories, features and release
- ❏ (If applicable) Complete the Lean Business Case template and submit to the Portfolio Sync for a go/no-go decision
- ❏ Prioritise the features using estimating poker and WSJF
    - ❏ Agree the cadence for this session during PI Execution
- ❏ Allocate features to teams

- ❏ Have Product Management and the System Architect(s) socialise the features with the teams

Setting the Timetable for The Train

- ❏ Set the Program Increment and Sprint cadence
- ❏ Send calendar invites for PI Planning, the System Demo (or ART Show), and Inspect and Adapt
- ❏ Establish the cadence for the following ceremonies and send the invites
    - ❏ ART Sync or Cocktail Hour
    - ❏ Unity Hour
    - ❏ Reunification
    - ❏ Epic Writing Workshops
    - ❏ Feature Auction
    - ❏ Prioritisation (WSJF) session(s)
    - ❏ Bubble-Up
    - ❏ System Demo or ART Show

All Aboard

- ❏ Arrange a suitable venue for the seven-day Quick-Start
- ❏ Mark arrangements for train members to co-locate (or book venues in other locations)
- ❏ Place the stationery order for PI Planning and the supplies for the Team Product Box exercise
- ❏ Deliver *SAFe Scrum Master* training
- ❏ If you plan to hold a Self-Selection event download the Self-Selection Pocket guide and use the checklist
- ❏ Build your agenda for Team Day
- ❏ Facilitate Team Day
    - ❏ Speed-Meet with Personal Maps
    - ❏ Choose a train theme
    - ❏ Choose a train name
    - ❏ Name the teams and build team product boxes
- ❏ Deliver *SAFe for Team* training
    - ❏ Find the chickens (Definition of One)

- ❏ Calculate Capacity for PI and apply the 30% discount
- ❏ Line up speakers for day one briefings and collect presentations in advance
  - ❏ Business Owners
  - ❏ Product Management
  - ❏ System Architecture
  - ❏ Development Management
  - ❏ UX/CX
- ❏ Prepare Planning Context Briefing
  - ❏ Capacity allocation
  - ❏ Feature Kanban
  - ❏ Program Board
  - ❏ ROAM Board
- ❏ Facilitate PI Planning
  - ❏ Hold Scrum of Scrums every hour
  - ❏ Collect "Dear Management" letters at the end of day one
  - ❏ Facilitate Management Review and Problem Solving
    - ❏ Gather positive feedback
    - ❏ Review Team Plans, Draft PI Objectives, Feature Kanban, ROAM Board and Program Board
    - ❏ Capture Actions and Decisions
  - ❏ Ensure Business Owners share positive feedback and the planning adjustments
  - ❏ Facilitate business value rating of Team PI Objectives
  - ❏ Facilitate the Confidence Vote
  - ❏ Facilitate the Retrospective
  - ❏ Ensure the Business Owners say thank you to the ART
  - ❏ Celebrate!
- ❏ Send out post PI Planning communication

Staying on the Tracks

- ❏ Design, build, and operate a Program Kanban for Epics and Features

Appendix

- ❏ Operationalise the ART Timetable
    - ❏ Cocktail Hour and ART Sync
    - ❏ Sprinting
    - ❏ Reunification
    - ❏ Discovery
    - ❏ Bubble-Up
- ❏ Operationalise the Chapters
- ❏ Plan activities for the IP Sprint
- ❏ Facilitate Inspect and Adapt
- ❏ Invest in removing bottlenecks with DevOps

Contributors

Maarit Laanti

Maarit Laanti, PhD, SPCT, has been a pioneer, practitioner, and researcher in large-scale agile for over twenty years. She was recently nominated to the list of one hundred top women contributors in Lean and Agile and is currently finalising a book on Agile Portfolio Management.

She is behind the first large agile transformations on SAFe before it was called SAFe, Nokia S30/S40 learning journey that became Leading SAFe training, portfolio management, and lean-agile budgeting that she contributed to SAFe 3.0.

She has published the first academic research on scaling agile methods, founded Nitor Delta, an agile consultancy company, and brought SAFe into Nordics.

Darren Wilmshurst

Darren is an Associate of the Chartered Institute of Bankers following sixteen years in Retail Banking culminating as a Senior Personal Banking Manager within the Guildford Group of Branches. A career change into IT in the late 1990s led to a number of senior roles within IT. He is also a Chartered IT Professional.

Darren is now a Director of Radtac, a Global Agile Consultancy Business. He is a SAFe Program Consultant Trainer (SPCT), a contributor to the SAFe Reference Guide 4.5, and founder of the London SAFe Meet-up Group.

Finally, he is a co-author of the BCS book *Agile Foundations – Principles Practices and Frameworks*, and a reviewer of *Valuing Agile; the financial management of agile projects*.

Aaron McKenna

Aaron McKenna is a director of McKenna Consultants, a team of professional computer programmers and agile consultants. Aaron is experienced in leading, transforming, working in, teaching, coaching, and consulting in agile methodologies since 2009. He is a Scaled Agile Framework (SAFe) Program Consultant (SPC), Management 3.0 Licensed Facilitator, Certified LeSS Practitioner, Certified Scrum Master, Certified Scrum Product Owner, and Certified Scrum Professional.

Claire Sanders

Claire Sanders has deep experience in software development and data analytics delivery. She is SPC4 certified with multiple site and multi-year experience helping companies improve with the Scaled Agile Framework. She's proud to be part of the Pretty Agile team training, launching and coaching Agile Release Trains.

Cécile Auret

Cécile Auret is an Agile change agent in a French government agency. She is going through the ups and downs of the transformation, helping teams and programs transition to agile to deliver more value with the use of Scrum, Kanban and the Scaled Agile Framework®.

Robin Yeman

Robin Yeman is Lockheed Martin Space Fellow with 26 years' experience in systems and software engineering building products from submarines to Satellites.

She has a CIS degree from Syracuse University, Master's Degree in Software Engineering from RPI, and is currently obtaining a PhD at Colorado State University.

Robin has been supporting Agile programs at scale since 2002. She is an SPCT candidate, CSM, CSP, CEC, PMI-ACP, PMP, and CSEP.

Contributors

Michael Stump

Michael Stump is a Lean-Agile Leader, mentor to executives on Business Agility and state-of-the-art SAFe® principles and practices. His extensive international consulting and management experience enables him to inspire, lead, manage, and advise companies through great organisational change. As an advisory board member to technology companies, his specialty is Lean and Agile transition journeys within highly distributed, multi-cultural enterprises.

Michael is a passionate helicopter pilot. A Zurich, Switzerland native, he regularly travels the globe and currently lives in Boulder, Colorado and New York City.

Melissa Hay

Melissa helps leaders and teams to deliver value using SAFe. She's launched and coached Agile Release Trains in the public and private sectors over the last 5 years both in Australia and abroad. Melissa is a certified SPC4, international speaker and trainer. She's proud to be part of the Pretty Agile team.

Carl Starendal

Carl Starendal is an Enterprise lean/agile trainer, advisor and Sweden's only SAFe Program Consultant Trainer (SAFe SPCT). He has served directly for Scaled Agile, Inc., the creators of the Scaled Agile Framework® for two years as well as having years of hands-on experience as an important part of several multinational Lean-Agile transformations across a diverse range of industries, in and beyond the software industry.

Carl also frequently speaks internationally about leadership, Lean-Agile transformations, and leadership in product development, and he is a highly regarded advisor, trainer, and facilitator.

Marc Rix

Marc helps large enterprises leverage the game-changing power of Lean, Agile, and DevOps at scale. He has been practising Agile for over twenty years and is an internationally recognised thought leader, consultant, trainer, adviser, and speaker. Marc lives in California and is a Product Manager at Scaled Agile.

Sonya Yeh Spencer,

Sonya Yeh Spencer, a passionate Agilist, was first introduced to Scrum in 2001. She is a certified agile professional and an experienced Scrum Master, currently working for PCCW Global. She sees being agile is more than just for software development but a way of living. She believes when a Scrum Master who truly believes in agile ways of working and embody these values and principles, teams will become more agile, quality-driven, engaged and productive. These days apart from helping teams and organisations adopting Agile practices and SAFe, she enjoys living out in the bush, finding the most efficient way to grow her own food and become self-sufficient.

Bibliography

Adkins, L., *Coaching Agile Teams: A Companion for Scrum Masters, Agile Coaches, and Project Managers in Transition*, Boston: Addison-Wesley, 2010. Kindle Edition.

Adzic, G., *Impact Mapping: Making a Big Impact with Software Products and Projects*, Provoking Thoughts, 2012, Kindle Edition.

Appelo, J. *#Workout, Games, Tools & Practices to Engage People, Improve Work, and Delight Clients.* Rotterdam: Happy Melly, 2014. Kindle Edition.

Ballé, M., D. Jones, J. Chaize and O. Fiume, *The Lean Strategy: Using Lean to Create Completive Advantage, Unleash Innovation, and Deliver Sustainable Growth.* McGraw Hill, 2017, Kindle Edition.

Bogsnes, B., *Implementing Beyond Budgeting: Unlocking the Performance Potential*, Wiley, 2009, Kindle Edition.

Bowman, S., *Training from the BACK of the Room! 65 Ways to Step and Let them Learn*, San Francisco: Pfeiffer, 2008.

Bowman, S., *Using Brain Science to Make Training Stick: Six Leaning Principles That Trump Traditional Teaching*, Glenbrook: BowPerson Publishing, 2011.

Campbell-Pretty, E., *Tribal Unity: Getting from Teams to Tribes by Creating a One Team Culture.* SpiritCast Network, 2017.

Cohn, M., *Agile Estimating and Planning.* New Jersey: Pearson Education, 2006.

Collins, J. *Good to Great: Why Some Companies Make the Leap and Others Don't.* London: Random House, 2001.

Deming, W. E. *Out of the Crisis*, Cambridge: MIT Press, 1982.

Derby, E and D. Larson, *Agile Retrospectives: Making Good Teams Great.* Pragmatic Bookshelf, 2005. Kindle Edition.

Grant, A. *Give and Take: Why Helping Others Drives Our Success.* London: Weidenfeld & Nicolson, 2013. Kindle Edition.

Goldratt, E. M. *The Goal: A Process of Ongoing Improvement.* Great Barrington: North River Press, 1984. Kindle Edition.

Gothelf, J. *Lean UX: Applying Lean Principles to Improve User Experience.* O'Reilly Media, 2013, Kindle Edition.

Hackman, J. R., *Leading Teams: Setting the Stage for Great Performances.* Boston: Harvard University Press, 2002), Kindle Edition.

Heath C. and D. Heath, *Switch: How to Change Things When Change is Hard.* London: Random House, 2010. Kindle Edition.

Heath C. and D. Heath, *Decisive: How to Make Better Choices in Life and Work.* New York: Crown Publishing, 2013.

Hohmann, L. *Innovation Games: Creating Breakthrough Products Through Collaborative Play.* Boston: Pearson, 2007. Kindle Edition.

Kersten, M., *Project to Product: How to Survive and Thrive in the Age of Digital Disruption with the Flow Framework.* Portland: IT Revolution, 2018. Kindle Edition.

Knaster, R. and D. Leffingwell, *SAFe 4.5 Distilled: Applying the Scaled Agile Framework for Lean Enterprises (2nd Edition).* Boston: Addison-Wesley, 2018.

Kniberg, H., *Lean From the Trenches: Managing Large Scale Projects with Kanban.* Pragmatic Bookshelf, 2011.

Leffingwell, D., *Scaling Software Agility: Best Practices for Large Enterprises.* Boston: Addison-Wesley, 2007. Kindle Edition.

Leffingwell, D., *Agile Software Requirements: Lean Requirements Practices for Teams. Program, and the Enterprise.* Boston: Addison-Wesley, 2011. Kindle Edition.

Bibliography

Lencioni, P., *The Five Dysfunctions of a Team : A Leadership Fable*. New York: Wiley, 2002.

Liker, J., *The Toyota Way: 14 Management Principles from the World's Greatest Manufacturer*. McGraw-Hill Education, 2004. Kindle Edition.

Mamoli, S. and D. Mole, *Creating Great Teams: How Self-Selection Lets People Excel*. Pragmatic Bookshelf, 2015. PDF Edition.

Manns M. L. and L. Rising, *More Fearless Change: Strategies for Making Your Ideas Happen*. Boston: Pearson, 2015. Kindle Edition.

Martin, K. and M. Osterling, *Value Stream Mapping: How to Visualize Work and Align Leadership for Organization Transformation*. McGraw-Hill Education, 2013. Kindle Edition.

Modig, N. and P. Åhlström, *This is Lean: Resolving the Efficiency Paradox*. Rheologica, 2013. Kindle Edition.

Patton, J. *User Story Mapping: Discover The Whole Story, Build The Right Product*. Sebastopol: O'Reilly, 2014.

Pink, D. H., *To Sell Is Human: The Surprising Truth About Persuading, Convincing and Influencing Others*, Melbourne: The Text Publishing Company, 2012. Kindle Edition.

Poppendieck, M. and T. Poppendieck, *Lean Software Development: An Agile Toolkit*. New Jersey: Addison-Wesley, 2003.

Poppendieck, M. and T. Poppendieck, *The Lean Mindset: Ask the Right Questions*. New Jersey: Addison-Wesley, 2013.

Reichheld, F. *The Ultimate Question 2.0: How Net Promoter Companies Thrive in a Customer-Driven World*. Boston: Harvard Business Review Press, 2011.

Reinertsen, D. G., *The Principles of Product Development Flow: Second Generation Lean Product Development*. Redondo Beach: Celeritas Publishing. 2009. Kindle Edition.

Ries, E., *The Lean Startup: How Today's Entrepreneurs Use Continuous*

Innovation to Create Radically Successful Businesses. New York: Crown, 2011.

Rother, M, and J, Shook, *Learning to See: Value Stream Mapping to Create Value and Eliminate Muda.* Brookline: The Lean Enterprise Institute, 1999.

Smart, J. F., *BDD in Action: Behavior-Driven Development for the Whole Software Lifecycle.* New York: Manning Publications, 2015.

Tabaka, J. *Collaboration Explained: Facilitation Skills for Software Project Leaders.* Upper Saddle River: Pearson Education, 2006, Kindle Edition.

Weinberg, G. M., *Why Software Gets In Trouble: Software Quality Series: Vol. 2.* Leanpub, 2017.

Womack, J.P., D.T Jones and D. Roos, *The Machine that Changed the World: The Story of Lean Production – Toyota's Secret Weapon is the Global Car Wars that is the Revolutionizing World Industry.* New York: Free Press, 1990.

Zuill, W and K. Meadows, *Mob Programming: A Whole Team Approach.* Leanpub, 2016.

About the Authors

Em Campbell-Pretty

SAFe® Fellow
Scaled Agile Framework Program Consultant Trainer (SPCT)
Scaled Agile Framework Release Train Engineer (RTE)
Extreme Leadership Certified Facilitator
Training from the BACK of the Room – Certified Trainer

Em Campbell-Pretty is one of the world's most experienced SAFe practitioners and the author of the Amazon #1 best-selling book, *Tribal Unity: Getting from Teams to Tribes by Creating a One Team Culture*. As one of the first SAFe Fellows and SPCTs, Em has been working with SAFe since before it was called SAFe.

After reading Dean Leffingwell's *Scaling Software Agility* she launched Australia's first SAFe Agile Release Train in early 2012. A couple of years later she went on to start her own business inspired by her hugely popular blog prettyagile.com. A true servant leader, Em is committed to building great teams and transforming culture whilst still maintaining focus on delivering business outcomes. At the heart of Em's success is her unrelenting focus on building a culture of transparency Lean leadership, learning, and innovation.

Em is an active member of the global Agile community and was invited to co-chair the Enterprise Agile track for the Agile Alliance 2014, 2015, and 2016 conferences. She is a recognised expert in Scaling Agile and sort after keynote speaker at conferences across the globe. She was recently recognised by LIA100 as one of the 100 top women influencers in Lean and Agile. Today, Em helps organisations across the globe implement SAFe and launch Agile Release Trains using her unique "culture first" approach to Business Agility.

How to contact Em:
Email: em@prettyagile.com
Blog: blog.prettyagile.com
Follow Em on Twitter: @PrettyAgile
Connect with Em on LinkedIn:
https://au.linkedin.com/in/ejcampbellpretty

About the Authors

Adrienne L Wilson

Scaled Agile Framework Program Consultant Trainer (SPCT) Candidate
Scaled Agile Framework Release Train Engineer (RTE)
Project Management Professional (PMP)
Scrum Master (CSM)
Aerospace Engineer (Bachelor of Engineering, Aerospace)

Adrienne spent the first 20 years of her career in a variety of technical and management roles building high-design assurance flight critical, telecommunications, medical devices and IT systems. Since 2007 Adrienne has been using a variety of agility development methodologies to deliver business and technology results starting with RUP, migrating to Scrum, and eventually embracing the Scaled Agile Framework (SAFe®).

During this journey of embracing agility, Adrienne has had a variety of roles focusing on delivery, business and agility coaching, and having the opportunity to build and lead several organizations Agile PMO/ Centres of Excellence. Further, she has had key SAFe® roles including the Release and Solution Train Engineer positions where she has been responsible for launching multiple release trains and multi-site release trains.

As an enterprise agile coach, Adrienne has successfully coached organizations in Aerospace, Telecommunication, Hospitality, Transportation and Insurance/Banking verticals in very successful agile transformations that are still operating today. As a part of Pretty Agile, Adrienne and Em Campbell-Pretty conducted the first SAFe Program Consultant (SPC) class and launched the first Agile Release Train in the Philippines.

Adrienne is an active member of the agile community. She has spoken at international agile conferences and meetups around the world. Through these engagements she is excited to share that while transformations are hard work there is no reason you can't have fun while participating in them!

How to contact Adrienne:
Email: adrienne@prettyagile.com
Blog: blog.prettyagile.com
Follow Adrienne on Twitter: @AgileCanuck
Connect with Adrienne on LinkedIn:
https://au.linkedin.com/in/adriennelwilson

Also by Em Campbell-Pretty

TRIBAL UNITY
Getting from TEAMS to TRIBES by Creating a One Team Culture

AVAILABLE NOW ON amazon & iBooks

"Every aspiring Lean-Agile enterprise can be no better than the culture that evolves to support it."
- Dean Leffingwell

A "culture first" approach to achieving Business Agility with the Scaled Agile Framework®